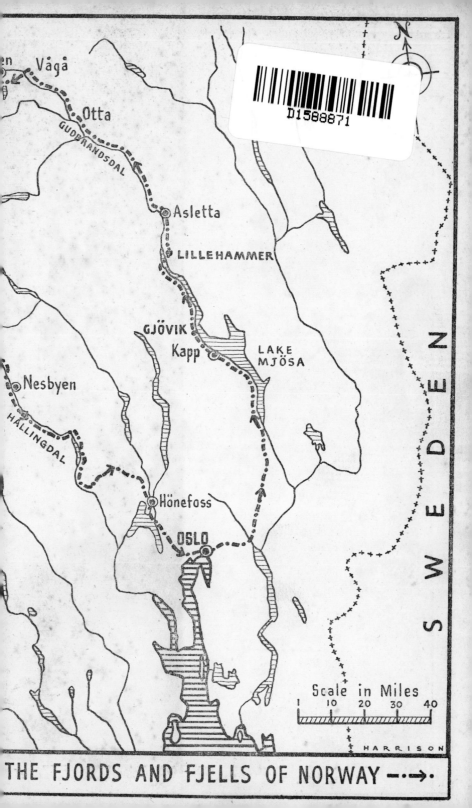

THE FJORDS AND FJELLS OF NORWAY --·-->

75 PJ

NORWEGIAN JOURNEY

Also by Garry Hogg:

. . . AND FAR AWAY
THE ROAD BEFORE ME
TURF BENEATH MY FEET

NORWEGIAN JOURNEY

BY

GARRY HOGG

THE TRAVEL BOOK CLUB
121 CHARING CROSS ROAD
LONDON W.C. 2

PRINTED IN GREAT BRITAIN BY
NORTHUMBERLAND PRESS LIMITED
GATESHEAD ON TYNE

For

the

" ELIZABETH "

of

this journey

CONTENTS

9

TO BEGIN WITH

I BROUGHT the car to a standstill and Elizabeth and I looked about us. We were on the brow of a hill, somewhere north of Manchester. The skyline north, south, east and west of us was a blur of smoke from a thousand tall chimneys upthrust from it into the uncomplaining air. Beneath us were a million granite setts, the floor of a great industrial area. Ahead of us the road dipped to bring us into yet closer contact with the terraced houses and shops and factories large and small, the pubs and cinemas and fried-fish-and-chipperies and police-stations and goods-yards and schools that still carried the word "Board" carved deep into grimy stone.

"I will arise," I said, "and get 'ence."

It is a line of verse that has always appealed to me. I cannot remember whether it is a line from Kipling, or the beginning of an uncalled-for parody on Yeats's *Lake Isle of Innisfree*; its statement anyway is uncompromising.

"Where to?" Elizabeth asked, knowing that I meant more than just that I proposed to drive away quickly from where the car then stood.

I answered, almost without thought: "Norway."

And then, of course, we began, as our way is, to turn the matter over in our minds.

Norway. Why Norway? But, *of course*, Norway. It was as though we had always known that next time we left these shores it would be for Norway. It remained only for us to find, or make, an excuse. . . .

The letter was awaiting us. The publisher of a series of books of mine for older children would like the next one to have a foreign setting. Had I any ideas?

"Why not a Norwegian one?" Elizabeth suggested.

Why not, indeed?

11

BERGEN TO ODDA

> *" To Noroway, to Noroway,*
> *To Noroway o'er the faem! "*

BUT there had been no *faem*. The deadly sea that had overwhelmed Sir Patrick Spens and buried him fifty fathom deep had lain glass-smooth beneath m.s. *Venus* for twenty uneventful hours, and now she was about to tie up at her berth. For the past two hours or so she had been winding up the colourful and ever-changing Krossfjord, between the bare rocks of Sotra and the hills of Midhordland.

Gay chalets perched like toys on any small level space that offered, the Norwegian flag waving lazily above each, at the tip of a high, slender flagstaff. Motor-boats darted hither and yon among the scattered rocks; bright-sailed yachts and dinghies cut the surface into criss-cross patterns that vanished and reappeared continuously: a herring-bone weave to the deep-blue water that took its colour from a cloudless sky.

A voice came to us over the ship's inter-com., pleasant, warmly toned, personal: " This is Bergen. The City of Bergen welcomes you. We hope that your stay among us, in Bergen and wherever you may be going in Norway, will be an enjoyable one, and that when you leave us you will take away with you the happiest of memories."

I thought of that greeting when, some weeks later, we drew in to the Tyne Commission Quay. It was not Newcastle's fault that it was raining; that the sky was almost as grey as the buildings over which it lowered; that a pall of smoke and soot lay over the land and extended well out into open water to greet us. Newcastle is a great industrial city, hub of a great industrial area; it cannot help itself. But as we stood on *Venus*'s upper deck, talking to Gerd and her sister, two Norwegian girls who were visiting England for the first time, and answering their questions, I wished that I could take over the now silent inter-com. for a few moments.

15

I should have liked to be able to say, in fluent Norwegian:
"This is Newcastle. The City of Newcastle is sorry that.
being an industrial city, it cannot offer you the immediate
and challenging beauty of its opposite number, Bergen.
Nevertheless, it extends its welcome to you, and hopes that you
will make haste to explore its hinterland. Behind and beyond
our deplorable slag-heaps and giant chimneys lie the Pennines, the Roman Wall of the Emperor Hadrian, the Lakes,
the Vale of York, the Dales; and beyond all these, the warmer,
gentler beauty of the South and West. May your days
be spent in pleasant places. Newcastle wishes you god-
speed. . . ."

"Jeg forstår ikke"

I find it hard to believe that there can be a lovelier approach
to any port than that of Bergen. In Bergen, water and solid
land are so intermingled that it is not easy to decide which
predominates. *Venus* seemed to be sailing straight into the
heart of the town; and beyond the main shopping area, as
we found within the hour, there lay further stretches of water
large and deep enough to float our liner and the rest of her
fleet, with room and to spare for the innumerable smaller
boats that seem as much a part of Bergen as her single-decker
yellow trailer-trams, her vast fleet of *drosjes*, her green and
sky-blue single-decker buses.

The voice had passed from its message of welcome to instructions about disembarkation. Surrounded by Americans
with expensive pieces of luggage and even more expensive
cameras, Elizabeth and I went ashore at last, and into the
Customs Shed. The Customs man did not look quite so
disdainfully at our rucksacks as the man on the Tyne Commission Quay had done, but he forbore to open them. He
scribbled a chalk mark on each, and waved us away: he had
larger fish to hook.

High above us as we walked along Skoltegrunnskaien
towered the black hull and triple-whitebanded smokestacks of
the vessel that had brought us to Norway. A few hundred

yards farther on she appeared again, in miniature: a black tug-boat with identical funnel markings, clean and trim as the vessel she had just helped to moor at the quay, now puffing silently away to her own berth on the opposite side of the water-way. Our nailed boots on the cobbles made almost the only sound to be heard, save the swish of the *drosjes*—the opulent American taxis—running a shuttle service between Customs and the hotels. The horseshoe of mountains, the lower slopes of which carried the residential district of Bergen, was the rampart across which later we must make our way into Norway. But in the meantime our first objective was to find a resting-place for the night. We had only one clue: Kong Oscar's Gate. This, having Bergen's railway-station at its far end, we thought likely to prove a good hunting-ground for different types of hotel.

It was, I suppose, sheer cowardice that prevented us from immediately asking the way. We had no street plan of Bergen, but had argued that in so small a town it should be easy enough to find one's way to the station, and thence along the street of hotels. But our cowardice perhaps needs to be explained.

For some time before setting sail, Elizabeth and I had been committing to memory not only a number of basic words— commodities we were likely to need during our stay in the country, and the essential verbs—but also a variety of phrases which we thought would serve us on our travels. As a safe-guard, too, we had committed to memory a certain number of, so to speak, courteous phrases; these, we hoped, would some-what modify our bluntness of approach. We had, at the very outset, been disconcerted to find that there is no brief Nor-wegian "Please". The circumlocution for this most neces-sary word is even longer than in French. Though we had practised it for some time, mainly at meals, we still felt self-conscious about using it. It is one thing to say, "*Vaer så snild* (or *god*) *å si mig* . . ." when the person to whom you are speaking has no more idea than yourself whether pronuncia-tion and inflexion are correct; it is quite another thing to go up to a complete stranger in the street and say, in Norwegian: "Will you be so kind (or good) as to tell me . . ."

We put off the plunge as long as possible, but time was passing, and we were no nearer our objective than we had been an hour before. We had intended to be much more enterprising, but had received a rude shock on board ship when we tried out a phrase or two on the purser. We knew that *takk* meant "Thank you", but we had received a kindness that seemed to call for something more than a bare "Thanks". So, I had uttered, with some emphasis: *Meget forbunden*. My little phrase-book told me this was correct for "Much obliged". So it may have been. But the purser's eyelid quivered an instant, and then he said to me, in impeccable English: "If you're more than grateful, then *Mange takk* is plenty. If you really want to let yourself go, try *Tusen takk*. A thousand thanks will get you anywhere in Norway! "

I asked him what a Bergen policeman would be likely to say if I sprang on him my cherished but clearly antiquated phrase. He answered with a grin: "He'd probably ask you in good American-English, 'What the hell's all that about?'! " Small wonder, then, that Elizabeth and I had somewhat lost faith in our phrase-book.

We ought, of course, to have known. Examined more closely, we found it contained among its "Useful Phrases" the Norwegian for "This is a capital hotel". The date of its composition could be fairly easily guessed at from that single clue.

"Why not try out a question in English?" Elizabeth suggested. "After all, Peter told us that everybody in Bergen speaks fluent English with a strong Tyneside accent."

"A Geordie's lingo is probably as difficult to understand as Norwegian would be," I said. "However, I'll try this fireman. He's probably conditioned to all known types of shock."

There was a row of them sunning themselves outside a red-brick building. I chose a plump individual with a rosy face and tightly fitting uniform. I decided to modify the "Please" gambit by using its longer form, so that any abruptness in my voice due to self-consciousness might be mitigated.

"*Vil De vaere så snild å si mig hvordan jeg kan komme til jernbanestasjonen?*" I asked, clearly and distinctly.

In what language he thought I might be asking him the
18

way to the station I do not know, but he certainly did not grasp a word of it. He shook his head, perspired freely beneath the peak of his cap, shook his head in a despairing manner, and gazed at me blankly. I repeated the question, a little more slowly, emphasizing alternate words and looking fixedly at him as I did so. I thought he was going to burst into tears. Perhaps the kindest thing would be to go immediately from his presence and try again, if I could summon the courage, elsewhere.

I tried a third time, slurring the opening words and concentrating with great intensity on the final word in my sentence, giving it a query-intonation as I did so. It was a kind of lingual acrobatics which was going to become a regular feature of our experience during the succeeding weeks; most exhausting!

But it worked. Or rather, it did and it did not. He caught the final, the vital, word: railway-station. Delighted and relieved, he burst into a flow of explanation. I was to turn to the left, to the right, to neither hand (like Launcelot Gobbo's instructions to his blind father), at this point, that point, the other point. . . . The spate was interminable. But Destiny intervened. A passer-by came up behind us, tapped me on the elbow, and in three adequate English phrases set us on our way.

It was the first experiment, and by no means an unqualified success. As always, ability to make oneself understood comes faster than the corresponding ability to understand. The more fluent Elizabeth and I became (through the simple expedient of linking together phrases whose validity we had proved) the more it was taken for granted that our command of the language was extensive. Five basic words, carefully uttered by us, would let loose a reply in a hundred not-so-basic words, of which only perhaps a couple would mean anything to us.

We found the station. But we could not find, even then, the street we were after. It was not, apparently, terminated by the station, as we had thought. We turned right instead of left, and once more clattered along a sun-baked street into the heart of Bergen. I glanced at my watch. It was five hours since we had eaten anything, and town-walking in nailed boots is most exhausting. If Kong Oscar's Gate existed at all, then it must be heavily disguised!

Then we spotted a tall, thin individual approaching us at a brisk lope, in build and manner much more the Norwegian type than the rubicund fireman we had tried before. "Here goes," I said. Turning smartly about, I dropped into step, Elizabeth following suit on the other side of him. I gave utterance to my inquiry once again, only altering it this time to the name of the street I wanted.

He was, manifestly, a highly intelligent individual. He slowed down and, enunciating clearly, repeated the name of the street. When I nodded and essayed a confirmatory "Ja", he said no more, but swung off at the same loping stride, as silent as a deaf-mute, gesturing lightly to left or to right when we had to turn, while we followed in his wake like a small procession behind a Pied Piper. He stopped. Then, pointing with a long bony finger to the street name on a wall, he nodded briskly and returned by the way he had brought us. He probably did not even hear the rather pathetic "Tusen takk" which Elizabeth and I called after him.

Thereafter, our experiences took on a slight note of fantasy. We walked the whole length of Kong Oscar's Gate, dismissing in turn hotel after hotel, until we stopped by mutual consent outside the last of all. This, we somehow knew, was to be *our* hotel. We entered, climbed two flights of slippery marble steps, and asked boldly in English for a room. The receptionist, a smiling girl in a bright blue frock, spoke to us rapidly—in Norwegian. We asked again, using the most elementary words and speaking very slowly. Surely a receptionist in Norway's second city would have that amount of English! She shook her head, broke into further speech, her eyes sparkling as though it were all the greatest joke in the world.

Laboriously, we tried again, in Norwegian this time. It had the effect I have spoken of already: a torrent of words impossible to stem. In the end she took a scrap of paper and a pencil, wrote something down in a queer, angular hand, and thrust it through the glass window with a look that said plainly: "Well, that'll make it clear, anyway!" But the only recognizable character on the paper was a figure which might have been 6.30. Elizabeth and I looked at one another, uncomprehending; then at the still smiling girl; then at one another again. Clearly, there was nothing to be gained by waiting here. We offered her a thousand thanks for what we had not received, and clattered off down the sweeping marble stairs to street level.

As we reached the pavement, edging our rucksacks through the swing-door, a middle-aged couple stood to one side and then entered behind us, making for the stairs. But, as we passed them, they greeted us in the manner of people who had known us all their lives. For a moment we stood still, dumbfounded. But when I darted back to find out who they were, for neither of us remembered having ever seen them before, they had vanished like a pipe dream. We never saw them again.

We stood, then, a little forlornly in the cobbled square near the hotel, deliberating our next move. Both of us were determined that the hotel we had tried should, in fact, be ours. But what was the next line of action? That was the question. We found it difficult even to think coherently; the sudden encounter with the now vanished couple had proved a decisive shock.

As we stood there, waiting for inspiration, a man's voice behind us hailed us in Norwegian, clearly asking a question. We turned, to confront an elderly little man who might, from his appearance, have been a retired village greengrocer. He had an umbrella in his hand, though the sky was as cloudless still as it had been all day. Beside him stood another elderly figure, his wife. He repeated his question. For the moment Elizabeth and I were paralysed.

It was Elizabeth who found the way out. Speaking for the first time, she brought out clearly and with emphasis a phrase which we were to find among the most useful we had conned in preparation for this trip. It had not dated; its meaning was manifest; its effect was always to break the spate of words and reduce the speaker's remarks to fundamentals. It consisted of three simple words, three gold coins which we turned

over in our pockets a hundred times in the early days of our
travelling:

"*Jeg forstår ikke,*" said Elizabeth, firmly. "I do not understand."

Blessed words, those! A confession of weakness, no doubt;
but better to confess the weakness than, foolhardily, accept
speech that we could not translate, and so, perhaps, find ourselves in a situation from which we should be too late to
extricate ourselves. It was the first, but a long way from being
the last, time that Elizabeth saved the day.

The little man's face lit up as though a lamp had been
placed behind it. Without more ado he broke into halting
American-English. Forty years ago, he told us with pride, he
had lived for a while in the United States of America. The
language he had learned in those far-off days had come to our
rescue now! Would he be so good as to act as interpreter
for us, we asked him. There was nothing he would like better.

Briskly he trotted up the marble stairs ahead of us, anxious
to be of service. Never did interpreter enjoy himself more,
or feel a greater pride in his ability. Norwegian phrases
flickered to and fro through the glass window of the reception-
office; somewhat more halting English phrases were exchanged
between us; and in the end we learned what the smiling girl
in blue had been trying to make us understand: that she was
merely deputizing for the official receptionist, who would be
back at 6.30, spoke excellent English, and would no doubt
find us just the accommodation we were seeking.

There is a tiny postscript to this. The following morning,
as we sat in our beautifully furnished room, there was a discreet tap at the door. I opened it, to admit the little man of
the previous evening, umbrella and all. Hat in hand, he had
come to inquire whether we had been comfortable, whether
there was anything else we might care to ask him to do
for us, and to wish us a pleasant trip when we set out on our
travels.

So charmed were we by his arrival, his old-fashioned courtesy, his insistence that what he had done for us was the merest
nothing, that neither Elizabeth nor I remembered what we
had fully intended to do: to ask him why he had accosted us

in the first place, and what was the question he had put to us. Now we shall never know. That, and the mystery of the couple who greeted us and vanished at a breath, must remain for ever a part of the fantasy which was our experience that first evening as we prowled the sunlit streets of Bergen.

BERGEN

Bergen has its parks and open squares, notably the Nygards-pårken and Ole Bull's Plass, but the meeting-place for every-one is, of course, the famous Torvet, the open-air Fish Market. Here, on week-days, under the eye of the statue of Ludvig Holberg and backed by the swaying masts of the small boats, the fishermen stand with their boxes and tanks of fish. There is a great flashing of oft-honed, broad-bladed knives, and heads and tails fly in the air and thud to the ground as the staple food of western Norwegians changes hands. In the tanks, fish are alive, swimming furiously or brooding sullenly at the lack of *lebensraum*, until a muscular forearm dips, strong fingers clutch, and the shining creature is withdrawn for approval and swift death. So swift are the movements of fingers and knife that it is not always clear whether the fish is gutted and wrapped before or after life has fled.

In the evenings, and at holiday times, men and tanks and chaffering customers are gone and the Torvet is given over to a series of hot-gospellers and others; it becomes, in minia-ture, another Hyde Park Corner. The only difference that we could see was that there is no heckling. The crowd, though eternally shifting its stance, its size and its shape, was good-humoured but non-committal. Elizabeth and I found a café with an immense window filling the whole of the seaward wall. From our table in the middle of it we overlooked the Torvet and, as we sipped the first of innumerable glasses of ice-cold milk and toyed with pastries of a quality we hardly remembered, we could watch all that went on.

A stout man sat on a stool plucking at a curious, wire-stringed instrument. The window was closed, and we could not hear what sort of noise it made; nor could we hear the voice of the stout woman alongside him, who alternately harangued the shifting audience and drew snatches of music from an instrument with which, for the rest of the time, she gesticulated. The only lookers-on who registered anything positive by way of interest were three diminutive boys, wearing knee-breeches and the blue-and-white knitted caps which are worn by all and sundry from two years old to middle age. These leaned their elbows on the corners of the small table at which the stout man sat and gazed impassively upwards into his expressionless face. At intervals one of them would reach over and pluck an additional note or two from his strings.

When this came to an end an immensely tall, rake-like individual with a skin-tight, navy-blue reefer jacket and trousers appeared magically from nowhere, brandished a small black book above his head and broke into speech so powerfully that we could hear his voice booming through the closed window, against the rattle of coffee-cups and the tinkle of the till. He had hardly begun to speak when a large-bosomed woman in a double-breasted coat and skirt unfolded a canvas stool, sat down upon it, conjured apparently from the air a small portable harmonium and, with her head upturned towards her companion, whom she never ceased to watch with a quite astonishing fixity, broke into occasional random chords. We could not hear these, but they attracted the immediate attention of the small boys, who approached without hesitation and propped themselves immobile along the back of the harmonium, their chins resting on its ledge. At intervals one of them would reach over with one hand and, we could only suppose, depress a key and extract, without the necessity of pedalling, a prolonged and high-pitched note.

This really was too good to miss, and we paid for our milk and pastries and went across to have a closer view. The tall orator was in full spate, his knuckles white as he clenched and brandished the book above his head, his voice carrying the resonance of water breaking into a cave on the sea-shore, urgency and passion dominating even his pauses. If ever there was an apostle of hell-fire-and-eternal-damnation, this was he; and in Norwegian it seemed even more frightening than it would have been had we been able to understand what he was saying.

Then, as suddenly as he had begun, he ended. The hollow thundering of his voice ceased as though turned off at some main; the black book was thrust into his jacket pocket; the stool was folded; the small boys fell away as the harmonium was gathered up and packed into itself; the Torvet was free to the next comer, whoever he might be.

A warm, glowing light lay over the water and the streets and buildings and open places of Bergen. It was hard to believe that this was, in fact, a city of more than a hundred thousand inhabitants: it had the air of a small seaport on holiday; there was a universal sense of leisure. Couples strolled, small families gathered to consider which way they should amble next; children walked with their parents, sedately, without noise; the only policemen we saw in all Norway, two tall men in dark cloaks, paced leisurely through the crowd, deep in quiet conversation; an occasional yellow tram jangled its bell as it took the turn by the Torvet, bound for one or other extremity of this city-in-miniature; silent taxi-cabs sped nimbly among the people strolling the streets.

The sun was setting out to sea and its warm radiance lit the tree-clad slopes carrying the funicular to the summit of Mount Flöien, almost a thousand feet above us. Looking back over our shoulders, we could see, silhouetted against the sky, *Venus*'s black funnels with their three white bands. We looked out for any of her passengers who might, like us, be taking a stroll in the lingering evening. Perhaps we might run into the couple whom we had dubbed "Gertie and Friend"—two twenty-five-year-old girls wearing kilt and windbreaker, knee-length golf-stockings, but light-weight shoes, apparently quite oblivious to the fact that, with their build, they could not have chosen a less becoming rig. But we did not see them.

Nor did we see any of the Americans who had been here, there and everywhere throughout the crossing. One we remembered particularly: a thin, scholarly individual wearing a sober grey suit, wide-brimmed hat and a most exotic tie of hand-painted silk. He had been drunk for the last long

25

hour before we tied up. Drunk, not with the spirits which could be bought so easily and so cheaply in the saloon bars, but with the riot of colours that made up the coastal scenery of Norway as we approached. He wielded the most expensive and desirable camera I have ever seen or hope to see (one that excited in me a quite frightening cupidity) and unceasingly muttered as he dodged about the ship that never again would he be content with monochrome. How many shots he took I do not know, but spool after spool of film recording the deep-sea greens and blues, and the reds and oranges and russets and purples and yellows, must have been taken and emptied into his capacious pockets in that last magical hour of the trip.

I, who had believed that no colours could ever match the exquisite blues and greens of the west coast of Eire, was forced to question my belief. Forced, too, to ask myself whether my own oft-stated conviction that colour is not worth using until it can be processed more truly was any more tenable. Rather wryly, I remember how I had come home from abroad some twenty-five years ago and declined to visit a cinema showing one of these new-fangled Talkies, firmly convinced that nothing could replace the best of the then current silent films.

The majority of *Venus*'s passengers had been decanted either into one or other of Bergen's big hotels, or into the train for Oslo. They missed something, in that latter case; for this was an evening in a thousand, with a warmth and radiance I think I shall never forget. Bergen is said, so far as weather is concerned, to be the " Manchester " of Norway. Lying on the seaward side of a curving range of high hills, it is a trap for all the rain-clouds that cannot be bothered to climb farther inland before they break. So, this radiant evening of our arrival must stand out as memorable even in the view of Bergen folk, who for once could leave behind them their umbrellas, their mackintoshes and their waterproof leggings, and sally forth in their lightest apparel.

This wearing, by men, of light garments has, I am sure, a strong psychological effect. It is seen at its most emphatic, I suppose, in the Americans, who seem (if we are to believe the cinema) to spend most of their time jacketless. Freedom of movement of arms and torso results when the jacket is hung up in the wardrobe; there is a sense of liveliness, of preparedness for anything. When the belt is substituted for the braces some new access of energy and resource is felt by the trousered male.

We noted, among the Bergen folk, this absence of jackets, this addiction to belts. We noted the prevalence of plus-fours —or rather, a modified plus-four. The garment suggested that all the thousands of pairs that had lain on outfitters' shelves when the vogue in England generally died away had been shipped to Bergen and donned by thousands of men who were slightly longer in the leg than English wearers. We noted, too, the longish hair worn by most men. Yet there was an extraordinary number of barbers' shops in Bergen, as in every other town we passed through. How do these barbers make their living, when hair is worn so long and cut so infrequently? Do Norwegians patronize them solely for shaving? That might explain how the barbers contrive a livelihood, for in three weeks I did not see a single Norwegian moustache. May be there is a governmental ban on the sale of razors to private individuals?

We slept that night for the first time in our lives in Norwegian beds. *On* Norwegian beds, might be a more accurate statement. All the softness was above, rather than below, the sleeper. These beds were the precursors of many beds in which we slept. Though the wood of which they were made, and their ornamentation, might vary between a Bergen hotel and a *gjestgiveri* in some remote country district, their basic principle remained the same: two side-boards and two end-boards producing a rigid rectangle not many inches longer than a coffin and only a foot or so wider at best. If the bedding was solid you did not feel the upper edges of those side-boards; if it was soft, and you were unfortunate enough to roll to one side or other within the strait limits of the bedstead, then some portion of you made decisive contact with that hard resistant upper edge.

All the luxury, if one may be permitted the word in a land so Spartan, is to be found in the *dyne*. This is a sort of eiderdown, not quite so awkward to deal with as the French *duvet*, but quite awkward enough. It is nearly the length of the bed, and about two-thirds as wide. When you have lain down you pull it up and over you and, if you are wise, thereafter lie very still. If you turn to left or right the eiderdown turns with you, to expose your back to any wandering draughts; if you seek to tuck it in behind you (no mean acrobatic feat), then your knees and chest are immediately exposed. You simply have to decide which part of you is most deserving of protection.

In hot weather, such as we experienced practically throughout our stay in the country, this did not matter over-much; but there were, among the Jotunheims, some chilly nights, and it was then that this devilish contraption proved most exasperating. Neither side would tuck in; if the end were tucked in, then one was bare half-way down one's chest; with feet drawn up, the confounded thing was not wide enough to do its duty amidships. I always meant to ask some Norwegian how, in really wintry weather, he manages to avoid frozen nose or toes, but the opportunity never came my way. In any case, almost every room we entered, either to eat or to sleep in, possessed a grandiose cast-iron stove: doubtless these were kept permanently stoked as soon as the cold weather came along, and with thirty or forty square feet of red-hot cast-iron, probably even these *dyner* would prove superfluous!

Elizabeth did not share my somewhat jaundiced view of the object I have been discussing. Slimmer than I by many inches, and shorter by nearly a foot, she found them ideal. At the end of a long day's walking, perhaps far above the snow- and timber-line, she would snuggle down with a sigh of utter content; long before I had worked out the latest-to-date scheme for mastering my *dyne*, she would be sound asleep. In the morning her *dyne* would be lying unruffled along her slim length, having slumbered as peacefully as she herself had done. If she had had her way (and the necessary *kroner*) she would have bought a *dyne* and packed it into my rucksack, at the expense of everything else I had carried with me for a thousand miles or so, and would be using it here in England with complete content.

I suspect that the average Norwegian, though perhaps not as hardy as his Viking forbears, despises luxury; despises even the warm intimacy of the connubial bed. I did not see one double bed during all my stay. Doubtless they were to be found in the bigger hotels, where the tourists spend their money, but they were not to be found in the small *pensjonats* where we put up. Twin-bedded rooms ordinarily had those forbidding pieces of furniture placed in diagonally opposite corners. We saw many of their prototypes in open-air museums such as those at Bygdöy and Lillehammer. In these, the bedding may have been hay, but they were snugger (if less hygienic) than those offered to us. On a really cold night, with snow swirling against the log walls and wind threatening to lift the turf from the roof and send the chimneys spinning across the wide valley, there must have been a good deal to be said for sleeping *en famille* in one of those old hay-beds, box-like and deep and dark.

When our saviour of the night before turned up after breakfast to ask us how we fared we saw that he still carried his umbrella, and this time with good excuse. The brilliant sunshine and great heat of the preceding day had given place to torrential rain and clouds so low that the last outliers of Bergen's residential quarter, climbing among the firs on the lower slopes of Mount Flöien, were hidden in mist. We donned our oilskin macs and sou'westers and sallied forth into the streets that, only nine hours before, had been bathed in sunshine. Water poured down the gutters, trickled in the cracks between the cobbles, overflowed from the eaves and, spouting above us, bounced off the flagstones like a million small transparent peas. The few people who were abroad that morning wore oilskins and carried umbrellas, too. The blue of last night's water was grey and stippled under the myriad shining rods of rain. Passing *drosjes* flung up wings of water from the road, and the tram-wheels squirted out in front of them little feather-edges of spray along the gleaming rails.

The Torvet, scene of such entrancing activity last night, was now a sheet of thin, grey water, across which an occasional figure sped. Our ears caught the sound of singing and we paused a moment, tilting our heads forward to throw off an accumulation of rain-water from the curl of our sou'westers.

"Let's find it," said Elizabeth, and together we made for the old Bourse, or Exchange, a stone's-throw from the Fish Market.

It is a fine, lofty building with flagged floor and high stone columns supporting a vaulted roof which carries a series of bold and imaginative frescoes depicting scenes of Norwegian life. As might be expected, the majority of these have to do with the sea. Viking long-ships, and ships more modern, bearded and modern figures, bright apparel, brilliantly painted sails and banners, fill the odd shapes of the roof and walls among the pillars. Beneath all this were gathered together some hundreds of the men and women we had been speculating upon only the previous evening—men and women wearing peaked caps like those of bus-drivers, who crowded the streets and seemed in a high degree of exaltation, for sober Norwegians. They proved now to be members of the far-flung choral societies which had gathered over the week-end to compete against one another in Bergen.

A rostrum was occupied by the conductor of one of these choral units. He was haranguing his members. Then, his remarks at an end, he raised his baton and they broke into a repertoire of national songs, unaccompanied, melodious, stirring. We could not understand anything of what they were singing, though in more than one of their songs the word "Norge" was reiterated, and with such intensity of feeling that it seemed to us to possess almost as much music in its compass as the British word for which it stood.

Other choirs, awaiting their turn, applauded, and took their place when the last song was ended. The conductor stepped down and exchanged a word or two with the next conductor. So, for a couple of hours and more, while the rain sheeted down outside, choir after choir rehearsed and applauded and rehearsed again. There was a constant coming and going through the wide doors; children approached as closely as they could, staring with fingers in their mouths at those singers from whom came such a wealth of music. Now and then, one of them, tiring of the music, would begin to play tiggy among the grown-ups, but some sober individual would check him and the momentary tumult would abate. High over our heads the boldly painted figures ceased hauling nets, launching ships, hewing timber, carving decorations, herding beasts or building log huts on mountain-sides, and looked down on the music-makers below, charmed into immobility.

The Norwegian language does not give the impression of being musical when spoken or sung. Nevertheless, Norwegians are musically minded. We realized this first in Bergen, where these numerous choirs sang such full repertoires, with such evident pleasure and to such a responsive audience. We were to find it again, long afterwards, in Hallingdal. Though we did not know the words, we could sense the pride, the nationalism, in their way of singing, in the idiom of their music; it is paralleled by the Welshman's love of song and his pride of birth, perhaps better than anywhere else.

Rute Bok

The day was immensely long. Mainly, I suppose, because of the steady, relentless rain. Every hour was precious to us, for Norway was not a country we could hope to visit often, with a return fare at little short of £20.

We had arrived with few preconceived notions, except that with the limited time at our disposal we could not hope to visit the much-publicized Land of the Midnight Sun. As usual, the whole venture had started with the collection of some large-scale maps. Spreading them over the floor, edge to edge, Elizabeth and I had worked out a rough route which, with a lot of good management and the sort of luck we usually have, might prove feasible. A curve-sided triangle (is there a geometrical name for this?) based on Bergen in the west, Oslo in the east, and the Jotunheim Mountains in the north: this, we hoped to achieve. With every passing hour of inexorable rain in Bergen our prospects were by that much reduced.

"Let's get to work on the *Rute Bok*," said Elizabeth, firmly, and went along to borrow the hotel copy from the receptionist. This is a most remarkable book. More remarkable, I am inclined to think, than the famous *Indicateur Chaix*, with which, many years ago, I used to plan the most elaborate journeys (some of which I later even made) the length and breadth of France. The Norwegian book has more to it even than the French one. It gives not only all train routes (which are relatively few, since the country lends itself so ill to railway engineering), but steamer routes, coast-wise and along the fjords, ferries, both long-distance on the fjords and short-distance between point and point, and buses. These last are perhaps the most remarkable, if not the most romantic, of the means of transport to be experimented with in Norway. Their drivers, I am certain, have no superiors in the world, and precious few equals, if any. We saw a good deal of them, during those weeks, and it was reassuring to know that all public service vehicles must have their brakes officially tested at frequent and regular intervals. We thought of this particularly during a trip down the hairpin-bends of the Sognefjell road, and up the hairpin-bends that end at Stalheim.

The *Rute Bok* offers most, if not all, of the charms of a well-planned detective story, even to a sort of code. Dark numerals for certain types of transport; lighter numerals for others; italicized numerals for yet others; all in addition to an alphabet-and-a-half of code letters and a splendid array of symbols. There is, of course, no English translation to all this, so that a further pleasant piquancy was given to the exploration we did among its hundreds of pages and thousands of diversified and alternative routes. We learned, too, quite a lot of the language in this hard school.

We learned, incidentally, that just as there are two basic languages in Norway, and variant spellings among the words of each, the spellings changed at two- or five-yearly intervals by some whimsical authority, so there exists a splendid variety of spellings of place-names. Often nothing but guesswork would serve, so that we travelled a section of our route as though in a haze. I think the high spot of all this was when, having decided to take a ferry to a place called Ullensvang, we arrived to find that it was clearly signposted Oppedal. Only the fact that these small ferries run with remarkable time-keeping, and that we arrived at the exact moment on the schedule, enabled us to be certain that we were, in fact, where we had intended to be. If Ullensvang is pronounced Oppedal, then I find increased sympathy for the French student in England who saw the theatrical poster which read: "*Hamlet*: Pronounced Success."

However, we got the hang of our *Rute Bok* after a while, and I think we never savoured a richer triumph than we did when, to make sure that we had not made some ghastly, fundamental mistake, we consulted a Travel Bureau with our planned itinerary and found that we had worked it out flawlessly to the last small detail. Even the man behind the counter was impressed.

The *Rute Bok* is a bulky volume, and renewed in the middle of each month. I carried it in the flat outer pocket of my rucksack untold miles throughout Norway, but we never thereafter used it in such detail. Ultimately, when I was faced with a more than ordinary climb, I abandoned it. I wish now that I had it by me here, with its gay, yellow border and its extravagant complications of routes. I would like to sit, here amid the flatness of Cheshire, and look up some of those routes that run well into five figures—into the six and seven thousands—and see what glorious fjord-and-mountain journey I could plan for Elizabeth and myself to take, in the comfort of two armchairs.

. . . .

Somewhere near Trengereid we got out and stretched our legs. For nearly two hours the long, sky-blue bus had growled its way from the gentle slopes behind Bergen to the steeper slopes that marked the cutting between Ulriken and Gulfjell and so to the snow-line and the watershed midway between Bergen and the little hamlet of Norheimsund, on Hardangerfjord. Growled, because not many miles out of Bergen the driver had stopped his bus, deliberately engaged a very low gear, and then sat back to swing us at an unvarying gait from sea level to something like two thousand feet.

He was driver and conductor in one, as were all the long-distance drivers we encountered. A dour individual, unsmiling, undemonstrative, as machine-like as the powerful engine he controlled. Indeed, the only sign he gave that he was, in fact, a human being was when he stopped the bus, half-turned, and pointed out of the window to the precipitous road we were about to take, downhill to Hardanger. It clung, this narrow, hard road, like an eyebrow to the sheer side of the hill from which it had been hewn. On our right, the slope of the hill continued, not far short of vertical, out of sight, separated from our vehicle by a kerb ten inches high, or may be just a foot. How great the drop was we could not tell from where we sat; but at least we knew that if we did chance to burst an off-side front-wheel tyre, or suffer a fractured track-rod, it would matter little to the twenty or thirty occupants of the bus whether the drop was five hundred or five thousand feet.

Ahead of us was the first road tunnel we had seen: hewn out of the solid rock to take our mountain road safely beneath the spring avalanches. It was bus width, hardly more, and dark as a whale's throat. When it engulfed us our driver switched on his side-lamps, and they made about as much difference to the darkness as if two tame glow-worms had been riding on his bumper tips.

"What," Elizabeth asked me in an ill-controlled whisper, "what happens if we meet another bus?"

It was one of those questions to which there can hardly be an answer. I was surprised to find that I myself was suffering no qualms—I who am the world's worst passenger, and critical of everyone's driving but my own. We were out of the snow-shed before I could think up a reassuring answer, and when we came to the next one we felt better because we had triumphed once over a hypothetical danger.

I suppose there must be some system of timing by which the drivers know that at a given hour they have right of way. Certainly we met a dozen or so of these powerful buses, but never once at a point on the road where it was impossible to pass. May be these drivers are gifted also with second-sight, and can see, through a million tons of granite, just where the reverse-direction bus is on the route, and at what precise speed it is travelling. Perhaps it was continuous calculation of this sort that accounted for the almost inhuman aspect of our driver.

He mellowed somewhat when at last, having left the snow-fields far behind us and branched away from the furiously tumbling snow-water, we ran into more level country. Here a farm or two, or even a cluster of small timber dwellings, gave us a change of landscape. Now the bus took on the character of an English rural bus. People waited at the road-side, collected packages from the bus and handed over others. A small, sealed mailbag was delivered to a small boy, who scooted up a path with it and entered a minute post office, in-distinguishable from other dwellings save that it carried the bright red-and-gold bugle which is the Post Office badge in Norway. Elderly people alighted or entered; children divested themselves of miniature rucksacks and deposited them on the ample racks which line the sides of all public vehicles, whether on road or on rail.

One thing only distinguished the atmosphere from the rural bus journey in England: here, as everywhere, there were the minimum of words and gestures. Soberness was upon us all. There is a certain innate withdrawnness about the Norwegian, man or woman, old or young. If the Englishman is accounted by Americans and others reti-cent and uncommunicative, he is garrulous and expansive by contrast here. It is particularly noticeable in all public places such as restaurants and buses and railway stations: it is most rare to see anyone making any sort of disturbance by gesture or by sound. Enter a café where a dozen men may be playing cards over their cups of excellent coffee: not one of them will look up, even though with a Union Jack in the strap of your rucksack you are most evidently a foreigner. No one listens to hear what you order, or watches to see how you handle your knife and fork, or speculates as to your destination. The temperature of the room, the quiet murmur of low-toned conversation, does not vary by a degree or a note.

A Dane whom we met at Haugastöl was visiting Norway for the first time. A native of a small, flat country, he was staggered by the mountain ranges, the gigantic indentations, of the land he was visiting. He was no less staggered, it appeared, by the taciturnity of its inhabitants. Compared with his own gay land, he told us, it was as though all these people were at a funeral. And then, warningly: "Sweden is many times worse!"

It may be so. We have not been to Sweden, and the only Swedes we know come much later into this story. But if they are really more sober and unsmiling than the Norwegians they must be a strange race. Nevertheless, I know that library shelves will show half a dozen light-hearted travel books on Denmark and Sweden for every one (if there yet is one) on Norway. I think particularly of those two delightful volumes, Monica Redlich's *Danish Delight* and Katherine and Romilly John's *Lodgers in Sweden*.

Eight *kroner* apiece, that three-hour bus journey of fifty-six miles cost us, and it was money well spent. Well spent because it gave us our introduction to bus travelling in Norway and a swift glimpse of the distant snowfields and mountain-tops that we were later to know more intimately and more hazardously; and also because it was exciting enough to compensate for the wrench we felt at leaving Bergen. We had fallen in love with the little town and were very glad that we were to return to England from the same Skoltegrunnskaien, rather than by the Oslo route. Throughout our inland journey we talked from time to time of the delights that awaited us there, and of how we should feel when, a thousand miles between our departure and our return, we once more trod its cobbled streets.

HARDANGER

As we approached Norheimsund we saw close to, for the first time, Hardangerfjord. Everybody who has ever written about the Norwegian fjords has his own choice among the many, and will defend this or that against those others. If Hardanger stands high in our memories it may be just because it was the first fjord we saw. Later we were to see Sörfjord and the much greater Sognefjord, and branches of these to which our map gave no names. Each had, and retains, its own especial claim on our affection, and this is no place in which to sing the merits of one over the others. Nevertheless, if some generous individual were to offer us a second trip to the Norway fjords, we should be hard put to it to decide whether to visit, this time, those which we did not see before, or to pay a longer and more lingering visit to those few which we saw for all too short a time.

In spite of the length and spectacular quality of the journey we had made between Bergen and Norheimsund, we arrived punctual to the minute at that little fjord hamlet, and were dropped outside the tourist hotel. The rain of Bergen had turned to thin snow at the summit near Trengereid, where buses from each terminus meet and drivers and passengers have time for a cup of coffee in the windswept restaurant. When we reached Norheimsund it was rain once more: thin, rather tired rain, a little shame-faced, perhaps, because it was doing so much to mar a supremely lovely landscape.

We took one look at the tourist hotel, turned our backs upon it, and walked through the rain to the little bridge the bus had passed by at the end of our journey. There we turned right, away from the little line of shops that made up the main street of Norheimsund.

How many scores of times things have worked out in this way for me I just do not know. I have written of them in *And Far Away* and *The Road Before Me*, and more recently in *Turf Beneath My Feet*. Occasionally carping readers have challenged me, and expressed a selfish desire that I would not so complacently (as they assert) describe my luck with stopping-places. I do not intend to sound complacent; but the fact remains that, perhaps more often than any one man deserves in half a lifetime of wandering about the country without taking any thought for day's-end problems, I have fallen—I was going to say upon my feet. I mean, rather, into the comfort and ease that a man looks for at the end of a hard day's cycling or walking or scrambling. I think now of Tan Hill, of Selattyn, of Etal, of Woolstone, of a hundred homely inns and farms and cottages where food was abundant and hospitality unstinted.

It was so again, in Norheimsund. Elizabeth and I walked three hundreds yards, not speaking. We bore right over the bridge, and came upon what I think is the only *pensjonat* in the village, the Nordtopp.

The word calls perhaps for explanation. The phrase *en pension* carries a certain connotation for holiday-makers, and not always a happy one. In Norwegian towns of any size there are hotels for tourists on graduated levels of splendour and luxury. Then come the *pensjonats,* where you may stay for a night, or a week-end, or longer. You have a bedroom, the use of a lounge and the usual offices, and a dining-room for meals: *frokost,* or breakfast; *middag,* or dinner, the main meal of the day and still so called whether eaten at two in the afternoon or eight in the evening; and *aftens,* or supper: a lighter meal to be had any time between, say, five o'clock and nine o'clock in the evening.

At these *pensjonats* you will sleep well, eat well, live well, if simply. Your bedroom will be spic and span, white painted, simply furnished, well lit by wide windows (how the Norwegians love window-spacing!) and by electric light. The linen will be spotless, whether on table or on bed. The floor will be polished wood, either varnished or painted, very often a battleship-grey which sets off well the gay, loosely woven native rugs. The only unsightly object will be the cast-iron stove, often standing almost ceiling-height, black-leaded to perfection, but hardly a thing of beauty or ornament.

Lower in the scale comes the *gjestgiveri,* and then the *hyrre-berge*: the Guest House and the—well, just what is one to call it? Clearly the word is cognate with *auberge,* but the *hyrreberge* is not the equivalent of the English inn or the French counterpart. These offer you the same sort of hospitality as the *pensjonat,* but on two lower grades of elegance. The linen is clean, the floors polished, the china gleaming, if perhaps a little thicker. The choice of dish may be smaller, but that is by no means certain. Throughout our wanderings we stayed at places such as these, and never once did we strike unlucky.

It has to be admitted that in England one cannot always be assured of cleanliness and hygiene if one goes elsewhere than to a listed hotel (and not absolutely always then). In smaller places, even before the problems of catering licences and staff wages arose, meals could be very inadequate, very dreary, and not always cheap at that. Among these lower-grade resting-places in Norway we found the standard uniformly good. The Norwegian Tourist Association grades these places, laying down prices for accommodation and for meals, and standards which are continually checked. This is an admirable form of control.

The Nordtopp was our introduction to these small country *pensjonats*, and typical of most. When we asked whether there was a room for us we were shown up a narrow, winding staircase into a spotless bedroom with wide windows on two sides and its own glass-surrounded balcony actually over the water, giving a view eastwards straight across Hardangerfjord to the snow-capped mountains that made the horizon. The floor, of highly waxed grey paint, had two small, bright, folk-weave rugs, one beside each of the two narrow box-beds in opposite corners. An electric fire was switched on for us. There was a reading-lamp at the head of each bed. A wash-basin (running water in bedrooms is uncommon, though we encountered that amenity in the unlikeliest of places) with decorated jug stood against the stove: snug washing in winter, no doubt, with the hiss of soapy water splashed on to red-hot iron! A small table, two basket-chairs and two bedroom chairs and a fitted cupboard completed the furniture.

There was a card pinned to the wall beside the door, indicating the statutory charge for the room, per night. Here it was eight *kroner* for the double room; we sometimes had to pay as much as twelve. Four shillings, or six shillings, per head per night, plus meals! Even though, once or twice, we stayed at a rather more spectacular type of hotel, we averaged throughout our stay almost exactly ten shillings for supper, bed and breakfast, each of us. There was a small item which we did not at first understand. An extra *krone* was chargeable for the first night only of a stay. This was a comparatively new supplementary charge to cover laundry, and did not vary whether one stayed at a *pensjonat* or a five-star hotel. It was thus possible to calculate in advance, to within a few *öre*, just what one's accommodation and meals would cost; and there was always the comfortable certainty that the standard would be excellent, wherever one found oneself.

The Nordtopp gave the impression of actually growing out of the water of the fjord. Leaning from the balcony window, we looked straight down into deep water. Raising our eyes, we saw rainbows forming against the distant hill slopes, for it was raining still; but by the time we had had a meal and returned to our room the rain had magically departed and the white snowfields on the far side of Hardanger had become visible. We could have leaned out over that window-ledge to the end of time, so entrancing was the view that evening. What wind there had been had dropped, and the smoke of my pipe curled upwards, unbroken, to disintegrate in the stillness of the warm evening air. To our right was the little bridge we had crossed not so long before; beyond it, the first houses of this one-street hamlet. And ahead of us, a couple of hundred yards distant in a straight line, was the little wharf, the timber warehouse, the toy crane, and the wheeled gangway used each time the ferry-boat serving Hardangerfjord made a call.

I have said that the house gave the impression of growing straight up out of the water. The impression is just. It was increased, however, when Elizabeth made her careful inquiries about toilet facilities. It is perhaps as well that we should settle this aspect of Norwegian life once and for all, and in clear-cut terms. The Norwegians seem to be an exceedingly cleanly race: clean clothing and personal cleanliness, whether in town or in country, are everywhere in evidence. There is, of course, water and to spare. But they retain one blind spot, and a visiting Englishman is likely to feel about Norwegian plumbing as the American feels about ours.

The *Norge Hoteller,* a volume second only in usefulness to the *Rute Bok,* has a clear entry in a special column showing exactly how many W.C.'s (if any) each listed hotel possesses. After the hotels come the *pensjonats,* but unhappily the rural ones are not included. We quickly learned that whatever the other amenities might amount to, that of indoor sanitation was so rare as to be an event. In one small *pensjonat* on the fringe of the Jotunheim Mountains we had running water in our bedroom; but the W.C. (or V.C., as the Norwegians rather startlingly call it) was hidden away, a grim wooden lean-to shed backing on to the byres in which the owner's few cows were tethered fifty yards from his back door.

Here at the Nordtopp it was not quite as bad as that. The toilets (there were two of them, companionably placed side by side) were in a little annexe. A path beneath some small birch trees led to them. Having shut the door behind one, and removed the wooden disc by its polished knob, one stared vertically downwards—to the fjord itself some twenty feet below! I had encountered this sort of thing before, near the condemned cells in (I think) the fortress on Mont St. Michel. The upward draught of water-cold wind was disconcerting, and inhibiting, even on a warm evening such as we enjoyed in Norheimsund; in colder weather I suspect visits to that little self-contained annexe were a formidable experience. Perhaps that is why, as so often, they were built in couples, so that one might have moral support from a companion in distress!

Even when, as in Odda and one or two other places, there was indoor, water-flushed sanitation, the chances were very small that the system would be operable. For all the wealth of water which Norway possesses, in running, static and descending form, the use made of it in this one intimate connection is quite deplorably inadequate. I remember a cameraman I once worked with on a story in a remote country district. He suffered from an unpredictable digestive system as a result of Army experiences out in the Middle East. Time after time he used to say, shaking his head lugubriously: "I've lost my inspiration again this morning," and resort to pills. I, with a finely balanced internal economy, can sympathize. Fortunately, Norway, or certainly those regions we were exploring, is notably rich in empty landscapes; a return to Mother Nature is preferable to accepting a makeshift human artifice.

FJORD FERRY

A brilliant sun flooded through the wide, deep windows of our bedroom at an astonishingly early hour. The previous evening Elizabeth, not to be outdone by some of the more spectacular Norwegian sentences with which I had bombarded people in Bergen, tried out a most elaborate inquiry about the morning ferry we intended to take along Hardangerfjord to Utne. She knew that she could never stand up to question-and-answer, and that her nerve would probably fail her unless she got it all off in one tremendous burst. I wish now I had written down the sentence she worked out, rehearsed, and eventually sprang on a woman in the doorway of a bakehouse.

I know it involved exact hour of departure, place of departure, route and destination and what-were-the-chances-of-its-being-before-its-time? How Elizabeth did it I have never found out. Organization has always been her strong point (and a weak one of mine); her mind works clearly, gripping essentials and ignoring irrelevancies. So for my part I stood aside, not wishing to confuse her either by ill-concealed mirth if things went awry or by admiration if she got away with it.

Get away with it she did. She returned to me, her face glowing beneath her gipsy head-scarf, to inform me that the boat might arrive before time, but would definitely not leave before time; that it hailed from Bergen and was bound for Utne and beyond and that there would undoubtedly be room for us on board; that we could if we wished get something to eat and drink on board; that the actual point of embarkation was the wharf we could see from our window. There were times, afterwards, when I was ungenerously inclined to suspect that she had been taking a long chance and relying on luck; that it was all a process of wishful-thinking, to be proved or disproved when morning came. Certainly it was many days before she undertook such a formidable piece of research all on her own again: perhaps the effort plumbed her resources to their modest depths and she needed time to stock up again.

Whatever the truth may have been, punctual to the minute the little fjord ferry *Voeringen* tooted her siren and swung round the bend to tie up at Norheimsund's quay. We, having settled our absurdly modest bill for 18 *kroner*, 95 *öre*—9/6 each—for a substantial supper, bed, and more than adequate breakfast, including the surcharge for laundry, were awaiting her arrival at the quay. We stood there in morning sunshine so bright that we could not look at the distant snow-clad hilltops towards which we would soon be travelling. Twenty yards from us was the tourist hotel. Its residents and guests were still in their bedrooms, missing the gold of the morning. There were no other passengers waiting to go aboard, but there was merchandise of various kinds, and two small, agile lads in knickerbockers and hand-knitted pullovers and tas-selled caps stood by the toy crane, prepared to load and unload.

Most of the merchandise consisted of sacks, wooden crates, barrels and drums, a roll or two of wire-netting and a bundle of hay-rakes. But a little apart from the rest of it there was a covey of brand-new spinning-wheels, made in butter-yellow wood, each with its neat label of origin and destination. I was glad that I had spotted these in time, for they made, with their queer assortment of circles and angles, of turned spindles and shapely treadles, a fascinating pattern of light and shade. Without comment or lifted eyebrow from the people on the quay, I had rearranged the four spinning-wheels to the best advantage, and I took my photographs without fuss or palaver, squatting low on a bale of fish-netting for one shot and balanc-ing on a crate for another.

There was an engaging absence of fuss about the arrival and departure of *Voeringen*. The tinkle of a bell, the soft hiss of a rope being thrown adoitly to a waiting crooked arm to be made fast to a bollard, the slight commotion of a screw put astern with the rudder hard over to swing the boat close alongside; that was all. No shouting, giving and counter-manding of orders, no hoarse instructions and yelled acknow-ledgments. Two seamen opened a rail to make room for the end of the wheeled gangway which was trundled competently to the edge of the quay by two small efficient boys. A youthful officer came to the head of the gangway, a few papers in his hand, exchanged a nod with the postmaster, who had just come down to the quay with a sealed mailbag and exchanged it for another, and then retired to his office below the bridge. A derrick was swung overboard and picked up in one haul the whole of the merchandise except for the spinning-wheels, which were carried individually on board. The two boys who had been hoping to operate the wharf-side crane may have been disappointed but they did not give any sign.

Perhaps the scene would have been livelier with badinage, the give-and-take of comment and ribaldry, that one would have listened to almost anywhere else; but this near-silent operation had something peculiarly satisfying about it, and though it was but the first of a dozen or more similar calls, the smoothness and adroitness of its working never ceased to fascinate me.

Elizabeth and I went aboard, bought two tickets from the officer, dumped our rucksacks on a seat and took possession. This was our introduction to what must be for most people, and certainly was for us, the most characteristic mode of travel in this generously watered country: travel by fjord ferry. For the next three hours or so we were to zigzag along the narrowing waters of Hardangerfjord, calling first at one small port and then at another, until we reached Utne, the next stage in our planned itinerary.

No sooner had we cast off and reached open water again than we became aware of snow-capped hills in all directions. There were those we had dimly seen during that spectacular bus trip the afternoon before; there were those we had gazed at, lit by a westering sun, from our balcony window—those which were the fringe of Folgefonna, one of our ambitious dreams; and there were others, continually appearing, vanishing and reappearing, as our little craft headed in and out of the creeks and inlets of Hardanger, at the end of which lay Öystese, or Herand, or Bjölvefoss, or Vines. Tiny hamlets, every one of them, and all put together, it seemed to us, out of the same box of bricks. A neat wharf with wooden piles, sleeper-floored and backed by a tiny waiting-room; a two-storey warehouse, with hoist and sill, obviously for storing grain; five (or it might be ten or fifteen) small wooden houses behind the wharf; a port-master with a peaked cap to distinguish him from the knitted-cap wearers young and old; a sprawl of merchandise to put on board; a gaggle of young boys, hands deep in the pockets of their knickerbockers, superintending after their fashion the activities of their elders; and, behind it all, colour.

There is always colour in Norway. I do not mean the rich blues and greens of water and sky and tree-clad hills; I mean the man-made colour which is so vital to their lives. Bright paint wherever bright paint can be applied: to walls and window-frames, doors and rails and steps—blues and yellows and lush-greens and signal-reds and a lavish use of white and cream and the darkest crimson. And, besides all this paint, the flowers. Gardens are small or non-existent where the hillside crowds the few dwellings almost off the quayside into deep water; but where there is a window there will be a window-box, or two window-boxes, bright with flowers nodding in the sun or bowing to the breeze. Iron-railed balconies at Öystese were bright with trim flower-boxes laid along the arm-rests, tended with care, riotously blooming.

I have nowhere seen such love of flowers and bright colours as in Norway. Elizabeth holds that it is because so many of the Norwegian winter months spread backward into autumn and forward into spring, and the lack of colour during those grim months, above all in the north where the days are hardly days at all but extensions of deep night, causes men and women to crowd into their all-too-short summer the greatest wealth of colour they can achieve.

One trivial incident at Öystese remains in my memory almost as clearly as the window-boxes (which, after all, we were to see everywhere we stopped, both in Hardanger and farther afield). Braced against the side of our boat on her arrival at Norheimsund were two long, wide thick planks of mahogany. May be they were later to be trimmed to shape and polished to serve as a counter in some bank or shop.

They called for skilful handling. The wharf crane was inadequate, and *Voeringen*'s derrick was called into action. A noose of rope was slipped along the heavy planks until their estimated point of balance was found, and then the winch was set in motion. Two warehousemen took the planks by the hither end and steadied them as they rose over the rail and were swung outboard. But now their control of the planks ended, and they were swinging too high for anyone on the quay to take over. They twisted like some gigantic weather-vane in the air between the boat's side and wharf level, and when they were lowered to the wharf they caught on a bollard, twisted violently with their own weight, and dropped at a dangerous angle.

No one shouted. A hand on deck gestured, and the noise of the winch ceased. But it was too late. Twisting as they descended to the wharf, they hit the solid concrete of which it was built, and I saw for the only time in my life a literal demonstration of the saying that used to fascinate me as a child when a sailor in a pirate story exclaimed: "Shiver my timbers!" One of the great planks, two inches thick and more than a yard wide, split at its lower end as though an invisible wedge had been driven into it. The split may not have been more than a couple of feet long, but its result was to release the pent-up tension innate in the tough wood, and the plank warped like a negative held in a warm, damp hand.

The waiting warehouseman contemplated the plank impassively. I do not know whether it was his, or whether he was merely taking delivery on behalf of someone else. Whoever was to receive the plank now, a quarter of it at least was useless. A plank can warp in no time at all; a warped plank can hardly be straightened and made true. Someone should have shouted, expostulated, apportioned blame, denied responsibility, cursed and sworn. No one did. No one even as much as made a note in a pocket-book, for reference. A man put a brown hand into the wide, twisting crack, vicious with its strands of warped fibre as a crocodile's jaws, shrugged and turned aside. The engine-room bell sounded; someone slipped the noose of the wire hawser off the bollard aft, there was a flurry of water astern, another coiled rope was thrown aboard, and a moment later Öystese with its gay window-boxes and its silent population slid astern of us as we headed in a wide circle for the snow-capped mountains on the other side of the fjord.

Emerging an hour or so later from one of these little secluded ports, we found ourselves heading straight for a lithe grey shape that was silently ploughing the deep water north-eastwards. She was too far away to identify, but one of the sailors, who had passed close to our rucksacks a time or two and fingered our Union Jacks that were stuck in them conspicuously, came for'ard to tell us that she was a British ship, a cruiser carrying eight-inch guns. We realized then for the first time what an ordeal it must have been for these quiet Norwegian folk to find, as they did so suddenly and unexpectedly ten years or more ago, warships bearing the Nazi flag steaming inexorably up these winding inland seaways and making the little deep-water ports their bases for punitive expeditions. We overtook her a day later: H.M.S. *Devonshire*, anchored off Odda at the head of Sörfjord.

We had still a call or two to make, and by the time we swung round the last bend and came within sight of Utne, at the head of the promontory separating Hardangerfjord from the pine-needle-like Sörfjord, the cruiser was out of sight. Even had she been in sight, however, I think we should have been unable to keep our eyes on her, for, as we approached Utne, we found ourselves drawing close to the most spectacular mass of snow-capped heights we had hitherto seen. Just past the entrance to Granvinfjord, one of the small, elusive arms of the mother fjord, towering to four thousand feet almost sheer from the water, was Mt. Oksen. Her immense weight had compressed the rock on which she was founded so that it was, so to speak, squeezed outwards, narrowing the neck of water until it seemed almost possible to leap across from her flanks to the little white cluster of houses, the point-steepled church and the modest timber wharf that made up Utne.

Voeringen tooted her siren and began to swing in towards the wharf. Standing in her bows we looked directly ahead at the mountains that buttressed Hardangervidda—an immense plateau averaging well over four thousand feet above sea level. The mountains, virgin white against the deep, cloudless blue

47

of the sky, passed across our bows to port. Just before we tied up at Utne we caught a fleeting glimpse of another of those alluring fjord arms—the one which pierces the rock masses in the opposite direction to Sörfjord. It leads to Brimnes and the little township of Eidfjord, through which runs the spectacular motor road from Kinsarvik to Haugastöl, though this was not yet opened for its two-month season of use. The water in this fjord is augmented by the ice-water flowing down from the great ice-fields of the Hardangerjökulen, on which Scott's men trained for their ill-fated Antarctic expedition.

UTNE

It would be hard to imagine a greater contrast to those distant ice-capped rock masses than the tiny port of Utne. Here was warmth and homeliness and the serenity, not of isolation amid the splendour of sky and snow, but of rural occupation. We were told that we were just too late to see the famous Hardanger blossom at its most beautiful. If that was really so, then that blossom must have been quite indescribably lovely. Even then, at the end of May, it rivalled the Vale of Evesham and all those celebrated blossoming acres of the south and west of England. Blossom was everywhere. It adorned the fruit trees with voluminous petticoats of whitest hand-made lace; it blew lightly across the lanes and fields at the least breath of air; a myriad soft sequin-petals, spendthrift and gaily air-borne. Utne's small church, with its sharp-pointed spire, was surrounded by blossoming trees, and its walls were so white that it was hardly an idle fancy to suppose that they had been coated by some kindly snowstorm of these same tiny white petals.

We dropped our rucksacks on the wharf and lingered to see *Voeringen* depart, bound for Kinsarvik and the long zigzag route up Sörfjord which we ourselves were to take on the morrow. Then we looked about us. Twenty yards away was a white fence, and beyond that the Utne Hotel. We had not booked a room, though we had known from our map that if we did not find a bed at Utne we should be stranded. There was no sign of life about the hotel, but we walked boldly up to the door and brought out, for the third time since *Venus* docked at Bergen, one of the most important of our phrases: *"Har De et vaerelse for oss?"*

Usually, of course, the time of our inquiry was at the end of the day's walking, and we would add, to round off the question tidily, the word *i-natt*, which seemed to us near enough to "to-night", though we discovered months afterwards that if our phrase-book was to be believed we should have added *i-aften*. Probably if we had known this at the time we should still have used the other word, for there was something more conclusive about it, both in sound and in rhythm, and it was in any case the night rather than the afternoon that was our immediate concern.

Curious, we thought, that at such a delightful spot there should be no visitors. The end of May was surely a most desirable time in which to visit Hardanger: were we the only people to have discovered this little place? It was hard to believe. So it was all the more surprising when the maid we spoke to shook her head dubiously and doubted whether there would be room for us in the hotel. She would, however, go and make sure. Elizabeth and I looked at one another in dismay. Perhaps the explanation was that the hotel was not yet open after the winter? Then the girl returned, with the good news that there was, in fact, one room available, though only for a single night. She led the way upstairs.

The Utne Hotel has character in every square foot of floor and wall. The wooden staircase starts from the middle of the well-windowed hall, spiralling upwards like a wide, painted corkscrew sticking through the rug-strewn floor. A three-quarter turn brought us to a landing lit by a soft lamp, with three short corridors leading off it, lined with numbered bedrooms. There was running water in ours, and a lavatory just along the corridor which functioned perfectly.

Middag was at two o'clock, and we filled up the intervening hour or so by wandering among the trees that filled the spaces between house and house and overflowed almost on to the jetty itself. There was a promising lane running out of Utne to the south-east, flanked by orchards that extended to the water's-edge and up the hillside to the right. Among the trees, hay had been grown, been cut, and was now drying. Not, as in England, drying in long swathes the length and breadth of the field, but draped over taut-strung wires between pole and pole, to catch the wandering breeze and throw off the untimely shower. The hay had been mown close, so that the green field from which it had been lifted to dry was a shaven green sward beneath the trees. Blossom petals had been caught in the fine, hanging hay: a wedding procession might have passed by and left that sweet record of its passing.

Other wires could be seen at the backs of the hotel and the houses, hung with snow-white linen. Never in Norway did we see the long-drawn-out clothes-lines to which we are accustomed at home. Instead, two stout poles, with cross-pieces at the top like low telegraph-poles. Strung between the opposing cross-pieces were four taut wires, and to them was pegged the washing. I am not housewife enough to know whether this would be as effective a manner of drying clothes as the more usual one, but it was certainly both more tidy and more picturesque.

We discovered when we returned for *middag* why there had been only one available room. As we were approaching the hotel a bus and a *drosje* arrived outside it and deposited a hotelful of men and women, mainly Norwegians, but including, as we were soon to find out, nearly a dozen English-women. They had been away all morning, doing a trip along the fjord-side, through the little villages that cling precariously between bastion and deep water, along the west bank of Sörfjord.

After lunch, because we had really done no walking yet worthy the term, and had a considerable amount to do in the next few days, Elizabeth and I took map and camera and a handful of boiled sweets to suck against the heat and dusty-dryness of the road, and set forth to get the feel of country walking. It was a lane that we would gladly have walked for a day and another day at the end of that, if we could have fitted it into our plans. White and dusty, had there been any traffic to raise the dust, firm beneath our feet but not hard enough to jar our heels: in fact, a typical Norwegian country road of the sort we were to come to know and like extremely well.

We walked first through the climbing outskirts of Utne, with its little sloping gardens and bright flowers, then into the more extensive orchards that bounded the road on either side. Men with lengths of hosepipe were spraying their trees with a sweet-smelling insecticide. Sometimes the hosepipes were carried in the fork of two long poles across the road from one side to the other and only the hiss of the spray told us where the men were working. A grey length of hose, motionless in the short grass, would suddenly be jerked by an invisible worker down the hillside or up the hillside among the trees, and a coil or two would come to life like a sleeping snake startled by our approach, straighten out, and vanish behind a hay-fence.

There was no traffic. We saw two bicycles lying against a bush beside the road, but we did not see their owners. We walked through a hamlet or two, each with its jetty and warehouse, its cluster of leisurely folk sunning themselves or occupying themselves with simple tasks in their own time. A sunburnt young man tarred a fence; a bearded ancient sat on a stump of timber, hatchet in hand, splitting small logs into kindling; a woman knitted in a doorway, two tiny children playing on a rug at her feet: this was the tempo of Sörfjord, as, indeed, of nearly all of Norway that we saw. Time has its own markings on the dials of Norwegian clocks.

It would have been fatal to linger in Utne, the atmosphere was too demoralizing. Everything about the hotel and the hamlet of which it was for us and others the focal point, spelt leisure. It occurred to me at one point that it might be an ideal place in which to stay for six months and write a book, but I know that I never should write a book amid such surroundings. How could one bend over a typewriter and quarto paper when there was a sunlit wharf on which to sit and smoke and contemplate an immense curving skyline of high mountain-tops? How bend one's mind to the producing of a daily stint of words when there was deep blue water to plunge into, rock or field or terrace to sunbathe on, stones with which to play an idle game of ducks-and-drakes?

And what could one do in the short hollow hours that intervened between the lavish *frokost*, the long-drawn-out and delectable *middag*, followed by coffee of such ravishing quality that one was ashamed almost to smoke while sipping it, in a deck-chair in the hotel garden or on a bollard on the quay, and the superb *aftens*, at which one helped oneself from one of the most lavishly spread cold-tables that we anywhere encountered? How often, afterwards, when walking along a dry, dusty road, midway between any two points where we could slake our growing thirst, we sighed for that *spécialité de la maison*, its recipe known only, I suspect, to Fröken Aga and her mother, that cordial we drank in unlimited quantities from ever-refilled carafes, in which red and black currant and apple and bilberry juices had been blended with a nice judgment to make a drink the gods on Olympus would gladly have taken in lieu of nectar!

No, we dared not linger. And so it was that, early next morning, Elizabeth and I planted on the wharf our two rucksacks, carefully disposed so that our Union Jacks would challenge the eye, and then sat down to a breakfast over which we would have been content to linger a great deal longer, had we not had the morning ferry to catch.

"AHOY, THERE, *Devonshire*! "

It was as well that we took that precaution, for it happened that there was no one to come ashore at Utne, no one but us to go aboard, and no cargo to be picked up or dropped. The ferry-boat hardly waited to tie up: she sounded her siren, slowed down, paused, and sounded her siren again. On which Elizabeth suddenly realized what was afoot and leapt like a gazelle down the wooden steps of the hotel, raced on to the wharf and uttered a loud and authoritative cry, what time I was still gathering myself together and trying to sip a little more of that delectable coffee which was too hot to swallow at a gulp.

What she called out I do not know, but by the time I arrived she was being helped on board *Skare*, rucksack in hand, having prudently hoisted mine aboard first. There was no gangway down, but the boat was small; in one stride I was over the rail and standing beside her on deck, surrounded by a mass of planking destined for Ullensvang. It would not have surprised me to find the handle of my coffee-cup still clinging to my crooked finger, so swift and impetuous had been our departure from Utne's memorable hotel!

We had thought *Voeringen* a small boat, but *Skare* could almost have been swung from her davits. The first, of course, was a long-distance boat which made a regular trip from Bergen, on the coast, inland among the wide fjords whose waters can be whipped by storms to a condition in which a small boat could easily be wrecked. We did not discover where *Skare* began her journey, but she was headed for Odda, at the terminus of Sörfjord, and I suspect she mainly plied between port and small port along this and other narrow branches of Hardangerfjord.

She was a trim, homely little craft, on which one felt almost any member of the crew could, and willingly would, exchange duties with any other. Indeed, almost as soon as we went aboard, the officer on the bridge vanished, presumably for a leisurely breakfast, and his place at the wheel was taken by a blond lad who cannot long have left his schooldays astern. He steered with assurance, but with just a little less skill than we had noticed on *Voeringen*; at one or two of the wharves he overshot his mark and had to call for reversed engines and indulge in a little manœuvring. As a matter of fact, having regard to his extreme youth, I suspect that this may all have been put on as an act: he would derive more satisfaction from tinkling his engine-room telegraph and making a show of elaborate ship-handling than from that silent, unobtrusive seamanship which had characterized *Voeringen* and was later to be seen here, too, when the officer responsible had downed his last cup of coffee.

A chill wind made itself felt as soon as we rounded the tip of the promontory and began the twenty-five-mile length of Sörfjord. Yesterday's trip had been with a south-west wind due astern of us; now, sailing almost due south, we had the wind on our starboard bow, and to reach us it had to blow over the frozen heights of the Folgefonna snowfield and the bitter glaciers descending from it towards Sörfjord—Buarbre and its lesser kinsfolk. The lad at the wheel motioned to us to come on to the bridge, to shelter behind the glass screens. For a while we did. But it was steam-heated there and we felt cut off from the landscape we were penetrating; we made our excuses, and left.

Sörfjord is little if anything more than a mile wide where it meets Hardangerfjord, just short of Utne. Thereafter it narrows steadily to the tip containing Odda, twenty-five miles distant and out of sight for all the straightness of the fjord. But it was a long twenty-five miles that we travelled aboard *Skare*, for she performed the same zigzag as *Voeringen* had done, from side to side of the fjord, calling at a succession of midget ports to drop a bale or two, pick up a hamper or small crate, deliver a consignment of paint-cans or floor-boarding or slates or coils of galvanized-iron wire. Lads with small trucks, a man with a pony and float, children with a box on wheels or a home-made sledge, would be waiting, each to collect his little load and take it away across the narrow street and up the hillside may be to one or other of the tiny small-holdings we could see from *Skare*'s deck. They perched among trees alongside swiftly falling water that was ice-cold from the glacier five thousand feet overhead; their occupants lived precariously, but, we believed, contentedly enough, remote from what many of us are inclined to call civilization.

We thought we should come in sight of Odda after an hour or two of travelling, for the sun was already high over the Hardangerfjord to our left. But we were almost at Odda before we caught a glimpse of it, for this is an industrial centre, with zinc and carbide works, and a pall of thick, dark smoke lay over the town, spreading on the wind outwards to meet us as we came up the fjord to end our voyage. It was a greeting we would willingly have forgone: a murky reminder that even in so pleasant a land as Norway there must be industry, that the Machine Age has to be recognized.

Odda Bay was alive with heavy whale-boats manned by young naval cadets pulling on the long sweeps under the jaundiced eye of their instructors. They were ploughing through the grey water as though it were thin gruel dragging at their keels. At the mast-head of H.M.S. *Devonshire* lights winked in Morse code, presumably directed at those boats' crews.

"We ought to wave our Union Jacks," said Elizabeth, seized by a surprising burst of patriotism. "Let's get them."

We extricated our six-inch flags from the straps of our rucksacks and flourished them bravely on their cycle-spoke masts, high above our heads. Answer there was none. We were piqued: here in alien waters was a British battleship, being hailed by two English travellers waving the national flag, and no one deigned to reply! We waved more vigorously, stirred to action by the unexpected indifference on board the long, grey vessel. At long last some member of the ship's company removed a hand from his trouser pocket, gave a languid response to our hail, and returned his hand to his pocket, satisfied that duty was done.

Alas! Where was the proud flag we had half expected to see run up to the mast-head in reply to our patriotic gesture? Perhaps it was being carefully preserved to drape the coffin when it should be slipped overboard with the last of Britain's prestige lying dead inside? Elizabeth and I looked at one another a little sadly: gesture calls for gesture, and answer there had been none. We felt a little foolish, as though we had essayed a witty remark and it had fallen wholly flat. We replaced our flags in their straps and slung our rucksacks on our shoulders, for *Skare* was already making fast at Odda's busy quayside. The gangway was run up through our rail; we went ashore.

ELIZABETH'S GLACIER

Already there was a flush on Elizabeth's cheek: we were on the threshold of an adventure that had loomed high in anticipation since we first began to browse through maps of Norway. Her imagination had been fired by a description of Folgefonna, an immense snowfield lying between Sörfjord and Hardanger, from which glaciers' tongues roved downwards, licking at the mountainsides: descendants of those titan ice-sheets that had carved the rock land of Norway into this fantastic pattern of valley, ridge and fjord during a sequence of Ice Ages. There was a track, it seemed, winding upwards from Odda. It would take us on to the snowfield itself by way of one of those down-thrusting tongues of ice, called Buarbre.

"We'd better have our nails renewed and hammered home," said Elizabeth, and we went in search of a shoemaker who would do this for us. In a pocket of my rucksack was a matchbox filled with spare nails, for we did not know what the country's resources would be when we got into the very wildest parts. Then, our soles well studded again, and a light meal beneath our belts, we set off for Buarbre and Folgefonna at two o'clock in the afternoon, leaving our packs in the *hospitz* where we had booked for the night.

As a precaution against dazzle from the ice we carried sun-glasses; we carried our trusty sticks, a sweater each as protection against the cold wind that would meet us as we topped the last rise and found ourselves confronting a waste of eternal snow, a bar or two of chocolate to fortify ourselves against exhaustion, and the usual paraphernalia of camera and exposure-meter and filters and extra film. This, we had been telling ourselves for days and weeks past, was to prove the expedition of all expeditions. Alongside it, that grim walk from Durness to Cape Wrath and back, over more than twenty miles of stony track, with rain falling and a blistered heel and not a scrap of food within us, would seem a mere summer afternoon's stroll. We were not far wrong, in the event.

The route started boldly enough, through the suburbs of Odda, past the zinc works, gently uphill all the way. For half a mile we were on the edge of what we should call a Council House Estate. It was most intelligently planned. The houses were in blocks of four, and no one block was exactly aligned with its neighbour on either side. Though they were all of a similar pattern they had been differentiated by a skilful and imaginative use of paint. The houses were of cream-washed cement for the first storey, with warmer-hued timber above.

But it was the paintwork that gave the houses their gay look of individuality: no two adjacent houses had the same-coloured paint on window-frames, doors or other woodwork, yet none of the colours jarred. They were soft colours: sage-green, dove-grey, a modest blue, a tawny yellow, a not too challenging red. Balcony-rails were painted to match, and there were the invariable gay window-boxes, and pots of flowers behind many of the windows.

As the road climbed the houses thinned out and at last we were clear of Odda, heading west-south-west into the hills, every one of which carried snow on its upper slopes and was linked to Sandven Lake by sheer waterfalls leaping from crag to crag. For a mile or two we walked alongside the lake, then turned away to the right to begin the second and more strenuous lap of our journey.

Here two mountains, Jordalsnuten and Eidesnuten, rise sheer from the gorge that the Jordalselva has been hewing for itself for untold thousands of years. The mountainsides are clothed with conifers wherever these can get a grip and find the earth they need for their roots; elsewhere it is hard, un-compromising rock. The river tumbled beside us all the way, curiously greenish-opaque in hue as a result of being glacier-water. Where it tore its way through the massive whitened boulders in its bed it was like milk-soda; there was a fury about its plunging that spoke of the steepness of its descent and the cruel conditions of its begetting. It levelled out for a short space where we reached the thousand-foot contour, near the isolated farm called Buar on the map; here the beaten track we had been following, wide enough for a pony-trap or jeep, came to an abrupt end. Except for two men working on the roof of an out-house there was no sign of life at all. We lingered, wondering whether, if need should arise, we might be able to get something to eat and drink there on our way back, for clearly it was the last habitable outpost among these forbidding hills.

"Come on," said Elizabeth, "I want to see 'My Glacier'!"

From the beginning it had been so named. The word Folgefonna was good enough for map-makers and ordinary travellers, but for us it was Elizabeth's Glacier. Looking back on it now, the hazards far behind us, I understand what fanaticism can do.

The actual summit, we knew, was about 5,400 feet. This left us a further 4,400 feet still to climb, for at Odda we had been only a few feet above mean sea level. The afternoon was still young and the few miles we had so far walked, on a firm surface gently graded, had but whetted our appetites for something more strenuous. At Farm Buar, then, we began the third lap of our expedition.

Almost as soon as we had left the farm behind us the grass track through a level field changed to a sort of dotted track: five yards of beaten earth, then a scramble over granite boulders, during which one guess as to direction was as good as another, then a further few yards of beaten earth, then more scrambling. As long as it was in clear country it was not difficult, though it became increasingly arduous as the gradient stiffened. But after a while we ran into bushes and stunted trees, and at once problems arose. The boulders increased in size and angularity: clearly they had been pitched down from the summit of the mountain on our side of the river through the action of frost, the weight of accumulated snow and the insistent leverage of tree-roots. The short stretches of hard earth came to an end and there developed a series of mild or difficult scrambles round and over and even under boulders as big as haystacks, but a good deal more resistant.

"Which way now?" I asked for the twentieth time. And for the twentieth time Elizabeth gave the only plausible answer: "To the right. That goes up more than the other, and we shan't get to my glacier till we get to the summit!"

It was exquisitely logical, and may be the very answer I should have given myself if she had put the question; but with every fresh decision of the kind the track, if it could still be called a track, became steeper and less distinguishable from the rest of the rocky terrain through which it supposedly led to the summit. We had lost sight of the sky for a long time past. The sound of rushing water which had been our companion for the first comparatively easy miles had long been lost to us, too, the river-bed having dropped so many hundreds of feet below.

"How's this?" I heard Elizabeth cry out exultantly.

She was twenty yards ahead of me, and going strongly. I got ready to catch my first glimpse of a glacier, though I could hardly believe that we had, since leaving Buar, climbed those remaining four thousand feet and more.

I overtook Elizabeth, poised on a little conical mound, clear of the trees and the vicious tangled undergrowth. Her stick was upraised and she was pointing to a mass of snow and ice that had spread down the corrie at the impulse of the vast snow- and ice-sheet on the summit that was Folgefonna. In the brilliant sunlight of that afternoon it was impossible to look for more than a moment or two at a time without discomfort and perhaps even danger. Elizabeth had donned her sun-glasses; I, slipping the deepest filter I possessed over my lens, prepared to take my first real snow photographs.

Alas, in my inexperience of such subjects those photographs never came within leagues of doing justice to what confronted us. Here, between the black sheer sides of mountain rock on which, under the impact of this strong and persistent sun, snow and ice could not retain their hold, there spread out before us the acres of glacier which was Buarbre. From beneath its lowest tip there crept, invisible and inaudible to us at that distance, the water that became the Jordalselva—that same milky-green torrent which we had followed for so long that afternoon.

We rested our eyes by turning them downwards at the kindly green turf beneath our feet, the first we had seen for many weary miles of rock-scrambling; then we looked again. Behind and beyond and above Buarbre was the Folgefonna snowfield: until we had reached that level we could not step on to ice-hard snow; could not claim that we had really done what we had set out to do.

"Come on," said Elizabeth; "next lap!"

"We'll have to travel lighter, then!" I looked up at the only conceivable route which we could take. "This really *is* going to be a pull."

Regardless of whether it was going to be bitterly cold or

not when we reached the summit we began to pull off much of
what we were wearing. We piled on that little knoll, weighted
down with a heavy stone, our sweaters and scarves, and we
topped the lot with Elizabeth's signal-red jumper. Then we
set out once more.

A smaller stream flowed down alongside us, from some gully
fed by the snowfield high up above us. For a moment we
had toyed with the wild notion of continuing our ascent by
first plunging across the valley to Buarbre itself and then
taking that route to the top. Elizabeth, if left to her own
judgment, would probably have done just that, regardless of
the fact that it would have involved first a steep stony descent
of many hundreds of feet to the tongue of the glacier, with
all those hundreds of feet to be climbed again when she
reached the other side; and then the remainder of the climb
on ice which, at that angle to the perpendicular, could hardly
have been negotiated without an ice-pick. Mercifully for us
both I did not, for once, give her her head.

In half an hour we reached the snow-line. It was nearer
the summit on this side of the valley than on the other because
we were facing south. When we turned to look back the
way we had come, the little cache of garments, with the
jumper flaming like a fiery banner above it, looked so close
that we could almost have reached backwards and touched it.
We had no means of knowing how much higher we had
climbed, but we were learning for the first time how deceptive
distances are, and gradients, too, in the comparatively rarefied
atmosphere of mountains.

I estimated that we had climbed to something over four
thousand feet from sea level, and with every successive twenty
feet there was another ridge to surmount, and no sign at all of
an end to our efforts. But there was, whenever she looked
round at me, a fanatical gleam in Elizabeth's eye; breathless
and clumsy of movement, I continued on my way, having long
ago surrendered to her the right of leadership. It was not for
nothing, I reflected, that she had once been dubbed " Argeli "
—Red Indian for Mountain-goat.

She clambered (it was not true climbing) with agility and no
apparent effort, carrying her neat eight stone with poise and

suppleness and making me feel that, with my thirteen or more stone at war with gravity, I was not cut out at all for this sort of thing. Snow lay in patches where a rock bastion cast a shadow for much of the day, and I tried the foolish trick of sucking a mouthful or two of cold crystals to slake my thirst. The immediate impact on tongue and palate was exquisite, but it turned to something merely clammy and repellent in no time at all, cold white ashes in the mouth.

Our stops to look about us, mainly at my cowardly suggestion, became more frequent, more prolonged. The track had by now become so steep that only by hand-hold where a root projected or an angle of rock was it possible to keep moving at all. We had to choose our points for resting, where a boulder jutted out and could be relied upon. The glacier looked no farther away than it had been when it first came into sight; but the summit which would be Folgefonna came no nearer, for all our frantic efforts to attain it. I wished I had an altimeter: it would, I told myself, be worth the extra effort of carrying it, if only to tell me positively whether we were within a thousand, or five hundred, or fifty desirable feet of the end of our journey.

"I shall sit down here a minute and get my breath back," I called out, more to my own surprise than to that of Elizabeth, who was now some way ahead of me.

I had not really intended even to say this, let alone to act upon it; but before she had turned to acknowledge my call I was sitting down on a steep slope, my stick between my legs, panting as though my lungs would burst through my ribs. Clearly I was in much less good training than I had thought I was.

Elizabeth waved back to me. "I'll go as far as the cleft in that rock," she announced. "If I can't see the summit from there, I'll"—there was a tiny break in the sentence—"come back."

I nodded, having no breath to spare even for a reply.

I turned and looked out across the valley to where the silent Buarbre streamed motionlessly down from the mountain-top, contained within those black, rocky flanks, curling round the boulders and clasping them to her icy bosom. If the going was hard here, where there was for the most part dry turf and rock with only intermittent patches of melting snow, what would it have been like on that ice-bound slope, I asked myself. If one were to stumble there would be no staying until one crashed over the last lip of ice into the waters of the Jordalselva, to be picked up by them and carried brutally down the valley, broken on jagged rock, squeezed through needles'-eyes, crumpled and riven and shattered. . . .

I do not think she called out, and she does not remember now whether she did or not. But something in my own morbid reflections was echoed by some sixth sense. I turned abruptly, to see Elizabeth, spread-eagled as though crucified on the brutal stony turf, descending towards me at a speed that was terrifying even to watch. I saw her long brown legs and arms flail the turf in a desperate attempt to check her progress, and in that instant I knew that there was nothing whatsoever that I myself could do to help. The slope of the track was both downwards and sideways—sideways into the narrow gully that contained the secondary tumbling rivulet. If she could not stop herself long before I could reach her she would plunge over the edge and down into the steep-sided gorge; and that would be the end.

She seemed to be slithering and tossing there for helpless minutes, but it can only have been a matter of seconds, as I knew afterwards, or she would have tipped over the brink and vanished once and for all. Suddenly the flailing of her arms and legs ceased; there was a slowing-up of motion; a hand clutched something, and she was still. By then I was working my way diagonally over towards her, not daring to hurry for fear I myself slipped and fell and should thus be unable to help get her back down the track if she were maimed. I was calculating distances and angles, calling out encouraging futilities in a voice that I knew was not my own at all.

Before I was half-way to her she cautiously sat up, looked about her, and gingerly got to her feet. "I'm all right," she announced. "I don't think I'll go any farther."

Whether she meant farther up, or farther down, it was a grim, unintentional jest for which, later, I was tempted to upbraid her. For the moment, however, I was too relieved to say anything at all. Soon I was by her side; and when we had steadied ourselves and surveyed our best downward route, we set off again, myself in front and walking with extreme circumspection, with eyes for nothing but that pile of garments on the little knoll far, far below us, our immediate and most desirable goal.

"So much for my glacier," said Elizabeth sadly, as she donned her red jumper and collected her things. "I'm sure we must have taken a wrong route, you know. It's supposed to be quite easy to get on to Folgefonna. I wish . . ." But what she wished remained unspoken.

It was not until we got back to England that we found out the truth about this allegedly easy trip up and across Folgefonna. It is possible between mid-June and mid-August. The ascent, through the Tokheim Valley, is by a bridle-path, and takes four hours at least. Thereafter it is possible to ski-run on Folgefonna by way of the mountain hut called Breidablik; after this there is another bridle-path steeply downhill to Sunndal, a tiny village hidden in an arm of Hardangerfjord called Maurangerfjord. We were, I suppose, lucky to get off as lightly as we did, having set off so casually and so ill-equipped. No thought of skis had crossed our minds. It was rather shaking to read later in cold authoritative print: "Arrangements for this excursion, including guide, skis, sleigh, etc., at a reasonable cost, may be made in Odda."

It is difficult with a small-scale map, and would not, in fact, be easy even with a large-scale map, to estimate what distance we covered that afternoon and evening from Odda to within five hundred feet (as we found out afterwards) of the summit, and back to Odda again. At a conservative estimate it was sixteen miles. But the effort expended in scaling rock after rock, thrusting through tangled brushwood, clinging to doubtful roots, crawling where it was impossible to walk, and tearing our way through thorn and bracken and armpit-high nettles on our return journey, was equivalent surely to a walk at least twice that distance on fair ground, may be more. Certainly neither Elizabeth nor I have ever come nearer to complete exhaustion than we did on those last long-drawn-out miles of the homeward journey.

We had remembered the first miles out of Odda as being steadily uphill but there had apparently been a stretch of a mile or so downhill, from the edge of Odda to Sandven Lake, and it almost broke our hearts when we were confronted on our return journey with this quite modest incline. We had eaten our small stock of chocolate and sweets; there had been no sign of life at Buar as we passed the farm, part way home, and I think we must have looked more than a little drunk as we staggered that last mile through Odda's outskirts to the *hospitz* in the main street.

In honour of the visit of the cruiser *Devonshire* there was to be a grand dance in Odda's largest dance hall that evening, but the very thought of people being willing to remain on their feet and perambulate round a dance hall was too much for us. We climbed, a step at a time, to the first floor, turned the handle of our bedroom door and dropped on to our narrow box-beds which, for once, seemed to us to be of the very stuff of heaven. We unlaced one another's boots, dropped them thankfully on to the uncarpeted floor, and then lay down to recuperate enough strength to go across the landing in search of the meal we so desperately needed.

Smörbröd

And what a meal it was, when at last we came to it! There is at once variety and sameness about the Norwegian *aftens* and *frokost*. It is, of course, a cold meal (though you can sometimes order something cooked, if you feel the need to do so), to which you help yourself from a table lavishly spread with variegated dishes.

There is cheese, and cheese: by this I mean that there is the inevitable massive cube of goat's-milk cheese, the hue of old cobbler's wax; there is a softer, milder cheese, of the consistency, say, of a Dutch cheese; and there is very often a more notable-looking cheese, a prince among cheeses, blue-veined, crumbling, pungent. To serve the first two cheeses there is a delightful tool, a cross between a heart-shaped fish-slice and a vegetable-parer. It has, inset in its shining blade, a curved slot with one razor-sharp edge. Drawn backwards across the surface of the cheese it produces wafer-thin curls, like wood-shavings, which can be spread on bread, or eaten neat.

An addict of bacon and eggs for breakfast all my life, I had not taken kindly to the prospect of cheese for that first meal of the day as a basic and inescapable commodity; and I have to confess that after one sampling I eschewed the goat's-cheese and concentrated on the others. This was probably foolish of me, for it is said to be an acquired and highly rewarding taste. Perhaps it is the first weeks of acclimatization that are the longest!

In addition to the cheeses there is a great variety of cold meats: liver and salami sausage, the speckled and somewhat embarrassing products of the *charcutier*, gherkins, sliced hard-boiled eggs, sardines and a smaller, rarer fish whose name we never learned. There is sliced ham occasionally (but only very occasionally in the country districts, though some of the most delicious I have ever tasted in my life was offered to us at a remote *pensjonat* near Åsletta in Gudbrandsdal and again on the fringe of the Jotunheim Mountains at Tessand). There are always various appetizing brawns and compressed jellied meats; smoked and pickled fish of varieties rarely encountered in England, for unlike the Norwegians we are not a fish-conscious race. And always, of course, several bowls of tart but exquisitely flavoured raspberry and bilberry jam.

It was a new experience to put on one's plate a variety of meats and fish and egg and cheese, and a good dollop of this most fruity jam as well. We found that it toned down the taste of some of the more exotic meats, but it did not seem to wage successful war against goat's-cheese. It was always available, as the butter was, in most satisfying quantities.

There is, then, at once sameness and variety in these Norwegian buffet meals. *Frokost* and *aftens* were much alike and varied but little from place to place (though I shall tell in due course of a certain breakfast in Oslo, and of an *aftens* in Uppheim): thus there was variety within monotony, or monotonous variety, whichever you prefer. I suppose that, after half a lifetime of the standard English breakfast of porridge or cereals, eggs and bacon, toast and marmalade, one has become conditioned to that menu and it proves actually less monotonous than a succession of breakfasts each garnished by a dozen dishes alien to one's experience and taste first thing in the morning. Common sense says: Why not restrict yourself, then, to a few dishes each morning and never repeat them two mornings in succession? An excellent notion, agreed. But just try sitting down to such a table and refraining from a comprehensive gesture embracing all the dishes from sliced eggs and liver sausage to smoked herring and blue-veined cheese, the whole set about with crimson pools of most mouth-watering bilberry jam!

Bread and butter were present separately, of course; and various species of *flatbröd*—a wafer-thin variety of our own asbestos-like breakfast-biscuit which I for one have never really taken to. And coffee, and milk.

Norway is a land flowing, if not with honey, then certainly with milk. Milk abounds everywhere, and though I would say that in general its fat-content is not quite so high as the best we produce in England, it is of a uniformly good quality, and incidentally much more thirst-quenching than if it contained more cream. Moreover, it is always served absolutely cold, and this is the only way in which milk will quench thirst. Tuberculosis was at one time very prevalent in Norway, but since stringent measures and pasteurization have been introduced this scourge has been enormously lessened in the country.

Milk is on sale everywhere. More interesting, it is automatically served at breakfast and supper, in quart jugs which are never allowed to run dry, however many people may be sitting at table. I remember particularly this meal at Odda to which we finally staggered after we had gathered strength for the short journey across the landing from our bedroom. We were the only occupants of the dining-room when we sat down, and I remember, perhaps with a suspicion of shame, that almost before we had loaded our plates for the first time Elizabeth and I (though I was the prime mover) had almost drained the quart jug dry. A surprised waitress, one of the most friendly we encountered anywhere, stood on tiptoe (for she was very short and plump) and peered over the edge of the jug, to find its level diminished to a quite startling degree. She waited until I had topped up my glass and then seized the jug and vanished, to reappear with it refilled to the brim and set it down in front of us with a comprehending smile.

In view of the abundance of milk it is surprising that neither porridge nor cereal figures on the *frokost* menu. We were offered the choice once, but there was no sugar or even syrup to go with it, and for me the experiment was not a success. I ought, of course, to have applied that panacea, the tart red-fruit jam, to my plateful: it would probably have been a memorable experience!

I think that buxom little waitress must have worn quite a channel along the floor between our table and the kitchen, before that meal was over. We told her, between our mouthfuls, that we had been attempting to climb Folgefonna, and she nodded understandingly and poured out a further cup of coffee for each of us. I remember that I used to drink cold milk until my coffee had cooled sufficiently to be swallowed almost at a draught, and then cold milk again until my cup had been refilled. My behaviour at that meal at Odda was deplorable.

Nemesis, however, overtook me almost on the spot. Towards the end of the meal, when I was casting about me for some fresh juxtaposition of unusual dishes, I began to feel in spite of the warmth of the evening a curious chill spreading over me. Nor was it imagination, for Elizabeth, who knows me well, spotted a paling of my tan and the advance-guard of an attack of sweat breaking out on my forehead. I rose somewhat unsteadily to my feet, tottered across the landing and collapsed on to my bed. Elizabeth wrapped me in all the blankets and *dyner* she could lay her hands on, and I lay and shivered uncontrollably for half an hour or an hour.

I told myself, when I could think coherently, that this was a delayed attack of minor sunstroke resulting from walking bareheaded on the snow-clad slopes of a mountain beneath a cloudless sky. I think it probably was; but in all honesty I suspect that I encouraged this state of affairs by indulging unwisely and inordinately in the generous table and inexhaustible milk-supply of the Odda *hospitz*! It was an hour or more before I dared throw off the piled blankets and, somewhat shamefacedly, sit up and look about me.

Elizabeth was busily writing up her diary for the day and obviously had something on her mind. "Do you think, darling," she began tentatively, when she had assured herself that I was almost myself again, "we might interrupt our itinerary, just for once?"

"In order to what?" I asked suspiciously. I felt there was something behind this innocent-seeming inquiry.

She paused to cross a "t" in the last line of her notes. Then she stood up and looked out of the window towards the heights from which we had lately descended. I pulled aside the curtain and looked out with her. The sun had dropped below those distant hills and the near face of them was dark in silhouette. They had a forbidding aspect which they had not possessed when, so light-heartedly, we had set out seven or eight hours before to climb them. I shuddered slightly, and let the curtain fall back into position.

"I thought," Elizabeth completed her sentence with studied casualness, "we might have another go at my glacier, to-morrow."

I do not remember what I answered. I was probably struck dumb, as I so often am by Elizabeth's more unexpected remarks. But I remembered that vision of flailing brown arms and legs rapidly descending a mountainside which ended in a ravine rock-strewn and boiling with ice-water from Buarbre. I wondered whether she, who had been actor not audience, even now realized how near she had come to destruction, and what had been the effect on me, impotent as I was to arrest the course of events.

I probably said something completely banal such as "Let's sleep on the idea". I know we went to bed, and slept like logs for all the tumult of naval men excited by an all-night dance thronging the narrow Odda streets and making the most of the last few minutes before they were due once more to go aboard the *Devonshire*.

In the morning, to my intense relief, nothing more was said about a repeat trip to Elizabeth's glacier.

ODDA TO OSLO

MIN FLAGG

IT was perhaps as well that our walking next day was on level ground; one of us, at any rate, had had enough of steep gradients. We took the road out of Odda along the east shore of the fjord, to find our way northwards as far as Kinsarvik and the ferry to Granvin. Remembering how the last few miles along the fjord into Odda had been marred by industrialism, we decided to take the bus until we were clear of Tyssedal, where a hydro-electric power station is operated by the water falling through multiple pipe-lines sheer down the mountainside from Lake Skjeggedal.

Half a mile out of Odda, and mercifully before we had been overtaken by a bus, Elizabeth discovered that she had mislaid her Union Jack. We are not an aggressively patriotic couple, but these flags had been bought at the very beginning of our plans for Norway: mascots which were to bring us luck when we became dependent on the goodwill of car and lorry drivers. Hitherto, we had hardly had occasion to make use of them, unless we count the foolish incident of our signalling H.M.S. *Devonshire*. But now at last we were upon the open road and unless we were to overspend our budget by using a public service vehicle where walking would be too slow, we must make sure of attracting attention. We remembered that Elizabeth had taken her flag from its straps when we unpacked and stuck it in a bedside lamp-shade.

"I'll go back and fetch it," I said, and dropped my rucksack at the side of the road, leaving Elizabeth to watch them both and keep an eye on passing traffic.

I walked back briskly, pondering what I was to say at the *hospitz* if the flag were not where she had left it. Someone obviously would have removed it, and, for the life of me, I could not think what the Norwegian for such an article might be. Absurdly, the singer's name, Kirsten Flagstad, kept

71

ringing in my mind, but I could imagine the ridiculous complications that would ensue if I took that line of approach.
Our phrase-book was in Elizabeth's pocket, and I was left to
my own resources. Flag; banner; pennant; bunting; standard: not one of these and kindred words rang any sort of
responsive bell within me.

I have the pictorial or photographic sort of memory that
clings limpet-like to anything of which I have seen the shape
and colour and style; words I never use remain imprinted on
my memory because something about their shape has once
appealed to me and impressed itself on the malleable wax of
memory. I carry in my pigeon-hole memory scores of regis-
tration numbers of cars belonging to people I have not seen
for twenty years. It is a ridiculous gift, almost totally worthless, wished on me at birth by a whimsical-malevolent fairy
who promised himself (or more probably herself) many years
of entertainment watching the pickles into which I could and
would get myself by exercising it. But it did not give me the
Norwegian for "flag".

I tried again a favourite trick of mentally turning over the
pages of our phrase-book. Even though fashions might have
changed in epithets since it was compiled and we might no
longer declare that "This is a capital hotel", nouns would
surely not have changed over-much. Had I seen that elusive
little word, flag? Was it among *Verden og dens elementer*
(The World and its elements)? At least in symbolism it was
a constituent portion of the world: what about the great red
splodges of one's childhood atlas over which waved the Union
Jack and on which the sun allegedly never set?

I then mentally ran down the columns under *Frukter,
traer, blomster og groensaker*, four self-explanatory words for
vegetable life. But the flag was not, so far as I could remember, among those, either. Later on, I tried for it under Dress
and Toilet, Town and Country, Mankind and Relations, and
even under Physical and Mental Powers, Qualities, etc.
(which offered the widest terms of reference and seemed even
more comprehensive when labelled: *Fysiske og åndelige
evner, egenskaper*); but it was not to be under these, either.

By the time I had exhausted the resources of my memory, I

was back at the *hospitz* and had run upstairs to our room. I entered and looked at the bed-lamp; but there was no flag. I looked along the corridor, but the girl I saw there cleaning a window at the end was not one I had seen before. I looked in at the dining-room, where I thought I might engage the help of the buxom little body who had so willingly trotted to and fro with replenished jugs of milk and kept an almost constant stream of excellent coffee pouring into one or other of our cups, but she was not to be found.

I returned to the bedroom, and there found another girl still, preparing to change some linen. I pointed at the lamp, uttered signs of distress, and, remembering suddenly that the word "forlorn" is a survival of an old word meaning "very much lost", pointed again at the lamp and gave voice to that word in a variety of intonations.

It is not surprising that she was at a loss to understand the wild-eyed Englishman so absurdly uttering the improbable word *forloren*, carefully spaced out and emphasized: *for-lor-en*, what time he pointed dejectedly at a lamp she must have seen a hundred or more times during her daily occupation. "Jack," this absurd Englishman tried next, ineptly drawing out the diagonals and verticals and horizontals of his national flag and waving an imaginary something at the end of an imaginary something-else: how was *she* to know this meant a flag on a little wire pole?

She shook her head, went out along the corridor and brought back a friend with her; the pantomime began all over again. "*Min . . .*" I tried to explain, fluttering my fingers as though only temporarily at a loss for a word I knew they both must know. And then, entirely without thought, dropping into my own language: "My flag . . ."

Comprehension was immediate. "*Oh, Deres flagg!*" And before I had fully realized the absurd fact that the word is practically identical in the two languages, the second girl pulled out from her overall pocket Elizabeth's missing Union Jack and, with the friendliest of smiles, passed it over to me. "*Engelske flagg,*" she said, delightedly. And then, to complete my mortification, she added in not half bad English: "Union Zjack!"

I thanked them both hurriedly, stuck the flag through my button-hole and sped back the way I had come to where Elizabeth was waiting by the roadside. Ten minutes later we were aboard a bus, spinning along the road to Tyssedal.

As with the trains, there is a sliding scale of charges on Norwegian buses: the longer the distance travelled the less, proportionately, you pay. Over a short stretch of road the fare seems unreasonably high; measured out over a long-distance trip it is not quite so bad. We alighted at Tyssedal and then set out along the level road to see what the still-young day might yet bring forth.

The sky was clear blue ahead of us, though tarnished by the smoke from the zinc works behind us. To our left, across the narrow sheet of water, the hills rose steeply to their snow-clad summit which was the near edge of Folgefonna. H.M.S. *Devonshire* lay at anchor, twin lights still winking brilliantly from her mast-head, so that we supposed those wretched cadets were hard at it (after their night's dancing) sweeping their cumbersome boats hither and thither on the water of Odda Bay. But ahead of us water and sky were clear, vivid blue, parted from one another by the steep sides of the mountains: Sörfjord was an elongated, blue-glass-topped-and-bottomed cas-ket, empty save for the small jewels that were bright-painted farmsteads high on those western hills and the occasional small craft plying, as *Skare* yesterday had done, between port and sleepy port.

Our road followed the corrugations of the eastern bank. The rock masses were sheer for much of the way and from time to time the road, instead of clinging to the precipitous edge overhanging the water, carved its way through a rock tunnel. Or rather, half the road passed through a tunnel hewn out of solid living rock, while the other half, narrowing to the limit of safety, clung to the water's edge. Travelling northwards, to Kinsarvik, one passed through the tunnel; in the reverse direction one would take the open road. Some of the vistas seen through the craggy framing of those tunnels carried a quite magical quality.

It was some twenty miles to Kinsarvik, where we intended

to pick up the late-afternoon ferry to Granvin. After spending so much time and such vast amounts of energy in climbing steeply up and down alongside the Buarbre it was pleasant to have an almost level road to walk on, with such alluring views ahead and to our left. To our right, of course, we could see practically nothing, for the hills rose sheer from the roadway; but behind us, and we stopped over and over again to feast on the beauty of the picture, was the wall of tree-clad mountain that wore the white justice's wig of Folgefonna and had defeated us but twenty hours before.

Alongside us, separated from our road by the still-narrow, silent waters of the fjord, were the northward extensions of that rock mass, with thinner snow upon them, mainly in sheltered crevasses, and waterfalls that thundered silently downward through channels they had been carving since Time was a boy. Ahead of us the water widened gradually, and at the end of it was the beauty of Hardanger once more, the blossom of Utne's orchard fields, the homeliness of the little wharf and clustered white-timber cottages, and the great sentinel Mt. Oksen, which stood at its point of vantage dominating the triple fjord pattern, its white head crowned by the blueness of the sky.

AERIAL ROPEWAY

About this time the previous day one of the crew had brewed for us in *Skare*'s small galley a large and welcome pot of black coffee. Sweet biscuits, too, he had rustled up from some unexpected source and laid on a plate for our pleasure. After a few miles along that dusty road we would have welcomed a cup of that coffee; or, better still, a long, cool drink! From some memory of verses learnt at school I used to quote, when our thirst became nearly unbearable: "Longing for a long drink, out of silver, in the ship's cool lazareet," and Elizabeth would groan in spirit and beg me to desist. There were no cafés or even scattered cottages along this part of the road, though it had seemed to us as we comfortably sailed along the fjord the previous morning that they were strung out like bright beads. Not till we reached Ullensvang (or Oppedal) did we find refreshment.

At intervals we came across those small aerial ropeways which are such a feature of the mountain districts of Norway. Though this country has no summits greater than that of Galdhöpiggen, which just surpasses 8,000 feet, it remains a fact that its average altitude above sea level is 1,600 feet; this is more than half as high again as the average for the whole of the European continent, which contains the Alps. Apart from one or two groups of fairly high peaks a surprising percentage of its 120,000 square miles takes the form of high plateaux, including the most extensive permanent snow- and ice-field in the whole of Europe.

The basic fuel of the country is, of course, wood. The combustion-chamber of the inevitable cast-iron stove is oddly shaped: perhaps eighteen inches long by less than a foot wide. It was not until I had examined one of them that I connected it with the ubiquitous stacks of fifteen-inch split logs by the roadside and against the outer walls of nearly all the houses and farms. These stacks of cleft logs are as much a part of the countryside as are the stacked turves of the Irish landscape; they stand, of course, in just the same relationship to the people. Where dwellings are surrounded by growing timber there is no problem: the man of the house takes his axe and saw and produces his own supply of winter fuel. But where there is little growing timber, or where the mountain-sides are so steep that one cannot just wander about on them with an axe collecting fuel, something more elaborate has to be planned.

It was so here, along this road between Odda and Kinsarvik, as it had been along the road that led eventually to Buarbre: one or more taut steel cables had been slung at an acute angle to the perpendicular, from a point of vantage near the road, upwards and out of sight to some terrace where trees grew and men also could obtain a precarious foothold. They were too far away for us to hear the ring of their axes or the hiss of their saws, but every now and then—and it could be most startling—there would be a sudden viciously increasing hiss, followed by a thud. We would pause in our stride, turn about, and see swaying gently against the anchoring-post at road level a little cradle slung from the overhead wire and carrying half a dozen or so logs that had been cut high up the mountainside. It was a simple, sometimes even Heath-Robinsonian device, but clearly efficient. Sometimes it was anchored in concrete, evidently a fixture designed for protracted and frequent use; sometimes it was an arrangement of strutted posts lashed with rope or bound with wire, set up for a relatively short period of timber felling, later to be removed and set up elsewhere.

I should have liked to explore the upper end of some of these aerial ropeways, but the prospect was daunting: the thin, gleaming wire, taut as a bowstring, pierced the thin scrub that had rooted itself in the granite clefts and vanished in a yard or two. Nor was it possible to step backwards in the hope of seeing where the upper end might be anchored, for the road was narrow and behind it was deep water. But I reflected that someone must at some time have had to shoulder a coil of thin, strong rope or wire and make the pioneer journey upwards, through rough terrain at an angle of perhaps 1 in 2, choose his spot, build his upper anchor, and then link the two ends together with the heavier steel cable, making it taut enough to carry a heavy, swinging load at high speed downwards. What kind of haulage system was installed at the top, I wondered. Man-power, of course; but was it a straight pull upwards or was there some sort of windlass? And if so, what expenditure of effort must there have been called for in conveying it all to that unseen height!

Perhaps the most remarkable of all these aerial ropeways that we saw spanned the Jordalselva between the roadside and one of the bastions of Jordalsnuten. Because the contour dipped beneath it we could follow the bright cable in its easy curve from the road anchorage to a point high among the thickly growing trees on the far side of the river. Curving away up there, it looked as gossamer-slim as the first long trial thread spun into position by an adventurous spider. By what art had it been conveyed across the forbidding valley filled with rushing, pale-green water? I should have liked to meet the man who, having decided what he must do, had set out

77

one day to descend from road level to that crevasse, cross it, and then begin the far steeper ascent on the other side, a thin coil of twine about his shoulder, his hands and feet in equal use as they propelled him ever upwards to a point at which he could halt, turn about and estimate the reward for his labours in terms of timber hewn.

One other such aerial ropeway we saw, much later in our travels. This time the little mobile trolley it bore was fitted with three stout iron hooks. For some time we puzzled as to what they might be designed to carry. They looked for all the world like the stout hooks which suspend home-cured hams from the kitchen-beams in isolated farmhouses. "How grand it would be," I said to Elizabeth (who is by conviction a vegetarian, though in practice it does not always work out that way), "if suddenly a hook-fitted trolley were to descend such a ropeway with a York ham suspended in triplicate!"

The mystery was solved for us soon afterward, though not as we had dreamed it might be: a similar trolley descended, bearing three milk-churns dangling from its hooks. Stepping a little farther along the road, we were able to see that high above us on a steep, grassy slope there was perched one of the small-holdings which Norwegian farmers have wrested from the rocky hillsides, with a cow or two grazing at a chancy angle and a hay-sled (for no wheeled vehicle would be possible on such an estate) leaning against the farmhouse wall.

"Milk," said Elizabeth (who, as experience has more than once proved, can do just as much damage as I can to a plateful of home-cured ham and eggs), "has a higher food-content than ham."

Just short of Kinsarvik we thumbed our first lift: a man driving a Vauxhall car slowed down, stopped, and welcomed us aboard. He was a Norwegian who spoke English with an American accent—not the first we had met and very far from being the last. The cloud of fine white dust still lay above the road for half a mile behind us, for there was no wind at all that afternoon; and when, a quarter of an hour later, we dropped down into the snug harbour of Kinsarvik that cloud had been further elongated by another eight or ten miles. We were grateful for the lift, but realized then, as we were

to realize more than once afterwards, how little a passenger
sees of the countryside he passes through.

It was on the car-ferry via Utne to Granvin that we were
accosted by an elderly Norwegian wearing the wide-brimmed,
Colonial type of hat which is always worn in Norway, if any
hat is worn at all. He wore, too, in spite of the heat, a heavy
overcoat. He spotted our flags and addressed us in English
with a particularly strong American accent. He introduced
his wife: a frail little body who did not speak a word, but
smiled amiably at us and was obviously impressed by her
husband's easy flow of words.

We soon heard their story. They had emigrated to the
United States before the first World War and lived there ever
since until that very week. Now, having sold up the home
they had built for themselves in Iowa, they had returned, in
their seventies, to spend the remainder of their lives in their
own country.

They were a quite tragic couple, for they had been back in
Norway just long enough to discover that all the people they
had known in their youth were either dead or so remote from
their accustomed way of life that they were stranger to them
than the Americans had been when first they landed in Iowa.
Already they were bitterly regretting the comfortable home
they had abandoned and sold in that far country. There
was sadness in the man's voice; and though his wife did not
speak, there was a corresponding sadness in her eyes.

Had it been possible, he said to us, he would even now pack
his things once more and return to Iowa, where for nearly
forty years they had been happy and prosperous, owning their
business and established in the house they had designed and
built. But now it was too late: they had fallen between two
worlds and felt hopelessly insecure. They went ashore at
Kvandal, midway between Kinsarvik and Granvin, where
this arm of Hardanger takes on a new name and thrusts northward to the rail-head. We waved to them from the deck and
they waved back, forlornly, strangers in their native land;
less happy, they who had so much looked forward to their
return, than we were to be among the Norwegian hills and
fjords.

There was light on the western flanks of Mt. Oksen; the tiny hamlet of Utne had been in shadow as we approached, but we still remember it as we saw it the first time, bathed in brilliant sunshine and flecked with petals from its cherry orchards. Then the fjord narrowed and the hills rose steeply from the water's edge. A flank was thrust out into the water, first from one side, then from the other, and it seemed as though our small boat was being shouldered out of her course. Half an hour later her siren sounded, her engines were stilled, and we drifted lazily to our berth alongside the Granvin quay.

There is a good (and we were told later particularly comfortable) hotel at Granvin, right on the station from which one takes the electric train inland to Voss. A single street contains at most a dozen buildings, all very small; a shop or two, a dwelling or two, and a couple of *pensjonats*, white-painted and attractive. But they lie behind buildings which screen from their view the tree-clad hills and the head of this narrow fjord. For that reason we took a chance on the *hyrreberge*, a wooden building not far from the water's edge, though separated from it by a railway-siding. Railway-lines, we felt, were preferable to a roof-scape opposite our windows.

It was our first inquiry at such a place, but we need have had no misgivings. Though its exterior was not quite as prepossessing as that of the *pensjonat* at Norheimsund, it was only because the place was about due for a repaint. We were shown upstairs into a spacious room with twin beds and a chair or two and a table. Its windows (on two walls) were large and had been open all day, so that the room was filled with sunshine still. It had a balcony, windowed on three sides, and we supped there at a table from which we could look down the darkening fjord beyond the quay at which our late ferry was tied up; and in brilliant sunshine we breakfasted there in our pyjamas, because the woman of the house had brought up our breakfast just an hour too soon.

It did not matter, for the morning was gay and we were embarking that day on a new and untried stage of our journey: no less than the most dramatic section of the famous Bergen-Oslo railway. The sun already was high above the hills on the east side of the fjord and even at that hour was uncomfortably hot through glass. It blazed on to our thin pyjamas, giving us the feeling that we were clad in thermogene.

It was our mistake, not the woman's, that our breakfast came to us so early. We had asked overnight that we might have breakfast at 7.30, so that we might comfortably catch the eight o'clock electric train to Voss and then our connection on the main line. The Norwegian, however, does not say "7.30" or "8.30". Like the Lancashire man, he will name the hour and precede it by the word "half". But with this difference: where the Lancashire man will say "half-eight" and mean "eight-thirty", the Norwegian will say *"Halv ni"* (nine) for "eight-thirty", meaning half-way-through-to-nine-o'clock. This is reasonable enough. But it also explains why, when we asked for breakfast at *"Halv syv"*, or half-past seven as we thought, we got it at half-past six.

It did not matter. We ate a good breakfast, packed our rucksacks, paid a very modest bill, and sallied forth to see what there was to see before our train left for Voss. There was no one about. The car-ferry on which we had arrived the previous evening had slept as peacefully throughout the night as the rest of Granvin had done. A thin plume of smoke now rose from the galley chimney where one of the crew was no doubt preparing coffee.

Stacked against a wall near the quay was a quantity of the roofing-slates used throughout Norway. They are of a greenish hue, not unlike Cumberland slates, but their charm lies mainly in their shape. They are all cut to a pattern which is best likened to a shoe-sole, or a fish-scale. Lying as they did just there, at an angle to the morning sun, they presented a most satisfying sight: a succession of graduated scales packed closely together, so that a pleasing harmony of curves and angles resulted. The pattern was further accentuated by the fact that, while the surface of the slates was pale green with a satiny finish, their curved edges were a lighter green, almost silver, and rough from contact with the edged tool that had shaped them.

It was the first time I had seen them at close quarters, though ever since our arrival in Norway I had admired the well-proportioned roofs of dwellings and warehouses and churches and schools on which these neat slates were laid. It is odd that so small a thing as the shape of an individual slate can make so profound a difference to the general effect of a roof-scape, even when seen from a moving vehicle or across a stretch of water amid sun and shadow. Multiplied a thousandfold, of course, the individual slate is lost, but the rhythmic pattern of intersecting curves, graduated from the small top slates to the largest ones along the eaves, is enchanting. The craftsmanship that goes to the roofing of small circular or octagonal turrets, curved dormer windows and branching gables of varying sizes and pitches even on one single main roof must be of no mean order. I should have liked to watch slaters at work in Norway, but never, alas, had the chance.

Bergensbanen

Two well-windowed observation-coaches, electrically propelled, constituted the Granvin-Voss train. A fifteen-mile run, occupying some forty minutes and costing half-a-crown each. It was a small enough train to give the feeling that it was one's private property and the temptation every few minutes to signal the driver to stop while one took a photograph was almost irresistible.

The line climbs steeply from sea level, the rails curving about the bastions of rock almost as though they are wire hoops to immense grey barrels. We slid unobtrusively into and out of midget stations that might each of them have come out of some well-chosen box of toy railway parts. As with the fjord-ferry halts, there was the minimum of fuss: one or two waiting passengers came on board, exchanged subdued greetings with acquaintances and relapsed into the near-silence that had brooded over the coach before their entry.

We reached the summit, paused and began the long declivity that ends in Voss station. Voss itself lies in a shallow saucer whose rim is made up of swelling hills and the mountains which are just visible on the outermost lip, snow-capped, silent, remote. Towards the highest of them, threading its way sometimes round, sometimes over and sometimes through, our train would soon be bearing us along *Bergensbanen* to its astonishing summit near the Hardangerjökulen, and to Finse, the highest of its stations, over 4,000 feet above sea level.

At Voss we found ourselves with an hour or so to wait for our connection. It is a pleasant station, with one long platform, modern buildings, and a hotel reached from the platform itself, but half hidden then by great masses of cherry blossom. We entered the station restaurant—a lofty, spacious room paved with smooth granite and lit by wide windows. The long glass counter had trays of varied cakes and pastries, cold poached and fried eggs, sausage and fish and ham and cheese: *smörbröd*, in fact, on the large scale. There was excellent coffee; and, of course, the tall glasses of milk, covered over like all the eatables with sheets of clear plastic. We made our selection, each item being lifted on to a plate with metal tongs, so that nothing was touched by hand. I do not know whether this is law in Norway, but I do know that even in the smallest and unlikeliest of cafés in the remote corners of the country cakes and sandwiches and biscuits were always transferred thus to our plates.

A dozen or twenty people were sitting about and we were part-way through the most delectable of custard-slices when Elizabeth spotted someone she remembered from *Venus* and darted outside to speak to her, leaving her sun-glasses beside her plate of half-consumed elevenses. I followed more leisurely and we chatted for a minute or two on the platform, exchanging notes. When we returned it was to find that our places had been cleared, the table swept clean of crumbs and everything, including the sun-glasses, removed. We managed to reclaim these, but the uneaten cakes and the uncompleted coffee had gone for ever.

Ten minutes before the train was due in from Bergen the ticket-office opened. The window was of plate-glass with an open panel through which one spoke. Inset in the wooden shelf which projected outwards to the passenger and inwards to the clerk was a curious recessed tray not unlike those partitioned dishes that hold cheese and butter and biscuits. There was a handle to it on the inward side.

I asked for two single tickets to Haugastöl. The clerk nodded, reaching to the rack beside him.

"*Hvad koster billetten?*"

It was ten *kroner*, fifteen *öre* each, he answered—a few pence over ten shillings—for the run of seventy-odd miles. He looked meaningly downward at the tray set in the shelf between us. I placed a fifty-*kroner* note in my half of the tray; he moved the handle, and my note passed beneath the window to his side. At the same time, lying snug in the other section of the tray, two tickets and just short of thirty *kroner* in change came sliding round to me.

It was neat and practical, and so designed that no sudden draught could flip either note or ticket into or out of the window. This is just as well, for there is so much small change in note form in Norway and, as on the Continent, the notes are used until the last vestige of stiffness has gone from them. I do not know what is their average period of circulation, but many of the notes of smaller denominations that we handled were almost as skeletal as leaves that have clung to their twigs through half a winter.

Then the train pulled in. A few people alighted and we, together with a good many others, piled on board, climbing steeply upwards from a very low platform. There are observation-coaches on some of the trains on this line, but there were none on ours. Fortunately, however, its corridor was on the southern, or more interesting, side; for this we were grateful, for there were no vacant seats. Nor would there have been much comfort if there had been, for the seats are hard and unyielding, even if there is sufficient leg-room: the Norwegians are prepared, it seems, to travel as well as to sleep hard! Double and triple racks are always loaded to capacity with rucksacks—apparently the only form of luggage the travelling Norwegian will recognize.

Elizabeth and I took up strategic positions in the corridor, which was roomy and unencumbered by luggage. The windows were so wide that they were to all intents and purposes unbroken for the whole length of the coach. Every other one could be lowered almost out of sight. At each end of the corridor a shelf carried two large carafes filled with fresh water carefully covered over against dust and flying soot. We did not hear any whistle blow on the platform or any answering toot from the distant engines; as silently as one of the ferry-steamers casting off from some fjord wharf, the long train drew away from Voss station and began the tremendous journey lying ahead of it.

For tremendous it really is. A more widely travelled writer than I has referred to it as one of the most spectacular feats of railway engineering in the world, and that is not hard to believe. The track rises from sea level at Bergen to over 4,300 feet near Finse in a distance of just over a hundred miles with gradients as steep as one in fifty. Then, for a further two hundred miles it gradually descends from these Alpine heights to sea level again at Oslo, twelve hours' run from the west coast.

One factor that makes the highest section of the railway, that between Mjölfjell and Geilo, sixty miles distant, so spectacular is that the line runs not only above the snow-line, but above the timber-line, so that the landscape lying about it is utterly barren, a waste of snow and ice illimitable. One has the sense of being on the roof of the world, for here are no peaks and intervening valleys; instead, there is a vast, undulating plain, a rolling sheet of dazzling snow and ice that might, for all one can tell, continue to the farthest limits of the world.

The general slope beside the railway-line is downwards to the right, or southern side; on the opposite side the mountains rise steeply close at hand, so that the metal rails cling to them, hooping them with steel. And because, though the mountains are motionless, their snow-apparel thickens in winter and is hardly doffed even in high summer, the slender rails that link city with city must be protected against the vast uneasiness that overtakes the snow with wind or change of temperature. When a mass of snow in which a whole cathedral could be contained begins to move, its line of travel crosses the railway; so for long stretches the single track must run through tunnels in the rock anything up to three miles in length, or through massive timber snow-sheds braced against the escarpment and skilfully designed to throw off any weight of snow travelling across it. Even when, as on the lower heights, neither tunnel nor snow-shed is called for, there must be mile upon mile of snow-screens. These make a herring-bone pattern on the white carpet, to check the wind-spun snow and keep it clear of the track whether the wind shift from north to south or from east to west.

The Bergen-Voss section of this railway was opened some seventy years ago, and the Oslo end of it some twenty years later. But this fantastic middle section was many more years a-building, and the first train did not run over it till shortly before the first World War. You may see, if the winter snow has sufficiently cleared, short stretches of road built in advance by the railway engineers to carry men and materials to the site: it must be one of the bleakest, grimmest service-roads ever put into commission.

It is of the very nature of the undertaking that its most astonishing features are the hardest to take in. For as the track climbs higher and ever higher towards that summit near Taugevatn, the snow-sheds and tunnels become ever more frequent. In the three hundred miles of the route there are nearly two hundred tunnels, and most of them seem to congregate just where you would wish them least. Some are so short that you are through them almost before you have thought to jerk up the open window; others, such as the Haversting, or the Reinunga near Myrdal, are a mile in length; the longest of all, between Myrdal and Upsete, the Gravahals, is three and a quarter miles in length. So, just where the journey achieves its maximum degree of wonder you are alternately blinded by a waste of unbroken snow or plunged into impenetrable darkness: the effect is most exhausting.

This was the journey on which Elizabeth and I were now embarking: the seventy-mile stretch between Voss, where we entrained, and Haugastöl, where we planned to alight and continue our journey on foot. There had been a time when we had said to each other: "Let's walk the highest stretch, shall we?" We even thought we would. But a more careful glance at the map showed that there was no road at all beyond

Upsete where the year-round snowfields crowd in on all sides. It was quite exciting enough to start walking when the summit had been passed, twenty or thirty miles farther on.

We were, luckily, in the rear portion of the train. It was thus possible very often to catch sight of our engines plunging into the square dark maw of tunnel or snow-shed beyond the curved length of coaches following them. The black of the coaches was impressive, seen against the pure whiteness of the surrounding snow; but the only element of beauty they possessed was the curve they made as they rolled along the track between our window and the head of the train. With Elizabeth clinging anxiously to my coat-tails I managed a photograph of our engines disappearing ahead of us into one of those cavernous tunnels.

In fairness to her I should explain the "anxiously". She has now long resigned herself to the fact that, whatever I may say to the contrary, my head for heights and precarious perches is certainly better than hers. You may think that to take a photograph from a window hardly necessitated her clutching at my coat-tails. It did not. But on this occasion our window had jammed. Rather than risk losing a shot I coveted I darted to the end of the corridor, jerked open the door, the window of which also was fast, and stepped out on to the top step.

It was a silly thing to do, but the impulse was strong. I had no time to fit a suitable filter or do more than guess quickly what the light-value was. I felt Elizabeth clutch my coat-tails at the same moment that I caught her involuntary and but half-suppressed gasp. Over my shoulder I said "Hang on!" and a second later I got my snap. Much less than a second after that the engines had vanished, and by the time I had stepped backwards and slammed the door to half the train was engulfed.

For sheer beauty, of course, it is the early stages of this Bergen-Oslo line that take the prize. For the first good many miles after getting well clear of Bergen the line clings closely to the edge of another Sörfjord, bounded on the farther side by the mountainous island of Osteröy. Then come the foothills, snowless at this time of the year and richly clad with trees. Then there is the saucer depression containing Voss, with its hints of grandeur to come. As the train climbs out of that saucer the rivers become swifter, the falls more numerous, the gorges they have carved deeper and more precipitous. The valley drops away, its houses and farmsteads shrinking till they are but toys, though their rich and varied colours remain to delight the eye through the smokeless air.

Sometimes the falling water, running in the reverse direction to the Oslo-bound train, comes so close that you involuntarily duck to escape the flying spray. A morbid imagination asks what would happen if at any point a fish-plate came adrift, a line snapped or buckled in the heat, and wheels ploughed through wooden sleepers till they sank into the ballast and the train turned slowly over. It is not a pleasant thought; for gradients and distances are all on the heroic scale even here, and an all-steel coach, hurtling to the depths of one of those gorges, would be ground by the action of swift water on immovable rock till it looked like a sheet of tin-foil that once wrapped an ounce of tobacco and had now been crumpled in the hand. The screams of the passengers would be no louder than whispers against the roar of the falling water.

At Mjölfjell, an hour's run from Voss, you are on the edge of wild country; snow-clad mountains such as 4,870-foot Hondalsnuten dominate the scene. Here is Norway's largest Youth Hostel, built and equipped very largely by volunteer working-parties of Hostellers from many countries, students and others. It was here that a number of sturdy young men and women with well-worn rucksacks alighted, bound for the hostel and some of the finest early-summer walking to be found. As for us, we took two vacated seats, just to be able to say that we had, in fact, sat down in a Norwegian train; then, swiftly, because the mounting grandeur of the scenery filled us with such waves of excitement, went back to our corridor positions.

We reached Upsete and plunged into the three-mile tunnel, the longest in the whole three hundred miles of the route; it was as we bored our way through the mountain that we remembered having been told that for one-sixth out of its grand total the line runs through either tunnels or snow-screens. Perhaps it is as well, for the accumulated impression of stark grandeur and vast isolation which is built up amid these snow-scapes has an almost numbing effect on the mind.

At Myrdal we stopped for ten minutes. And as we did so, music burst forth and we emerged from the train in company with all but the most blasé of our fellow-passengers to find that a band was playing us in on the platform. A real band, in a smart, gold-braided, blue uniform, with a conductor whose quick gestures and rhythmic movements took them through a varied repertoire of vigorous native music.

It was as exciting as it was unexpected, and all the more so for its perfect timing. Behind the station, on its north side, the mountains rose in an unbroken sweep; there was a comforting look about the station buildings from which passengers were issuing with steaming cups of coffee. On the widest part of the platform those twenty brass-bandsmen played lustily and with the most evident relish, for our delight. Applause broke out at the end of the first number, to be drowned by the opening bars of the second: it was as though they were trying to crowd into those brief ten minutes as much bright music as they could.

Then, as suddenly as they had begun, they ended; a whistle sounded—not imperatively enough to make us feel that we were being ordered about, but enough to warn us that the train was awaiting our pleasure. The figures scattered about the platform thinned out; cornets and trombones were down-tilted and emptied; music was neatly folded away and the music-stands perched on the instruments detached and slipped out of sight; we were aboard, and the train was once more in motion. There is still some climbing to be done before the watershed is reached and the long descent through Hallingdal to Oslo begins.

There is one remarkable station between Myrdal and Finse, lying almost midway between the three notable snow-fields, Storskavlen, Usaskavlen and Hardangerjökulen itself, which reaches something over 6,200 feet. It is the station called Hallingskeid. This station is unique in that the railway engineers, knowing that the forces of nature were, at that height, unchallengeable, built the whole station within a snow-shed. It is a dark, damp and dismal station, a nightmare of a station, in which engine smoke lies over such snow as has seeped in through the massive timbers and melted snow lies in long, grey, treacherous puddles the whole of the platform length.

Leaning out of our window we could look downward on the station staff, who were wearing gumboots to a man. The only gleams of brightness in that cavernous building were the gold braid on the officials' caps and sleeves, which just now and then caught a reflected ray from the white snow beyond the ventilation-slots. A man condemned to act as porter at Hallingskeid would need strange reserves of buoyancy if he were not to succumb to the inevitable gloom and dankness of that place. We were glad when the alternating light and shade of the outward wall of the snow-shed revealed that we were once again in motion, bound for Finse.

And how different was Finse station! Here all was lightness and brightness. We emerged from the last long snowshed into open country backed by the gigantic rampart that is the Hallingskarv—that nineteen-mile-long rock wall that is three miles thick and rises to between six and seven thousand feet. The railway-line here is two thousand feet above the conifer-line: the only evidence of man's hand in an apparently limitless waste of snow and ice.

What thousands of bleak, laborious man-hours must have gone to its making we could only conjecture; and it calls still for constant and unremitting supervision, day and night. Finse is the headquarters of that sturdy band of permanent-way men whose duty it is to hold the line against the relentless attacks of storm and piled snow, landslide and rock disintegration, that could at any time, and in a matter of seconds, destroy the inspired handiwork of decades. A whole colony of these men has its centre here in Finse, living the year round at a height of 4,070 feet, on call by day and by night each to their several sections, whither they travel on their great power-driven rotary snow-ploughs if the weather is severe, or on their quaint little pedal-tricycles that ride the rails like swift tight-rope walkers, minute black specks amid the white waste that is the only landscape they know.

At Finse station there is a monument of hewn stone most

impressive in its simplicity. Here Captain Scott brought his
men to train on Hardangervidda for the rigours of the Antarctic. It was an ample training-ground, for here are steeps
of snow and ice, barren outcrops of rock, treacherous water-
ways, and lakes such as Finsevatn, on whose milky-green
waters ice-floes drift even in midsummer. Here, with their
skis and snow-shoes, their sleds and teams of dogs, they could
practise manœuvres, harden themselves for the ordeal that lay
ahead in those even more inaccessible wastes, and learn the
ways of wind and blizzard in near-Antarctic conditions.

Robert Falcon Scott did not return. The granite pillar,
rough-hewn, four-square and perhaps fifteen feet high, was
erected here in his memory and in memory of his fellows
by the Norwegians who knew so well what such exploration
could mean. I was looking at it in silence when the silence
was broken by a voice and I turned round to see one of the
party of Englishwomen we had met at Utne. Utne: it seemed
to belong, and indeed did belong, to a world quite other than
this of Finse.

"I wonder if you would mind," she was saying, "if my
friend stood beside the monument. I see you're going to take
a photograph of it." She proceeded to introduce her friend.
"You will have heard of Dr. Wilson, who was with Captain
Scott? This is Dr. Wilson's sister. It is the first time she has
seen the memorial."

There was just time to take one photograph before we were
summoned back to the train. We were descending now,
though only very gently. Ahead of us there gleamed in the
painfully strong sunshine the ice-floes on Lake Finsevatn.
The station dropped behind us and once again we were a
crawling man-made contraption limited to narrow movement
west or east, while all about us were the snowfields on which
we could imagine ski-borne giants disported themselves in
winter among the screaming winds.

At Haugastöl half an hour later we disembarked. It did
not at the time strike us as odd that we were the only passengers to alight. We stood in the sunshine on the platform,
our rucksacks between our feet, and waved to the departing
train. It was one o'clock or thereabouts on yet another day of

cloudless blue. Above the station door the figures told us that we were still 3,290 feet above sea level. We might have been three hundred thousand feet, for all we knew or cared just then: there was snow and ice about us; blue sky was above us; we had so far done no walking at all that day. A quick meal at the station hotel, and we should be ready to set out. The echo of a cry in English, "Good luck, both!" remained with us as we turned about and made for the station buildings.

Middag AT HAUGASTÖL

"I wonder what that is," Elizabeth said, pointing.

At the far end of the platform there was a mass of crumpled brickwork, bearing every sign of destruction by fire.

"Probably a warehouse," I said, and asked a railwayman who came out of a door just then which way it was to the hotel.

He registered a moment's surprise. Then he pointed to where Elizabeth had been pointing. "That," he told us, "used to be the hotel. It was burnt to the ground some time back."

"Where then do we eat?" I asked him.

He shrugged and shook his head. "Not at Haugastöl," he answered casually, and went on his way.

Elizabeth and I looked at one another in silence. By the station clock it was nearly one. We had eaten breakfast at 6.30 and had a cup of coffee and a cake (half a cake in Elizabeth's case) at Voss round about half-past nine. We had from time to time talked of the substantial *middag* we would encompass before setting out on what our map told us would be a most arduous road walk, second only to the projected crossing of the Sognefjell. It was sixteen miles to our next stop, Geilo, though there was a possible midway stopping-place at Ustaoset. But to set out to walk hungry as we were and without the slightest prospect of a wayside café would be folly.

"Someone or other will find us something to eat," said Elizabeth. "Let's go and see."

We entered the station building, but it seemed completely deserted. Returning to the sunbaked platform, we saw a man with much gold braid on his uniform: though a porter had told us we could get nothing to eat at Haugastöl the station-master would doubtless be more helpful. Elizabeth put on her most winning air and told him of our plight. Could he, she asked hopefully, suggest where we could get a meal before setting out along the mountain road for Geilo?

Like the porter, he shook his head. The restaurant, he regretted to say, had been burnt down. There was no village of Haugastöl. What we could see—he pointed eloquently to the little block of buildings which stood on the platform like the superstructure of the Kon-tiki expedition on its balsa raft, surrounded on all sides by a white and shimmering sea—was all that there was.

Elizabeth was persistent. Though she herself can go for surprisingly long periods on the minimum of food, I have, as she frequently reminds me, "a big frame to keep up". She knows how I can flag, quite suddenly and unexpectedly, when the last calories have been burnt away. "Perhaps," she asked, "we could get a pot of coffee?" Her gestures served for the body of the sentence, but the emphasis on the final word, and a movement of the hands to indicate what sized pot she had in mind, made our needs quite clear.

The station-master looked doubtful. In all probability he was dependent for all foodstuffs, including milk, on the twice-daily train, and had little if any margin to meet demands such as these. Certainly there was no grazing for a cow, or even for a goat, that we could see. Then he nodded: he would see what his wife could manage. Would we please wait in there—he indicated a small, spotlessly clean waiting-room.

We waited, as hopefully as we dared, and rummaged among the small pockets of our rucksacks to see if by any miracle there was some food we had overlooked. Chocolate had proved very difficult to buy in Norway and extremely expensive when it could be bought. We had relied upon "iron rations" of raisins and sultanas, but, alas, these were on sale only upon production of a ration-card, and this we did not have. No, the bitter fact remained that our joint supply of food was half a bar of not very good chocolate and half a dozen peppermint-drops bought in Odda in mistake for fruit-drops, and thirst-making rather than thirst-quenching.

"She'll just *have* to produce a meal for us," Elizabeth said.

Almost as she spoke, the door opened and the station-master's wife appeared with two very small glasses of milk. We paid her fifty *öre*—sixpence—and thanked her, hesitating a little over the "*tusen*" which we now almost habitually used. When she departed we looked despairingly at one another and wondered how to make half a bar of chocolate and a few sips of milk do duty for a substantial *middag*.

We might have set off on our walk very depressed indeed had it not been for a most entertaining sight that met our eyes as we emerged on to the platform. Drawn up alongside it was one of the three-wheelers the permanent-way men use for maintenance work. It was a flimsy-spidery contraption like a trick-cyclist's machine, with long handlebar-stem, low saddle, small flanged wheels and triangular wooden platform sticking out to the right, supported by a third small wheel which runs on the right-hand rail. Mounted on the saddle of this contraption was a uniformed porter. Standing beside him on the platform were a man and a very tall woman. Squatting at their feet was a small boy. What space was left among their feet was occupied by baggage.

As we watched, the porter lifted himself from the saddle, pressed heavily on the pedal and set the little vehicle in motion. Under the pressure of his pedals it gradually got up speed and was soon spinning merrily along the line in the direction of Oslo, in the wake of the train which was for us now only a memory. Enchanted by it, I dropped my rucksack and sped along the platform, overtook it, passed it, turned and ducked low and snapped the little party as they approached me.

"If only," I said to Elizabeth, "we could commandeer one of those, how easy the remainder of our day's journey would be!"

"You've always said it's easier to walk than to cycle on an empty stomach," she reminded me.

It is true. I do think so. There is something about the continuous turning of a pair of pedals when one is hungry that is far more exhausting than swinging one foot in front of the other, upright on turf, or even on a hard, unyielding road.

"But we've passed the summit, the watershed," I reminded her. "It's all downhill, now. Just think what it would be like: get up steam and then let the thing rip all the way to Ustaoset, to Geilo, to——"

"—To Oslo and beyond," she finished for me. "Delightful! And what happens when, half-way through a snow-shed or tunnel, we meet the Oslo-Bergen train? It's a single track, remember!"

Elizabeth is at times uncomfortably practical. I had not thought of that. Doubtless, she was remembering that first hectic bus journey from Bergen to Norheimsund, when we speculated as to what might happen if we met a bus bound in the opposite direction; there is hardly room in those tunnels to pass a cyclist.

"True enough," I hastened to agree. "Never mind. I'll store up the idea for my next children's adventure book. I'll be able to put into that all the bits that would give you the horrors!" And I reflected as the little machine vanished into the distance that this stretch of country was one we had been resolved to walk ever since we began to formulate our plans. So, it would really be cheating to borrow a tricycle!

But I continued to ponder the problem of encounters like that as we walked away from the station. Tunnels have to be surveyed just as carefully as the open stretches of the line. How does a permanent-way man manage when, half-way along a three-mile tunnel, he becomes aware of the muffled tremor on the line that heralds an approaching train? He can tilt his machine off the line, no doubt, but it is a clumsy object to secrete about one's person in a constricted space. A protruding handlebar, caught in the steps of a passing coach, could jerk him and his mount from his shelter in a rock hollow and carry him thudding and dangling against the moving wheels until he was torn to ribbons or smashed to pulp.

It was as we were leaving the station precincts that we

were overtaken by a car bearing the Danish flag, which emerged from a narrow lane beyond the platform. The driver stopped and we chatted clumsily in a mixture of English, French and basic Norwegian. It was his first visit to the country, too, and he had not yet recovered from the shock of seeing mountains so stupendous and unrelenting in their snow-clad uniformity. He was a bright, cheerful individual, and it was easy to understand his comment on the taciturnity of the average Norwegian. He wished us luck, and drove away, heading for Geilo. His car was filled to capacity with his family, his baggage, and the paraphernalia one always seems to pile into a roomy car when setting forth on a holiday. Had it not been for that, he said, he would gladly have taken us with him. On the whole, hungry as we were (and we were sorely tempted to ask him for something to eat), I think we were glad that the car was too full for us to be given that lift. It would have been difficult to be strong-minded and refuse; yet if we had accepted we should have been false to ourselves and our resolution to walk this splendid mountain road.

"Anyway," said Elizabeth, " it shows that, whatever we've been told, there *is* traffic on this road. If we get absolutely stuck, or collapse in the road from hunger and exhaustion——"

"—Or die from exposure," I added, taking off my jacket and tie and wondering whether there was likely to be any relief from the blistering sun between here and Geilo.

"—We'd always be able to accept a lift as a last resort," she ended, cheerfully ignoring my interruption.

There were times, later in that day, when we remembered with a certain grimness the buoyancy with which she had uttered those words. For a moment or two I wondered whether to introduce stark reason into the conversation. What I had to say had little of comfort in it. Would it, then, be better to leave it unsaid, so that one of us at any rate walked with the comforting thought of a probable lift at the back of her mind? But Elizabeth does not like being left out of the reckoning in this way, and I decided to share the point with her.

"There's one thing we mustn't overlook," I said as casually as I was able. "This road, behind us, crosses Hardangervidda to Kinsarvik. When we were in Kinsarvik—only yesterday— it was bright and warm at fjord level. But the road between the two places isn't open yet. It's still snow- and ice-bound."

"But we're going the other way," Elizabeth objected.

"Yes. But because this road isn't open west of Haugastöl there'll be no traffic on it except in the opposite direction to the one we're taking. That Dane had been to Haugastöl station to meet one of his party and he's now on his way back to Oslo. Any car that could possibly give us a lift in the direction we want will have to meet us first, going *to* Haugastöl, and then (unless it's being put on the train for Bergen) turn round and overtake us. If we meet nothing, we'll *know* there's nothing coming up behind us which could give us a lift; and that'll be that!"

"It's a thought," said Elizabeth, and she squared her shoulders to the road.

GEILO-BOUND

Road and rail run almost parallel eastwards along the mountainside from Haugastöl to Ustaoset, the road on the left and a little higher than the railway. On the other side, extending the whole way from Haugastöl to Ustaoset, is the lake named after that railway-halt: Ustaosetvatn. It is an oddly shaped and forbidding sheet of water which gives the impression of being what, in fact, it may well be, a sort of sump collecting the water, ice and snow off the north side of the Hardangervidda.

In early June it was beginning to melt and the milky-jade water was patterned fantastically by ice-floes and whitish-grey melting snow-pancakes which were somehow rather horrible. How deep the lake was we did not know, but it occurred to us both that an inexperienced skier exploring during the mid-season when snow and ice begin to become treacherous might choose to have a long ski-run downhill to this level expanse, thinking it to be firm territory—and plunge to the bottom beneath what would, in fact, be only the thinnest of unbroken crusts. Perhaps only a week or two earlier those jaggedly angular divisions between floe and floe, which showed up now as shadowed pale-green lines, might not have existed on the surface, and the whole of Ustaosetvatn would have been, in fact, an icy quicksand from which there was no return.

The railway descends to 2,650 feet at Geilo: a fairly consistent decline throughout. The road, running on its left, rises and falls at the bidding of the forces that built the rock mass on which the engineers had to work. We were walking almost due east, and the great expanse of whiteness was almost more than our eyes could bear. Now and then, even though we knew it was asking for trouble, we would turn and look back the way we had come, following the now dazzling milky water on the far side of the line to the little black huddle of rectangles that make up the station of Haugastöl. There was something curiously impressive about the thin blackness of the line itself: as though skilled fingers had laid down a long length of straight tacking in black thread across the centre of a vast sheet of white satin.

The road made good walking. I have written elsewhere, scornfully enough at times, of road-walking as opposed to walking on turf. In England the choice lies between hard macadam and the pleasures of turf or rock, and no one would choose the hard smoothness of tarmac in preference to anything else. In Norway the choice hardly arises. Except for the outskirts of the bigger towns (and how delightfully small they in reality are, and how very modest the dimensions of their suburbs!) there is practically no tarmacadam at all. You will pass from the well-laid setts of the town, by way of a furlong or two of tarred road, and then, gratefully, on to what is in effect a dust road.

I have said "gratefully", and I mean it. For these roads are firm beneath the feet without having the hardness that hammers at heels and makes any lengthy walk a purgatory. Gritty, yes; but no one minds grit, and it is excellent when boots are nailed. These roads are not soft enough for one to sink in, even with the weight of a rucksack to help; and they are not hard enough to jar the ankle. They hit the happy mean—an excellent thing in roads as in other matters. In very dry weather, though, they have their disadvantages. I am old enough to remember when the majority of English roads were of this type, and I think I can savour still (and without relish) that thirst-inducing, fine, white dust disturbed by the passing cart or wagonette, which lay in the still summer air and parched the tongue and throat.

It would be the same thing in Norway, no doubt, when traffic abounded. It was partly for this reason that we chose to visit the country before the spate of tourists went the same way. Commercial traffic, except on one or two long-distance main routes, like that between Oslo and Trondheim, is pretty sparse, and cars are not two-a-penny in that country either. We found when we did get on to more populous routes that these dust-clouds could be distressing. Some of the private cars in which later we were given lifts were driven with their windows tightly closed, the only fresh air to circulate being that filtered up through a meshed ventilator under the dashboard. It was not always comfortable, but it was better than being suffocated! When we travelled aboard a lorry we managed to perch outside and the movement of the air was swift enough to disperse the clouds of dust; if our own cloud plagued some other traveller it was not our concern!

On the Haugastöl-Geilo road the problem did not arise, for, though it was a dust road, it had not yet emerged entire from its winter overcoat of snow; the hard, beaten earth and grit had that nice resilience so often found on roads that have long been under snow and ice. It was cool to the feet, too; an excellent thing, for in the early afternoon the strength of the sun was great and we were nearly two thousand feet above the tree-line, so that there was no prospect of shade.

The road wound quietly enough, rising and falling, sometimes level with and sometimes a hundred or more feet above the railway-line. Where there was a hollow into which snow could be funnelled by transverse winds, elaborate snow-fences had been erected: tall plank screens braced by massive stays on the leeward side of the prevailing winds, plank-and-space, plank-and-space, rather than an unbroken surface, so that the force of the wind might to some extent be mitigated as it filtered through.

The patterns made on the snow by these screens were infinitely varied, a constant delight to the eye. Not only was there the over-all pattern of the straight lines of these screens intersecting, branching and forking away, meeting and vanishing in perspective; there was also the lesser, more subtle, pattern effected by the light and shade of the sunshine. And this pattern had the added beauty that it was stencilled over an undulating or corrugated surface produced by the wind-blown snow that had penetrated the gaps between the planks, arched and rounded and tapered off like miniature drumlins, till they became mere ripples on the surface.

I essayed to photograph one of these snow-screens at close quarters, and was paid out for my folly. The snow looked hard and firm, but one step from the road and I was up to my knee, to my thigh, to my groin, in snow which proved to be about as substantial as a meringue. My heavy boot felt about, meeting no resistance at all. But for the bulk of my stern and the rucksack just above it I might have continued to sink. I lay backwards, the snow striking chill through my thin flannels, and rolled myself out, while Elizabeth chortled at my antics.

Sometimes the road passed through what must have been an immense drift of snow. The section of the drift showed clearly on each side of the road: a high, rounded wall, reminiscent, except for its snowy whiteness, of the great earth rampart, Offa's Dyke, of which I wrote in *And Far Away*. Here there would be a softer, more water-logged stretch of the road, and the surface would squelch beneath our boots. But the snow was indeed melting, more especially because this was a southward-facing slope and the sun had been hot for many weeks past.

We came every now and then to a cluster of the small, squat, substantial, timber-built mountain-huts or chalets which are used by the Norwegians from Oslo and Bergen and elsewhere as week-end ski-ing bases. Many were of dark, creosoted timber, built in the old style, with the butt-ends of the great pine logs projecting at the corners and heavy roofs holding them down against the fury of wind and snow. Others were of lighter, though still substantial, build, smoother-faced, with window-frames and doors painted in bright tones of yellow, red and blue. Red indeed is a favourite colour all over the highlands of Norway, and the reason is evident: from a distance, over empty snow, no colour will catch the eye more reassuringly than red, no colour will defy the deadening pall of white with more success. Nor, of course, need you go as far afield as Norway to find this custom of painting the woodwork red: in the Welsh hills, in the Lakes and the Pennines as well as across the Border, the dark rich red rectangles of door and window-frame, barge-board and gate and fence, will stand out boldly against the whiteness that Nature can lay so thickly on, and be the means by which the returning farmer or labourer or housewife finds the safety of roof and hearth.

We did not talk much as we walked, Elizabeth and I. Partly, I think, because this stupendous landscape almost forbade words. When we did speak it was to discover that each of us was more tired already than we were willing to admit, but though we had been walking for what seemed a very long time we were apparently no nearer the habitations of man than we had been when we had just left Haugastöl. The tyre marks ran along the middle of the road, and we thought of the cheerful Dane and his car-load of family, of the food and drink they would almost certainly (being wiser than we) have brought in hampers with them, and of the resources open to them in the form of hotels and cafés so quickly reached in a large and powerful car. But no car came our way. Nor, when we stood still and listened intently, was there any sound as of a car approaching.

"I can feel my rucksack knocking at my navel," I said, vulgarly. "It is quite imperative that we should find something to eat; and soon."

"If only some kindly-looking body would suddenly swing back the locked shutters of one of these log-huts," said Elizabeth, "and beckon with crooked finger, calling out—in Norwegian or in English, or in Sanskrit if it comes to that—'Come hither, little ones, and eat and drink at my table,' how swiftly I should leave this road and accept the invitation!"

"I should probably reach the door before you, ignoring all those good manners which were inculcated into me by fond and loving parents," I said. "I should have scoffed half the contents of the table before you'd got your rucksack off your back!"

But there was no likelihood of our being put to the test. These were week-end chalets, but this was not a ski-ing season. We did leave the road once or twice and struggle across a few yards of rock and snow-soaked bog to see whether by any miracle a door or window had been left unlocked and there was anything on a shelf that we could snatch and eat. How willingly we would have left a few *kroner* in the lid of a tin, and a tiny note beside it to say that two starving walkers had been saved by their carelessness in the very nick of time!

After what seemed an age of walking we reached Ustaoset, an ugly named ski-ing centre with a gigantic (and very much closed) hotel. There was a railway station nearly opposite, and a man we spoke to told us, though without much conviction, that he believed there might be another train passing through it, bound for Oslo. We debated whether we should sit down on the fence and wait for a problematical train, or walk on to Geilo.

On our map the remaining portion of the road looked less than the portion we had already walked since leaving Haugastöl; we had not then discovered how very casually the points are marked on this map and how dangerous it could be to estimate even quite short distances along its roads. Long distances between centre and centre were printed in red and seemed reasonably accurate; but the intermediate distances, when totalled, always came to considerably more than the over-all distance. We proved time and time again that, so far as the map was concerned, the sum of the parts was considerably greater than the whole. It never worked the other way about.

Beyond Ustaoset the road dipped more steeply, the falls exceeding the rises by a good deal. We left behind us the now familiar waters of Ustaosetvatn and entered upon a stretch of road over which snow-sheds had had to be built. It was evidently a more exposed portion than we had already walked, for once again the railway-line down on our right was swallowed up at frequent intervals by long, straight snow-sheds. With their snow-piled roofs they gave more than ever the impression that the thin single-track railway was nothing more than a black tacking-thread sewn through this un-broken sheet of white. To the northward of our snow-sheds the snow was still piled high; on the other side it was melting and draining away; the sun painted hard, black lines across the road where it ran through the timber tunnels. The blue sky ahead was framed within the jet-black timbering till the moment we emerged, thankful to be in the open once again.

We were almost light-headed as we walked those last, inter-minable miles, fortunately in the main downhill. The association of hot sunshine, crystal-clear air, too many mouth-fuls of unsatisfying snow, empty stomachs and sheer fatigue had a most deplorable effect on us. We had long given up speaking. Once, Elizabeth gallantly essayed a phrase we sometimes used when we were more than ordinarily tired—a quotation, I think, from *Le Voyage de M. Perrichon*, in which that odd and irascible traveller remarks: *"Les jambes me rentrent dans le corps."* It evoked no response in me; Eliza-beth did not try again.

A mile or two short of Geilo we saw our first car on the road since the Dane had vanished from sight. It was a large, sleek, fast-moving *drosje*, travelling in the opposite direction to us, and full. I did some rapid calculating. At most it could not be going farther than Haugastöl, say fourteen miles; it might be going only to Ustaoset, say five or six miles. It would be in Haugastöl in twenty-five minutes, and so back here within the hour. If its destination was only Ustaoset we should have even less time to wait for it.

"Let's sit down till it comes back for us," I said. Elizabeth was sitting by the roadside almost before the words were out of my mouth.

Only one crumb of consolation had come our way in the last miles: no train had passed along the line, Geilo-bound. At least, then, we had been wise not to linger waiting for it. We were that much farther on. I said as much to Elizabeth.

"On the other hand," she said dispiritedly, "if we'd waited a bit we'd have been picked up by that *drosje* a bit sooner."

Only the fact that she had collected a blister, and said nothing about it until then, accounted for her attitude, an unusual one with her.

The sun was still hot and to sit by the wayside with the near certainty of a lift the last few miles into Geilo was to savour delight. It may seem that our pride ought to have made us walk that last stretch, but pride took a bad fall in the joust against hunger and fatigue.

Sooner than we had dared to hope we heard in the still air the hum of the returning car. I stood up, and saw our *drosje*—it was already "ours"—approaching rapidly on the other side of the hill on whose crest we were waiting for it. It can have gone no farther than Ustaoset, for not much more than a quarter of an hour had passed.

It slid down the farther slope and breasted the rise on which we now stood conspicuously, our Union Jacks prominent, our every look bespeaking our need; it breasted the rise and, empty but for its driver, shot by without swerving an inch. If we had not stepped back on to the grass verge we should have had our toes clipped off. Swaying in its slip-stream, we saw it disappear down the hill that led to Geilo. I was, for a moment, speechless; and even Elizabeth, who is not given to the habit, uttered a naughty word. Then, light-heartedly, "Who'd want to take taxi-rides round Norway, anyhow?" she asked challengingly, and set off down the hill in its wake.

So stimulated were we both by our rebuff that we allowed the first two or three possible houses to go by, unapproached. Better, we thought, to get into the heart of Geilo, where the choice would be after our own hearts. At least, we knew that we should not have to go any farther that night. On the fringe of the village we spotted a likely looking *pensjonat* and went up to the door. They were sorry: they were in the midst of decorations in readiness for the tourist season. They had not a single habitable room.

Only moderately disappointed, we walked on right into Geilo and tried again. But luck was against us. At some of the *pensjonats* we heard the same tale; at others there was no reply at all. Doors were locked, windows shuttered, everything spoke of the mid-season between the winter sports and the summer tourists. Elizabeth's burst of energy—spiritual rather than physical, I am pretty sure—had by now petered out. I settled her against a wall, with my rucksack as well as her own to look after, and began a tour of Geilo.

It was a Saturday evening, which may have to some extent accounted for my drawing a blank at every door. Finally, I was told, after a man had kindly made a telephone call on my behalf and refused to accept payment, that if we would retrace our steps a mile or so beyond the village we should definitely —and he emphasized this—find bed and board. He named the hotel.

Disconsolately, I returned to Elizabeth who was half asleep against her wall, wedged between the two rucksacks. "We've passed it," I said apologetically. "On the outskirts of the village. The very first one we saw. Where we didn't even bother to inquire! "

Elizabeth smiled a wan smile and scrambled to her feet. She did not, as she might so well have done, remind me that it had been my idea to ignore that place and try down in the heart of Geilo, where the choice, I had told her, would be better. She never reproaches.

I remembered that we had walked quite steeply downhill into the long, level street that is Geilo. We had welcomed the slope, for it had meant that we had merely to let our legs swing and the weight of our rucksacks carry us automatically forward. Now we had that same hill to climb! We followed the railway-line for a hundred yards or so, and there was a certain irony in the fact that just before the road branched away from it the train that had been hinted at in Ustaoset drew into the station. But any sense of irony was quickly swallowed up: at least we had done what we had set out to do: we had achieved Geilo under our own steam.

The last stretch of road, though it was steep, passed easily beneath our feet. We found a hotel and were allotted one of the most attractive rooms we had throughout our wanderings. There was good food and drink in the dining-room; there was all the hot water we could use, running in our bedroom basin; there was a toilet along the corridor that worked to perfection. Could we ask more?

HOODOO AT TORPO

"That," said Elizabeth, "is the slow movement from Grieg's Piano Concerto in A."

We had been decanted from a car that had conveyed us from a point two or three miles east of Geilo as far as Ål. It was eleven o'clock on Sunday morning. There was no traffic about. Windows were wide and men and women and children sitting in the sunshine, listening. From one wide-flung window there came in full strength a concert which we were loath to leave. How long it had been in progress when we arrived, midway through the Concerto, we did not know. We heard it through to the end, and then a selection of lesser music by the same composer; then, reluctantly, we got to our feet and continued on our way. We had heard Grieg on the radio in the first Bergen café we had entered, and again in that bigger café from whose window we had overlooked the Torvet. It would have been difficult, even if we had wished to do so, to get away from the music of Grieg.

Before leaving Geilo we had taken the precaution of stocking up with food: the memory of the previous day's experience was yet with us. Now we sat on a grassy bank to eat our packed lunch, washing it down with water from a well in a field beside the road. There was a pole standing erect by the well; a slighter pole was balanced across the top of it, a weight at the thicker end. From the other end there hung a third, much slighter, pole, suspending a bucket. We opened the well lid, worked this pole downwards through our hands till the bucket hit the water, then drew it up and, because we had no drinking-receptacles, knelt down and sipped at the cool, thin rim of the bucket. I have drunk much less well at table.

It would be hard to find a greater contrast to the terrain over which we had walked the previous day and this to the east of Ål. Very soon after Geilo the landscape begins to change basically: it becomes warmer, more lush, more gentle; the ski-runs that criss-cross the high ground all about Geilo are things of the past. Here now are fields and trees: a homelier countryside. Water flows quietly, and has lost its icy tinge. We could look back over our shoulder and still catch a glimpse now and then of the snow-capped mountains that had surrounded us only twenty-four hours before; but ahead of us the landscape smiled welcome and we stuffed our paper-bags beneath a heavy stone, took one last long drink from the well, replaced the cover on it and set foot to the dusty road once more.

To right and to left there was meadow-land, but there hung in the still warm air a smell we were unable for a while to identify. It was strongest, and by no means pleasant, as we came level with a series of small-holdings, at each of which we noticed structures like outsize rabbit-hutches. They were covered with fine-mesh wire-netting and mounted well clear of the ground on stilts. Just occasionally an odd barking sound could be heard. Then we came close to one, to leeward of it, and we solved the mystery by the nose: these were silver-fox farms. In future, when we drew level with one, we walked more briskly.

We were entering now the wide valley known as Hallingdal and said by many who know Norway well to be the loveliest of all its valleys. The broad Halling flowed leisurely between our road and the railway-line on the other bank, now no longer a hard, black line on a snowy landscape, but sheltered and concealed by trees and hedges, modest and inconspicuous. We were more than half-way between Bergen and Oslo at this point; and because in the mid-afternoon sunshine Hallingdal was sleepy we felt sleepy, too. So, at Torpo, a village appropriately enough named for such an afternoon, we threw our rucksacks down by the roadside, flags well in view, and settled ourselves down to sunbathe. Time had ceased to matter to us. If necessary, we would sleep that night at Torpo. If we chanced to get a lift we would continue eastwards as far as the lift offered. Oslo was a long way yet, and already a week of our time was gone.

We shall always remember Torpo as the only place in Norway where we were conscious of a sense of hostility. It is hard to explain. I would not like to say that there was, in fact, hostility abroad in that small, sunlit village, but there seemed to be a hoodoo over us so far as the village was concerned, and we were unable to break it.

We dozed for an hour, tanning almost visibly, and then sat up to look about us. Gol, the next village on our route, was a dozen miles or more distant. Why were we thinking in terms of Gol? It was because both of us, though we had not spoken of it to one another as yet, were becoming conscious of this emanation of unfriendliness.

It is hardly possible to explain it, but we *felt* it. To begin with, for the first time since we had arrived in Norway we found ourselves being stared at. Small boys on ramshackle bicycles came along the road and proceeded to circle round in the dust slowly, deliberately, staring at us fixedly, first over one shoulder and then over the other. When they went away their places were taken by others no less inquisitive. We did not like it. We became uneasy, sat up, muttered vaguely, tried to look as though we really quite enjoyed being the object of this concentrated, silent attention; and failed.

We decided to move on, and stood up beside our rucksacks, prepared now to hail the first vehicle approaching in the right direction. There had been a number of these: family parties east or west bound, *drosjes*, a milk-lorry or two, a small car empty but for the driver. We had ignored them, content to lie in the sun and cook. Now that we had stood up, however, the thin stream of passing vehicles dried up completely and we began to wonder whether perhaps it had just been wishful-thinking on our part. We waited a quarter of an hour, half an hour, and then decided to give ourselves another ten minutes at the outside before going off in search of accommodation. To start walking on into such an empty stretch of road at this hour would obviously be absurd, though we did not relish the idea of staying on in Torpo.

The ten minutes passed and we set off down the village street to find a *pensjonat*, but we could not find one. If there is a *pensjonat* in Torpo it is certainly well secreted: another example, we told one another ruefully, of the village's latent hostility. We came at length to a small house carrying a board with a word on it easily translated into "Lodgings". It was the first house we had seen that could be fairly called dingy; we did not like the look of it. I hammered at the door and a seedy individual emerged, wiping a bleary eye on the back of his hand and then his hand on the seat of his trousers. He gave us to understand that there was a room available, but no food.

Even had there been a promise of a good cold table I think Elizabeth and I would have turned the offer down; the place just was not the sort we expected to find in Norway. Had we shut our eyes tightly and then opened them it would not have surprised us in the least to find that we had been transplanted suddenly to, say, some dingy industrial suburb and the notice: Beds for Transport. In a week of this clean, bright country we had been spoilt. We shook our heads, and he did not seem to care one way or the other. Without a word we turned east and set off along the dusty road, leaving all that was Torpo behind us.

But Torpo had one more small trick to play. It is hard, now, to describe the impression made on us soon afterwards by our reception at a small wayside café. We entered and approached the counter. No, there was no coffee. No, there was no milk. No (as a last resort) there was no tea, either with or without milk. We could have a bottle of mineral water. The apathetic girl placed a bottle containing some technicoloured fluid before us, and jerked off the cap. No, there was no *smörbröd*. But there were cakes: she placed before us two objects that looked harder and drier than ship's biscuit, and took our money.

Meanwhile, we had become conscious of eyes boring into the backs of our necks. When we turned about with our cakes and the bottle and sat down at a small table we found that the rest of the room had filled up with half a dozen youths in heavy sweaters and knickerbockers. They were regarding us in silence beneath lowered brows.

We brazened it out—just. Elizabeth poured the liquid into two small glasses, essayed to break the iron-bound biscuit into two portions and was defeated by it, smiled engagingly at me and took a sip from her glass. The effect on her was such as to make me stay my own hand. I saw a look of horror spread over her tanned face. She got up. I slipped my biscuit into my pocket so that if the worst came to the worst we should have something to gnaw upon, and followed her through the doorway, down the steps and on to the road, never more thankful to be out of a house than I was just then. The eyes that had bored into us from the start clearly had telescopic lenses, for we felt their impact on the backs of our necks till a turn of the road mercifully put a spinney of trees between us and them.

Then, of course, cars began to overtake us. At first our hearts lifted, for there was not just one car, or even two or three, but a steady stream of them, even if widely spaced. Every one of them was full, but people now waved cheerfully as they overtook us and melted into the distance.

"They seem friendly, at any rate," said Elizabeth.

There followed a succession of empty cars: by empty, I mean having plenty of room for us and our packs. Surprisingly, the occupants of these cars, whether *drosjes* or private, did not wave to us as they passed. Car after car we hailed, with a variety of gestures ranging from the casual to the suicidal; but the result was always the same. They sped past, roomy and comfortable and sure of their destination, while Elizabeth and I, our buoyancy-temperature dropping a degree or two with each rebuff, plodded on into the unknown.

Where, we asked ourselves, did these innumerable *drosjes* come from, and go to? Who used them? Did their drivers— those opulent-looking individuals with peaked caps who gazed so stonily ahead of them as they shot by—just drive them for pleasure at week-ends? Why, they did not even slow down to see if they could squeeze a fare out of us!

Then the discouraging thought came to us that perhaps in the week since we had left our native shores England and Norway had fallen foul of one another over some matter of imports or something; perhaps our very flag was anathema to the honest Norwegian? For a moment or two we even contemplated hiding our Union Jacks. But we forbore. Instead, we slumped forward more resolutely, our flags coming to life in the breeze of our motion. Perhaps this gesture of courage would break the hoodoo that had lain upon us for so long?

NESBYEN CHOIR

A bus overtook us, travelling briskly. Wildly we flagged it, taken by surprise at its advent, and began to stumble after it. A bus, after all, was a public service vehicle: it was obliged to stop on being signalled.

It did not stop; or not at first. It ran on for a hundred yards, followed by its own private cloud of dust and giving no sign that we had even been noticed. Then a red light flashed in the rear, a hand signalled that it was slowing down, and a moment later it came to a standstill. A man hopped out and beckoned to us in the most unexpected fashion. Instead of a vigorous wave or an inquiring lift of the hand he fell to miming our own movements, staggering from foot to foot in mimicry of our own clumsy movements as we ran with our rucksacks hammering on our backs. Only then did we realize that there was no further need for us to hurry. Our run dropped to a trot, to an easy walk. By the time we reached the bus its occupants had alighted: a party of some twenty-five women, almost every one of them in national costume, the richly embroidered Hallingdal dress. They proved to be the Nesbyen Choir, returning from a concert they had been giving higher up the valley. This was their private coach.

There were one or two men in the party, including the man who had leapt out to mock our plight—a waggish individual with a ready tongue and a twinkle in his eye; but the majority of the party were middle-aged women who in ordinary garb might well have passed unremarked, but who now caught and held the eye, every one.

Each wore a full-sleeved blouse of snow-white cotton and a long black skirt which fell from a breast-high yoke and broad shoulder-straps. No two of these were embroidered in the same way, but there was something common to them all in manner and inspiration. Large flowers and petals and twining stalks covered the fullness of the black material and spread, skilfully reduced in scope and pattern, up the wide shoulder-straps. On their heads they wore natty little embroidered velvet caps, close-fitting, set back on their sleek hair, some of them with velvet straps or bows tied under the chin. Buckled shoes completed the costume.

Though the dominant note was black there was such a richness of gay colours, such fancy and imagination in the interwoven decorative designs, that it could not be called sombre. Most of the women wore large brooches, either at the neck or clipped to the square yoke. Some wore in addition pendants and little bright-ribboned medals, further evidence of the Norwegian's love of bright things.

We were talking, Elizabeth and I, to the man who had hailed us, when we realized that something was afoot. The coach had drawn up at the water's edge for the party to look at the view across to the farther side of the valley. As though by mutual tacit consent the score of singers had formed a flat horseshoe on the grass verge of the road; then, without pre-amble, they broke into song. Sweetly on the still evening air rose the women's voices, soprano and contralto, warm and clear and bell-like; and in the background the bass and tenor of the three men of the party gave it weight and substance. No other sound came to break the magic: the last of the cars and *drosjes* seemed to have gone by and we were now too far from Torpo for anyone to overtake us on a bicycle and spoil the scene.

Entranced, Elizabeth and I stood there, listening. I caught the eye of the choir leader, their priest, and indicated my camera. He inclined his head gently, and I took my photo-graphs. The choir ended one song, paused a moment while I took another picture, and then without any prearranged signal that I could detect broke into song once more. The last song was sung to the tune of our own National Anthem; this took us by surprise, for we had not known that the tune was common to both countries.

It was time to move on. The Nesbyen Choir began to climb on board. By then Elizabeth had found that several of the women spoke English, and while I was ramming our ruck-sacks into the capacious boot in the rear of the coach she had been seized by two of them and taken on board. When I arrived I found only one seat free, at the very back of the coach. The place beside me was occupied by a tall young man who, even at the end of this long day of song, could hardly control his innate urge to sing. In a deep and beautifully modulated voice he sang softly to himself Norwegian songs such as we had listened to at Bergen. From time to time his voice was raised, and row by row the occupants of the coach took it up; before long the whole coach was alive with music once again.

Snugly ensconced midway along the coach, Elizabeth was in animated conversation with women all round her. Tantalizing snatches of sentences floated back to me from time to time, but I was too far away to catch most of what was being said. She had blossomed, since being swept on board by these middle-aged and friendly women, and a flush of happiness and excitement lit her face so that when she was half-turned towards me it was as though there was a light in that part of the coach.

The young man next to me appeared to have no English, so after one or two attempts to engage him in conversation I gave it up, content to listen to him singing. But suddenly, to my surprise, he broke into a vigorous version of " John Brown's baby's got a pimple on his nose! " and sang verse after verse of slightly ribald matter with immense relish. Then his voice died away and more decorous singing broke out; the whole way to Nesbyen the journey was enlivened and made rich for us by the inexhaustible capacity for song of this happy choir.

As we approached Nesbyen, which is, so to speak, the " Capital " of Hallingdal, the coach slowed down and stopped from time to time to allow one or more members of the choir to alight. Through the windows we could see them tripping up lanes and footpaths to their small homesteads set among the fields: farmers' wives, mothers and, in more than one case certainly, grandmothers, returning from their festival of song.

We stopped at last in Nesbyen itself, a clean, neat little valley village with a hotel, a *pensjonat* or two, some small, tidy shops and a superb backcloth of tree-clad hills on either side of the Halling. I went round to the back to collect our rucksacks, so that we should have them on our backs when the moment came to thank our hosts for their kindness, and thus be able to make a quick, clean exit.

Elizabeth's eyes were sparkling as I came up to her, holding out her rucksack to slip it on to her shoulders. "Fru Eide Svenkerud has invited us," she announced in a voice that almost trembled with excitement, "to spend the night at her farm! "

An hour later we were sitting round a big refectory table in Rud Farm: Fru Bergliot Eide Svenkerud, her massive and taciturn husband, a lanky teen-age son, Elizabeth and I, and Pröst Djuvik, the leader of the Nesbyen Choir. He proved not only to have fluent English, but to be a most accomplished pianist; before we all went to bed he sat down at the Blüthner and for a long time played Grieg and Chopin and Debussy and Bach, by ear and faultlessly.

I find it difficult to describe Rud Farm; there was so much to see, to ask about, to try to remember, in its tradition and symbolism. It was one of the oldest in Hallingdal: a building in which every corner, every piece of substantial and satisfying furniture, every ornament, spoke of tradition lovingly cherished. There was warmth and colour in the folk-weave curtains and table-runners, the upholstery of the chairs, the loose mats on the waxed pine floor and the hanging tapestries on the spruce-plank walls. In simple wooden frames pictures of the Norwegian scene confronted us between the windows; through the windows we looked out on to the wide lawn in front, the orchard behind, and through a vista of fruit trees to the paddock and fields that lay in the flat valley-bottom between the hills that enclose Hallingdal.

TIMBER-BUILT

It is only now that I realize what skill must have gone into the building of the great room in which we ate our meal, listened to music and had such good talk. It spanned the breadth of the house, yet there were no pillars to obstruct the view between window and window, though this was a two-storey house of unusual size. Here were no brick-supported beams, no steel girders: just the massive timber framework which the Norwegians understand so well how to assemble, and the sturdy quality of the country's native building material: fir and pine.

In Ireland, the homestead man builds for himself is the single-storey, whitewashed stone dwelling, snugly thatched with turf or straw. The long, low cottages seem to spring out of the bog and rock which surrounds them, as though they are born of the soil—as indeed they may be said to be. In Norway man builds from his native materials, too. But because the stone is somewhat intractable, or perhaps because the hills of granite are less ready to hand than the thousands upon thousands of acres of conifer, he builds as he has always built, in wood. Perhaps, too, because the Norwegians are essentially a race of sea-faring men they choose the material which has been tried in the sternest conditions: the timber that has carried them over wide and pathless seas, and carried them safely home again. If further confirmation of this theory were needed it could be found in the dragon-heads that challenge the winds and snows at the gable-ends of the *stavkirkes*, of which I shall write all in good time.

It must in part be this building material that gives such a sense of life and lightness to the Norwegian landscape. Solid and permanent as the buildings are, they give the impression that they could without much difficulty be transported bodily to some other site and set down for a further span of life amid new surroundings.

Above all this, of course, the material they are composed of is alive. The trees that went to their making grew on the steep mountainside not so long ago; they have reached the building-site, not by way of quarry and merchant's yard, but water-borne in ones and twos and threes and occasional circular rafts like gigantic water-lilies glowing rich yellow in their moving lake of deepest blue or ice-green water. And when they have come to the site the stoutest of their number are erected once more: corner-posts and newel-posts standing proudly as they once stood on the mountainside, to brace the lesser timbers that lie one upon the other to form the walls.

Trunk and stem and branch: once again they have taken up their natural relationship, and so the house is a living thing, not so many tons of quarried stone or moulded brick.

We became increasingly aware of this "living" quality of houses as we journeyed through Norway, but perhaps never more so than when we slept that night at Rud Farm, Nesbyen. Apart from the earthenware and glass and cutlery on the wide table and the panes in the windows there was hardly anything but wood to be seen in the dining-room-lounge where we spent the evening. The floor was waxed yellow; walls were yellow, unstained, glowing warmly when the lamps were lit— not to give real light, for it never became truly dark, but to give that extra sense of cosiness and intimacy which is theirs to bestow. The ceiling was a paler yellow: narrow planks with hardly a knot, and beams showing the grain, the occasional adze-marks where a knot had been smoothed off, and the hint of resin that bespoke their origin. There was no wallpaper or distemper, no paint on the essential wood-work—which is perhaps why the unglazed pictures looked so particularly well in their solid wooden frames.

When the last piece of Grieg had been played and the priest—so evidently a welcome and well-loved visitor, with the dignity and forthrightness of the best of his type—had shaken hands with us and taken his departure, we went to bed. Up a flight of bare, wooden stairs with handrail polished by genera-tions of use, along a bare wooden landing, then a corridor, and into one of the spare rooms. There were two beds, snug with deep pillows and *dyner* stuffed, we guessed, with feathers collected on Rud Farm. Folded over the foot of each bed were two thick blankets with an unexpected Red Indian design upon them, soft as velvet to the touch. How welcome they would be, we thought that hot night, in winter-time!

It was light enough to get ready for bed without artificial light, for, though the windows faced north, up a twist of the valley, and looked out on to grass and fruit trees and an infinite vista of farmland, there was a radiance in the sky that never, even in that latitude, entirely deserted it. Eliza-beth and I, leaning out through the window together in our thin pyjamas, were conscious of the subdued life that was present all about us: the little trees growing modestly in the orchard above their carpet of grass; the conifers higher up the hill-slopes, silent because there was no breath of wind to stir them; the Halling, in quiet motion eastwards, the great urge of the ice-fields and mountain torrents dissipated into wide, shallow places where the current was so slight that one would have been forgiven for thinking it to be just another of Norway's innumerable lakes. And, not least of all, the sense of life in the house under whose roof we were now to sleep: the kindly master and mistress and others who were now settling down in their bedrooms; the others of the household, each in his or her room, perhaps speculating as to what those English visitors were thinking; and the house itself, no less quietly conscious than its occupants.

We knew this without doubt when we had withdrawn from the sill over which we had leaned and supped our fill of the warm stillness outside. For, unlike a stone- or brick-built house, this wooden house remained alive throughout the night. It breathed with us, so that we did not feel, as we might do within walls of stone or brick, that we were imprisoned. We heard the faint creaking and whispering of its timbers accustoming themselves to the hours when there would be no mortal movement among them; the stretching, as it were, of wooden limbs which could change their positions; the muttered words and phrases of relief or comment or query from the planks and beams and joists and trusses and king-posts which had been silently performing their duties throughout the day and could now relax from them for a while.

I have never elsewhere felt this same sensation of being among living material—except perhaps on board ship. And that, after all, is basically very much the same thing. It only strengthens what I have already said about the Norwegians and their shipwright conception of the builder's craft.

We saw next morning, when at last we could tear ourselves away from Rud Farm, a close-up example of this timber building. In Norwegian towns, it is true, you will see stone buildings, and in their suburbs you will see buildings with a stone or concrete base and a timber superstructure. But not so often in the country.

In a field on the outskirts of Nesbyen two men were leisurely at work erecting a wooden house. Lying at haphazard about the site were scores of straight timbers, shorn of their bark, gleaming in the strong sunshine like sticks of butter-yellow toffee. The two men were placing them in position, inter-locking their butt-ends with skilful blows of the axe, so that stage by stage the walls rose, dead true, four-square, close-knit. At intervals shorter timbers would replace the longer ones, and the rectangle for a window or door become apparent. The butt-ends varied from timber to timber, often marked with the sawyer's or grower's sign.

But we had seen elsewhere the finished article and knew that when the essentials had been completed someone with a saw would come along and cut the tops and tails off those timbers so that the interlocking ends made a pattern that pleased him. They might be left round in section, or shaped at the sides until they were elliptical, or flattened top and bottom and side and side, with the resultant corners shaved, or lozenge-shaped: there is no end to the variations that can be played on the timber theme when a man still has pride in his work, the gift of imagination, and not too keen a sense of the swift passage of time.

The fundamental principles of handling and ornamenting timber are few and still persist. After examining the Folk Museums of Oslo and Lillehammer and elsewhere you can trace the modern variants on the old-time practice by looking about you in any country district. A few sturdy tools, handed down from father to son and to grandson; a native sense of proportion and balance; a rein-loose imagination: the results are to be seen in their hundreds and thousands the length and breadth of this smiling, uninhibited land.

They love paint and bright colours, and the reason for this has already been suggested. But they understand also that timber, whether in the round or in plank form, is in itself a thing of beauty, its grain infinitely varied, its light and shade and depth hardly twice repeated, and subject to the influence of sun and wind and cold. So, the builders often

leave their timbers to receive their decoration at Nature's
hand, and Nature has nothing to learn, even from the most
skilled Norwegian artists in colour. Elizabeth and I never
tired of running our fingers over the wood we encountered,
marvelling at the glossy, satin smoothness of bare wood from
which bark had been peeled, at the texture of timber that had
long forgotten the touch of axe and adze, but still knew the
caress of summer breeze and the stern chisel of winter wind-
borne ice. Small wonder that the Norwegian housewife is
house-proud to a degree hardly known here: there is no end
to the polishing and waxing and loving attention she will
devote to the woodwork which makes up so great a proportion
of her home. . . .

After breakfast we went with our hostess to see what con-
stitutes a true Norwegian farm. We passed from her own
part of the house, where the furniture included books and a
piano and *objets d'art*—for she was a travelled and highly
cultured woman—to the original farm building which adjoined it: a low-slung building of two stone-floored rooms
with an upper floor reached by a ladder that rose from the
floor of the main room and rested against a half-floor like a
minstrel's gallery without its balustrade. Here, two hundred
years ago and for many years to come, the man of the house
and his wife slept, withdrawing the ladder when they retired
to their great box-bed for the night. This "room" stretched
over about half the floor of the main room. From it the occupants could, if they wished to do so, keep an eye on what went
on beneath them.

This is called the *Hallingstua*, and at Rud Farm it had
been carefully preserved in its original state. On the walls
were large panels gaily and strikingly painted in the local,
Hallingdal, idiom by an old man who had been, like his forbears, the painter of such panels for the dale community.
I know of nothing quite like it here in England; the nearest
I can suggest is the painting to be seen on the few surviving
canal narrow boats so well described and brought to life for
us by L. T. C. Rolt in his book of that name. There is the
same florid boldness, the same conventional, somewhat
stylized quality in the panels large and small. They are not

easy to describe in words, but gay and stimulating to encounter unexpectedly on a canal passing through and under the back streets of some dingy town.

From the *Hallingstua* we passed to what is perhaps the most important single building in any Norwegian farmstead: the *stabbur*. This is a massively constructed storehouse. Here are kept the essentials for the community that is based on the farm, in quantities sufficient to see them through the grimmest of prolonged winters. It is approached by a sort of drawbridge or ramp, and elevated well above ground level so that, though snow may lie about it, the main fabric will be clear. More important than that, perhaps, is the danger of rodents; the *stabbur* is therefore raised on great timber cotton-reels (the equivalent of our Cotswold and other "staddle-stones").

Here, in this Rud Farm *stabbur*, was everything you would expect to find in a well-appointed farmhouse in Norway. Slung over beams were bearskin rugs almost too heavy to lift single-handed: used when the occupants of the farm had a journey to make by sleigh in mid-winter. Amongst the fur rugs was a long fur coat for driving a sleigh which had been handed down from the husband's grandmother. From hooks there dangled hams and dried fish, most unappetizing to look at, indeed almost surrealist in appearance, resembling the time-worn skeletons of monstrous bats dried and pickled and stowed away. Here were the smoked salmon, the salted leg of lamb, the bin upon bin of corn, the reserve of powder and shot, the rat- and other traps, the kegs of vinegar, the horse-blankets, tarpaulins, skis and ski-ing kit, the leather harness and coils of spare rope, heavy oilskins and sou'westers, hanks of twine—a hundred and one objects which must be on call in emergency, objects which belong, one would have said, rather to some pioneer community staking its first claim in the backwoods or prairie.

Indeed, this is very nearly true, for here in a country ruled for the long dark months by weather conditions that offer no quarter, all must be self-contained, self-supporting, with a margin for safety and succour rather than a knowledge that in an emergency one can call on the outside world for help.

Hence the skins and other raw materials which seemed to us, with our comfortable background of artificial amenity, so surprising; but which might well be the difference between life and death to those who had call to make upon them.

It was in the *stabbur* that we were shown the bear-proof key used to lock the *saeters*, or upland farmsteads used in the less inclement weather. The *saeter* has not only the ordinary type of key, massive and intricate as an old-fashioned church-door key, but also this unique instrument of wrought-iron designed to outwit—of all individuals!—the prowling bear, who is so much more cunning than we may be led to think as we watch him catching buns at the zoo.

It is like a small ship's anchor: a shank perhaps a foot long, with a ring at one end and two curving claws at the other. The claw end of the "key" is pushed through a slot in the thickest part of the heavy door of the *saeter*, which may be six inches thick or more. When it has been pushed through it is given a slight twist and then pulled outwards. The claws engage in a set of wards that cannot be engaged from the outer side of the door at all. With the exertion of a good deal of strength this additional lock is then turned, and the door can be opened. The *saeters* are far removed from the valley farms, in use only in the better weather of the short summer months. During the remainder of the year they are deserted, though fodder and other commodities may be left there in store. The bears know this and, hungry and enterprising, prowl the lonely highlands for what they can steal.

Now, as the brightness goes out of the sky and the first chill wintry winds begin to sweep down upon us, I remember the warmth and light and colour, the extraordinary sense of life, that permeated everything at Rud Farm, Nesbyen: the gaiety of that first evening, with the black-coated priest at the piano, pipe in mouth, playing piece after piece, while Fru Eide Svenkerud looked among her songs for the one she would sing to us next, and then slipping easily into her accompaniment and out again at the end of her song into some Grieg dance till she was ready to sing again.

We were lucky, of course, Elizabeth and I, to find ourselves among three English-speaking people, for there was much that we should never have come to understand if we had been dependent upon our own poor store of Norwegian. Nevertheless, so warm and generous was the feeling there that I think we should have come away with almost the same full sense of intimacy even if no English had been spoken. We tore ourselves with difficulty away.

LOG RAFTS

East of Nesbyen, or rather south-east, the valley is wide and the river flows quietly, hardly lower than its banks. On each side the valley-bottom extends level for some distance, to change into steep, well-wooded hillsides soaring to a fine, undulating line against the sky. Snow no longer covers them. In the valley, half hidden by the copses of silver birch, are the red-painted or weathered timber farmsteads, small and neat and self-sufficient, midway between road and flowing water. The river bore upon its shining bosom rafts of felled timber destined for the saw-mills farther downstream.

We did not see the rafts at first, but early on we had noticed, a few yards out from the river bank, a continuous line of logs floating motionless in the water, linked end to end with chain or twisted rope. Later we found out what purpose this served. Logs began to appear, drifting in the current in ones and twos and threes, scattered haphazard as though strong-armed Scots had tossed their cabers away from them at random and looked elsewhere for sport. They floated, not always end-on, but sideways and diagonally; had it not been for this smooth, unbroken fender of tethered logs they would often have drifted spear-like into the soft mud of the bank, there to pile up and be lost to the sawyers.

Farther downstream we saw them in greater numbers. Timber-men had knit these slim, solitary travellers into companies a hundred, a thousand strong. They had been tethered and girded about by linked logs in round and elliptical rafts which slid with an easy idle motion downstream until they were cornered by waiting sawyers and impounded alongside the water-driven or electrically-driven saw-mills.

I have said that they looked like gigantic water-lilies, but there is a more apt analogy. I would say rather that they were (except for their buoyancy) like immense millstones floating between bank and bank. This was because, though the hoop of timbers binding the whole together was uniform and unbroken, the contents of that ring consisted of clustered timbers short and long, lying parallel to one another, but at an angle to other clusters. There resulted a pattern such as may be seen on the chiselled millstones that once ground our corn, but now stand discarded against mill walls, or are incorporated by enthusiasts into crazy-paving schemes, or turned into door-steps or what-have-you. Particularly when the sun was low over the bordering hills, as it was during the latter part of our journey down Hallingdal, this pattern of light and shade, this angular grouping of yellow timbers within the tyre of the raft, reminded us of millstones: the whole raft surface appeared to have been chiselled and fluted into the eccentric lines of the millstone-wright.

I was never able to examine closely one of those travelling rafts. I should have liked too, to see how they were assembled, to watch the men, nimble as cats on their toes as the logs spun and rolled beneath them, forming and breaking up these sticks of frozen honey. I may seem ungrateful, but the fact is that, a few miles out of Nesbyen, just when we were beginning to wonder whether it would be possible on this empty road to get to Hönefoss and so on to Oslo before the time came for us to embark once more on *Venus*, we were overtaken by a fast-moving light truck. The driver stopped alongside us. His companion got out, went round to the back and rearranged an assortment of canvas, spare tyres, mackintoshes and waders, sacks and other gear, for our convenience, carefully re-stowed two fishing-rods, and helped us on board.

We travelled swiftly down the lovely Hallingdal valley for between two and three hours, and very soon our necks were stiff from turning our heads left and right and left again to snatch at some new beauty, some hardly descried wonder of crag or tumbling water or high-pitched farm, before a turn of the narrow road hid it from us for ever. We followed closely the river, and at every turn in the later stages a log raft came into view. But though I tried and tried to take the picture I wanted, always a tree came between me and my quarry, or the truck lurched and a picture was spoiled. The best of the rafts drifted down the Halling, but it was not until some days later, and on another river, that I got my pictures. It was a lesser raft altogether, and the sun was too high for me to capture the full effect of chiselling.

We drank in our impressions through the sense of smell as well as of eye and ear. For every now and then, at some bend where the road came close to the water's edge, the sharp, warm smell of newly sawn timber, the fragrance of still living saw-dust, invaded the air, and we knew we were passing one of the innumerable little saw-mills which are the middlemen between the growing timber and the craftsmen who build the houses. An expert may be able to distinguish between tree and tree by the smell of its fallen dust. I cannot. But if there is a more unforgettable smell, or one harder to describe, than that of a saw-mill where pine and spruce and fir have been worked, then I do not know of it.

Man's hand is not prominent or obtrusive, in Hallingdal. His houses, as I have said, seem living things: a collaboration between himself and Nature. One other feature stands out, surprisingly without offence. Curving and rising and falling against the background of trees along these hillsides are the immense sweeps of power-cables, from pylon to giant pylon. There are some who would say that wherever these appear they mar a landscape, and I myself am inclined to agree when the setting is, say, the Sussex Downs. But not here, in Hallingdal. There is something so majestic, so heart-stirring, in the grandeur of conception that one is not troubled but filled with admiration. The cables do not, even away from the valley-bottom, stand out against the skyline; they rise and fall in tremendous, sweeping, gentle curves, grey-white against the dark or light green of the conifers and the dark grey of the rock, glinting where they catch the sun at the right angle.

Because of their position they invite wonder and admiration. Men with tools must have climbed to those gaunt heights, quarried in the rock, mixed and run cement, erected the steelwork of the pylons and embedded it for ever in the living mountainside. And then, with their drums and tensioning-tackle, they had to fight their way up among the trees to lift the cables to the tops of the pylons and establish them as lines of power-communication between source and consumer. If the swift movement of the open truck made it impossible for me to appreciate fully the floating rafts it added something, I would say, to the impressiveness of those sweeping lines of twin and quadruple cable, for they seemed to come alive as the angle from which we watched them changed, and the trees and skyline moved behind them.

As we drew nearer to the east of Norway, approaching Hönefoss and Oslo, we found that passers-by on the road, cyclists and men and women and children going about their tasks and play, began to wave to us. We had been told that the people who live in western Norway are dour and uncommunicative, and we had noted rather regretfully that very few of them acknowledged our gestures of greeting, let alone volunteered any themselves. But now it was different: people waved, called out a greeting, followed us with their eyes, called to one another to come and look at two people with rucksacks displaying Union Jacks speeding by in a light truck. The friendliness was progressively more and more marked as we approached Oslo and persisted until we got into the Jotunheimen, where we entered another Norway altogether, the Home of the Giants.

A mile or so short of Hönefoss our truck stopped and the two men got out. This was the end of their run. We scrambled stiffly down from our perch among tyres and canvas, shouldered our rucksacks and set off downhill into the town. Hönefoss is marked large on the map, but is, in fact, a small township of some three thousand inhabitants. There was a roaring of water on our left just short of the town and we went across to inspect the giant falls over which the river tumbles foaming into the heart of the town. Baulks of timber, logs and scattered heavy planks tossed in the water above the falls and then plunged desperately downwards. Alongside them was a massive timber-chute, graded to carry the logs end-on and at a less immoderate speed to the backwaters in which they were collected for the saw- and pulp-mills. Even in early June there was a thunderous quality to that roar; what it must be like earlier in the year, or in late autumn and winter, when the river is in spate, it is hard to imagine.

Having found somewhere to sleep we went out in search of something to eat and drink, for this *pensjonat* supplied breakfast only. Very soon we were eating *smörbröd* and drinking cold dark beer. I had been surprised at the cost of the beer when I paid for it at the counter, but had thought merely that prices were this way in a country where so few people seem to drink anything alcoholic. We ourselves had drunk nothing but milk or coffee since our arrival, if we ignore that hectic fluid at Torpo, which we sampled and abandoned.

Elizabeth, after one tentative sip, put her glass down on the table and turned to me. "This," she said, "is a very remarkable beer."

Now, Elizabeth is even less of a connoisseur of beer than I am, and drinks only when it is extremely hot and beer is called for to accompany cheese and tomatoes on a picnic lunch. There was, admittedly, one occasion when, in default of anything more orthodox being available, lunch consisted of four bananas, a box of Black Magic chocolates and two pints of mild, taken on a canal bank where we were looking out for material for a B.B.C. feature programme we were working on.

When I had tasted the beer, however, I was quick to agree with her. This was beer such as I do not remember having tasted for ten years and more. And as if to strengthen the impression, the girl who had served me appeared at our elbow.

"Have you," she asked, "a motor-car?"

Not in Norway, we told her. She nodded, satisfied. Then I asked her why she should have come and asked this apparently irrelevant question. But it was not irrelevant, it seemed. Had we been in charge of a car, and proposing to drive it again that evening, it would have been against the law for her to serve us with this beer, and a punishable offence for us to drink it. The penalty for being found at the wheel of a car with even a fraction of one per cent alcohol in our system was a term of imprisonment without the option of a fine. We only learnt this afterwards.

We were drinking Norway's famous "Export" beer. I have not discovered to what countries it is exported, and there are doubtless regular beer-drinkers who will sneer at my inexperience and reaction and tell me that there are places in England where I can drink an even stronger beer, at a less price, and drive myself away afterwards (if I am capable of pressing the self-starter) without fear of imprisonment. There may be; and I may one day be glad to sample such beer. For the moment, however, I am content to remember that tall cold glass of Norwegian "Export" beer which we drank in Hönefoss.

Elizabeth tells a foolish tale of how, unwilling to see her waste the bottom half of her own glass, I took hold of it and drained it after I had drained my own, and had then the utmost difficulty in making my way back to the counter to return the glasses. Do not believe this: it is one of her quaint fancies, without a shred of foundation, bless her!

OSLO TO TESSAND

BREAKFAST IN OSLO

OSLO was celebrating the 900th anniversary of its foundation and was chock-full when we arrived there from Hönefoss. One-sixth of Norway's entire population lives in this capital city which is hardly larger than Bristol and smaller by a good deal than Sheffield.

It was, in the brilliant and almost overpowering sunshine, a gay and stimulating city, with flags flying, new paintwork everywhere, bright flowers wherever flowers could possibly be planted or stood in bowls and vases. Low on the wide, thronged pavements of Karl Johan's Gate there was a sequence of shallow bowls into which there splashed discreet jets of crystal-clear water. The disturbance they made on the surface made a kaleidoscope of the quaintly patterned-and-painted inside surface of the bowls. At night, by a subtle use of hidden electric bulbs, each bowl with its little jets was lit up from underneath, and Karl Johan's Gate became a promenade of magic beneath its graceful trees.

In the late evening we walked through the grounds of the king's palace. Oslo men and women, boys and girls, strolled along its walks, sat about on its lawns, talked quietly and intimately in the shadows of its high buttresses. There were no iron railings to keep them at a distance, no warning notices to drive them away. A young sentry paced briskly between his sentry-box and his rendezvous with his opposite number, turned smartly about, and endlessly repeated the performance: the only sign that the palace was under guard. Behind and below us, for the palace stands on high ground, were the lights of Oslo's centre: the street-lights, the coloured fountains, their soft glow irradiating the under side of the trees along the boulevards, the winking red and amber and green traffic-lights, the darting sidelamps of the cars; ahead of us was the quiet of the residential district in which we were to find a small *pensjonat*.

It was owned by an apple-cheeked old lady who proved to have less English than any other proprietress we encountered. Worse, she had more difficulty in understanding our slender store of Norwegian than anyone else we had met except the girl in Bergen we always referred to as the Blue Girl. In despair at her inability to make head or tail of what we were saying about breakfast in the morning, she fetched out another resident, who had a few words of our language and acted as interpreter. I suppose it was she who unwittingly paid us the best compliment we received in Norway. On our breakfast table each morning we were there she placed two morning papers: she must have taken it for granted that we read the language sufficiently well.

One thing at any rate she had certainly grasped, and that was our nationality. After a night spent in our well-windowed bedroom, in the two narrow box-beds placed oddly enough head to head along one wall, we were summoned to breakfast. We sat down to a table spread for us and no one else. There was the usual cold fare, in great abundance and variety above average. But just as we were beginning to make our selection she came in with an oval dish containing three fried eggs and eight rashers of excellent smoked bacon. They were small rashers, it is true, but there were eight of them on that dish. Elizabeth did not fancy a cooked breakfast: she had seen the best prepared salad she had been offered since landing in Norway, and knew that I should not be interested in that.

The coffee was well above the standard we had become accustomed to, though that had always been beyond reproach. There was marmalade as well as the usual fruit conserves and various jams. I ought, I suppose, to be ashamed to confess that I ate all that was placed before me; and with the greater relish in that I had almost forgotten the taste of bacon and eggs. Perhaps it was on account of the havoc I wrought that the following morning I was offered a dish containing three eggs and ten, let me repeat, ten, rashers; and with that an omelette which must have contained four more eggs at least. Perhaps it was as well that we were spending only two nights in Oslo: I should not have liked to insult that generous woman by leaving anything on the dish that she offered me, and there is no calculating the proportions the meal might have attained in, say, a week's sojourn! When at length we came to leave we sought out a *blomsterdame* and bought from her a bouquet of flowers. These we presented as we paid our very reasonable bill. We were thanked in an incoherent flow of Norwegian.

It is perhaps ungrateful after such a welcome not to pay tribute to Oslo's much-vaunted new Town Hall. We cannot honestly do that. Inside, it may be all that a Town Hall of this century should be; but outside, it looks, with its dark brickwork and uncompromising lines, as though it has been hewn solid from a block of Norway's own *gjetost*, that ubiquitous goat's-milk cheese. It stands well, it is true; looked at from the Pipervika, where the ferry-boats are moored, it has a certain presence. Its gilded clock-dial with its well-proportioned hands dominates the right-hand tower, and the bold bronze figure beneath it is impressive. But for us, at any rate, and I think for many other visitors, there is something just wrong about this Town Hall: a certain coarseness of conception, and always the ill-chosen material of which it is fashioned. We preferred to stand with our backs to it and look outwards at the wide water and the ships large and small, whose lines were so much more pleasing to the eye.

THE WORLD OF GUSTAV VIGELAND

Towns, even such clean and spacious towns as Oslo, were not for us on this trip, and we only stayed that second night because we did not want to leave without visiting Frogner Park and seeing for ourselves the controversial Vigeland statuary. Much has been written about this and you meet many even among the uninhibited Norwegians who say that this *tour de force* should never have been permitted, let alone sponsored. Elizabeth and I cannot agree. For here the whole is greater than the sum of its parts. Individual figures among the hundreds to be seen may not be Gustav Vigeland at his finest; his conception of the human form may not be that of the sculptor of the Elgin Marbles on the one hand or of Epstein on the other; the suggestiveness of some of the poses and the emphasis of some of the anatomical features may not be to everyone's taste; but when all is said, this remains one of the most astonishing conceptions ever to be gestated in the mind and heart of a single individual and executed to the last detail under his inspiration.

Vigeland died in 1943 at the age of seventy-five, and I suppose that in the whole history of sculpture there is no more astonishing page than that which he wrote. When he was little more than a boy he was working for an Oslo wood-carver at a wage of less than a shilling a day; when he was twenty-five he held an exhibition of sculpture which evoked the critical comment: "This is Vigeland's feeling for life expressed in a unique personal art. It is pessimistic if one considers the outward form, but genius has baptized it with fire." He had lived the first third of his life.

At the end of the second third of his life, so potent had his genius become that the Municipality of Oslo offered him an income for life, a studio to his own designs and a site extensive enough to accommodate whatever gigantic scheme he might have in mind. Their only condition was that he should devote the remainder of his life's work to them. He worked uninterrupted for the last twenty-five years of his life and left behind him plans and drawings and models which would enable skilled workers to complete the scheme. The result is to be seen to-day in Frogner Park.

The handbook to his work consists of more than sixty packed pages of text and photo and diagram. The only way to assess truly the aims and achievement of Vigeland would be to spend days on end among his statues, handbook in hand. We had not time to do this; nor would it, in fact, have been profitable, for one could quickly be surfeited by such a wealth of imaginative three-dimensional work. There is a magnet-like power to most of the sculpture, whether in bronze or in granite, which makes it exhausting to linger: the figures demand an intellectual rather than an emotional response.

I remember reading many years ago, in a book by either
Buchan or Rider Haggard, a first-person account by a man
who had been taken prisoner, tied to the back of a horse and
then led in procession through a vast concourse of people in
forest darkness. I forget his name; I forget all the details,
except this one: the utter exhaustion that supervened as a
result of a myriad casual touches of hand or shoulder or body.
It was akin to the death of the thousand knives. Here in
Frogner Park there was something of the same experience.
Too close contact with the fantastic bronzes of the Tree
Groups, or even with the reliefs in the Fountain Group,
the oldest unit in the whole conception, or the Figure Gates,
or the Lizard Groups—lizards play an important part in
Vigeland's work, symbolizing the dangerous world in which
puny man can hope in vain for mercy or salvation—produces
that same sense of prostration which is a sort of little death.

It is hard to convey any idea of the stupendous fertility
of fantastic invention which was Vigeland's. Some hint of
it, perhaps, may be offered by a set of captions taken at ran-
dom from the individual figures and groups. In the Tree
Group: Flying Girl descending through the branches; Man
and Woman entangled in the branches, their heads down;
Skeleton sitting in the tree. Among the Fountain Reliefs:
Foal kicking little boy through the air; Boy fighting Eagle;
Woman sitting in the horns of a reindeer; Dwarf lifting Girl.
And in the Lizard Group: Naked Man fighting big Lizard.

It is this emphasis on nakedness, and the frequent deliberate disproportion in the anatomy, which in the main distress
the sightseer who goes to Frogner Park unprepared. Gustav
Vigeland was clearly at war within himself between the
Christian and the pagan approach to life, and so vigorous was
his thought that it achieved crystallization almost before its
primal urge was cooled. Then tenderness of the man-woman,
man-woman-child relationship is balanced against the cruelty
of primitive and untutored beliefs; one turns from one to the
other in bewilderment, at a loss to assess the sculptor's true
philosophy or creed.

The Park is dominated, of course, by the 55-foot granite
monolith which is the sculptor's greatest achievement. We

are told that as a child Vigeland used to carve wooden knife-
handles in which human figures were interlocked; in this
Column, focal point of the whole vast world of his sculpture,
we have the apotheosis of his inspiration. There are many
who say that the inspiration is undeniably phallic: the mass
of stone thrusts upwards into the sky, carrying with it, or
propelled by, a vast concourse of curving and writhing figures
large and small, which could, without much twisting of the
truth, be regarded as symbols of spermatozoa. Vigeland himself emphatically denied this interpretation, but it has to be
said that he never substituted a satisfactory alternative explanation. He contented himself by saying: "The column
is my religion." We may, perhaps, leave it at that.

The writhing figures—how many there are we were unable
to count, and I do not truly know how one would set about
the task—consist of men and women and boys and girls and
babies in every conceivable posture of anguish and rest, sup-
plication and despair, fury and resignation, terror and delight.
Some of them, particularly at the base of the column, seem
inert, static; in others there is a terrible dynamic quality that
would make one expect to see them really break away from
the tangle of limbs in which they are enmeshed and seek
their own territories, singly and in twos or threes. I am not
sure that I would care to spend a night at the base of the
column in Frogner Park.

Higher up the column movement begins—a spiral movement that seems to twist the column itself, though it peters
out in a welter of static figures part-way up. Here is anger
and effort and self-seeking, with victory for some and defeat
for others. Towards the summit the broken spiral of movement is resumed and there is again the sense of futile upward
surging which had so powerful an effect in its initial stages.
But this, too, peters out and, so far as one can see, the uppermost figures are mainly those of children, but children in
whom a terrible maturity can be detected.

It is a tragic piece of symbolism rather than an exalting
one. I do not know a tithe of its meaning, nor ever shall. But
I do not see why one should feel disgusted by it, or indeed by
any of the innumerable figures which crowd that sculpture

park. Many of them, I am sure, do not do full justice to Vigeland's genius. I think he allowed that genius to become overlaid at one period of his work by influences that ought not to have affected a man of his calibre.

This seems to be particularly the case among the thirty-six granite groups which radiate outwards from the base of the column. Men and women and children again; young and old, grave and gay, static or dynamic. An old woman blesses a young woman, laying her gnarled hand on the younger woman's hair; three kneeling boys watch a bird flying; a man kneels behind a woman, embracing her; a man and a woman sit facing one another, their foreheads touching; two old women kneel, listening: the variations are endless. But among these granite figures there are too many who have massive torsos, bull necks and disproportionately small heads. There is, in a word, too much that is reminiscent of the Mussolini pose: the challenging mass of muscle, the sheer bulk, the square, bald, uninspired head.

Not all the figures, even among the men in their prime, are so executed. There are many whose features are clearly, even delicately, chiselled from the granite block. We were there at a time when the sky was overcast and there was little light and shade. With a strong, clear sun such as we had enjoyed till that morning almost ever since we had left Bergen, brows would have cast shadows, muscle-ripples would have been thrown up and the impression of solidity modified; a little mystery would have been wrapped about the more complex figure groups.

One mystery, however, there was even in such poor light conditions. At a yard range the granite surface of these figures appeared rough like gritstone; to the touch, however, it was satin-smooth. It was an experience I had over and over again during the hours we spent there. I never ceased to be surprised by the contrast between what my eyes saw and my finger-tips felt.

The sculptures in Frogner Park are not, of course, all the work of one man. Even in twenty-five years no worker, however ardent and however muscularly endowed, could hew from granite blocks or cast in bronze more than a small

137

proportion of this world of figures. Vigeland was given all the skilled masons and sculptors he asked for, all the facilities he could possibly need, an inexhaustible supply of the best materials. He himself worked with an energy which can hardly have been exceeded by the most prolific sculptor before or since his time, and the men who worked with him can have worked hardly less urgently. They shut themselves off from the rest of their fellow-men, to live a life of almost monastic seclusion. Year after year went by, but they paid no attention to what was going on in the world outside them: the only world they knew was the world of studio and foundry, of granite, plaster and bronze.

The monolith is perhaps the best example of this absorption in their work. The block of granite itself, weighing not far short of three hundred tons and between fifty and sixty feet in length, was quarried near the Swedish frontier and brought to Oslo by water. Thence it was man-handled to its site. I spoke with someone who had watched it being drawn through a small village on the outskirts of Oslo: it had taken a full day to do that short stage. As soon as it had been set upright on its raised terrace a vast shelter was erected round it, the full-scale plaster-casts, in three sections, were brought into the shelter and set up alongside, and work began. Three highly skilled stone-masons began at the top of the column, working their way downwards to the base where, fifteen years later and midway through the German Occupation, their work was completed. It was in the year of Vigeland's death.

To stand gazing upwards at the innumerable figures which, in fact, compose this column, and with this knowledge in one's mind, is a humbling experience. It was Sir William Watson who wrote:

"The Statue, Buonarotti said, doth wait,
    Thrall'd in the block, for me to emancipate. . . ."

He was speaking for Michelangelo. But the Frogner block thralls a vast number of individual if interlinked statues, each of which had to be brought to the light of day singly and in relation to its fellows. And Vigeland, part-way through the uncasing of these statues, changed his conception of the whole and called for fresh figures to be carved: not from the virgin block, but from the figures which had already been laid bare and completed. This, it always seems to me, is one of the great wonders of this work; and in one's admiration should be included, surely, those unnamed Scandinavian stone-masons—Danes and Swedes as well as Norwegians—who wrought so finely and for so long, that Gustav Vigeland's powerful dream might be made a reality.

In all more than a million pounds was spent on this enterprise. Some will say that the money was ill laid out; others that a million seems little enough for such a display of genius. We would gladly sacrifice almost all the granite groups (though not the soaring monolith) but not one single bronze figure. Certainly not the furious small boy who stands on one foot, his other raised in uncontrollable passion, his small bronze fists clenched in impotent rage. Certainly not the fine, striding male figure with the boy riding him pick-a-back. Not even the figure which, of the bronzes at any rate, seems to arouse most anger among sightseers: the great bronze figure of a man with one diminutive child on his left shoulder, two toppling off his right forearm and a fourth being projected football-wise from his right foot. "Man chasing four genii," says the translated caption. But is that it? Or is he, as is suggested elsewhere, "protesting against fertility"? It is the explanation which we would prefer to accept. Certainly the babies seem to be enjoying themselves, while the man is in an agony of frustration.

It is hard to leave this fascinating subject, and I am aware that I have said nothing of the elaborate scheme of lay-out which links figure with figure, group with group, gate and column and bridge and fountain and labyrinth, in such a way as to intensify the total significance. This must be done by an expert who has grasped the symbolism of the whole, or else merely be hinted at, as I have done.

But when at last you leave the sculpture park and make your way down the long avenue of trees towards Kirkeveien and the trams that will take you down into Oslo's centre, leave yourselves time to examine the superb gates. Here we have

Vigeland's lizards again, and there is deep symbolism in these struggling creatures, the tortuous knots that bind or fail to bind them, the twisted metal ropes, the vicious, stinging tails, the geometric designs, the dragon-like masks, the darts and hooks and star-like patterns so intricately fitted into the rectangular frames that constitute the gates.

THE VIKING SHIPS

We passed from the strange world of silent figures in stone and bronze to the outside world of living streets and throngs of people. In a little shop up a side-street just off Kirkeveien we ate pastries and drank milk and through the open window watched the people go by. Something clearly was afoot: crowds were collecting and there was an approaching blare of trumpets and other wild music. Curiosity triumphed over the half-forgotten delicacies, and we went out into the main street to see what it was all about.

Oslo's students in their brilliant red berets, their red-striped trousers and jackets and blouses with designs in appliqué-work on back and front, were demonstrating on behalf of the Lifeboat Institution. It was a cross between a well-organized Rag Day and a modest Lord Mayor's Show. Wagon-loads of attractive girls in fancy dress or national costume alternated with ramshackle cars driven or pushed by strangely garbed youths who clearly hailed from Ruritania, Bolonia, Mars or Jupiter—anywhere other than Oslo itself. Teams of huskies harnessed with the strangest rigmarole of ropes and leather traces hauled curious vehicles bearing challenging placards. Individuals came along the road in weird guise, dancing fantastic dances, performing acrobatic feats, dodging from car to car, from wagon to wagon, leaping on to horseback, seizing a husky's place in front of a wheeled sledge, riding roller-borne skis, uttering outlandish cries.

Tableaux on some of the big flat wagons came suddenly to life, pleading in eloquent mime for larger and ever larger donations to their most worthy cause. Bells and rattles and popguns broke upon our ears, antiquated car-hooters were blown, throaty klaxons croaked at us, strident blasts and curlicues of sound were extracted from the unlikeliest of instruments. It was all very surprising to two people who had by now come to look upon the Norwegians as a most undemonstrative race; we could have wished our Danish friend of Haugastöl had been there to watch with us and wonder. Perhaps he was, for the last we had seen of him—was it really only four days ago?—was his disappearing stern as he set off comfortably along the Haugastöl-Oslo road, leaving Elizabeth and me to our momentous walk.

There was a lot more in Oslo that we knew we ought to see. After the motley procession had passed out of earshot we sat considering whether we should go and wander through the many acres of the Folk Museum at Bygdöy, or look at the Viking Ships not far away, or at the Kon-tiki raft a little farther away than that; or merely relax—and then perhaps regret our lack of enterprise.

"There's an Open-Air Folk Museum at Lillehammer," Elizabeth reminded me. "And that's on our way after we leave Oslo. It'll probably be smaller, so there'll be fewer sightseers and we'll do better there than here."

We washed out Bygdöy, so far as its Folk Museum was concerned, with its 80,000 exhibits, its extensive acreage of ancient buildings—a hundred and fifty of them at least. But we could not see the Viking Ships anywhere but at Bygdöy, so we went there first thing after lunch.

These Viking Ships are, I suppose, Norway's greatest treasure. The earliest of them to be dug out of the mounds in which all three lay, alongside Oslo Fjord, was named *Gokstad*, after the farm near which it was discovered some seventy years ago. Buried in her, some time in the reign of Harald Fairhair, was a Viking chieftain, together with twelve horses, several dogs and, oddly enough, a peacock. Their remains were found inside this 77-foot vessel just as they had been deposited a thousand or so years before.

The second ship is *Oseberg*. In her had been buried, round about the year A.D. 800, not merely a Viking chieftain, but Asa, a Viking Queen. And this queen, who was buried at the early age of thirty, took with her to the Viking after-world her gold and jewellery, an ox, sledges and dogs, and even her carpets—a possession only of the wealthiest and most distinguished of twelve hundred years ago. A pleasing touch of the trivial kind which I myself find outweighs most historical fact is that a supply of fruit and nuts was buried with her, that she might not want for her favourite dessert. Nor did she lie alone in the long-ship. Beside her was found the skeleton of another woman, presumably her favourite handmaid, done to death that her mistress might not arrive unaccompanied on the threshold of the unknown world to which death had sent her. Her treasures may be seen to-day in Oslo's Historical Museum.

The third ship was called *Tune*. With the discovery of these ancient craft it became possible to write a more certain chapter about the high level of culture and achievement which legend and intelligent deduction had till then only suggested. Here was a collection of representative implements and personal belongings in use well over a thousand years ago. It is touches such as these which bring ancient history to life. Is there, to parallel this story, a better indication of life among the legionaries on Hadrian's Wall in England than that series of scooped curves, that scalloped edge to the stone water-cisterns, which reveals how the soldiers sharpened their swords after a skirmish with the wild Northerners against whom they had to defend their conquered territory?

Gokstad, *Oseberg* and *Tune* are most intelligently housed at Bygdöy in great, white, vaulted chambers that set off their fine lines to perfection. Built into the curved walls of these radiating chambers are high galleries from which it is possible to look down into the interior of each ship in turn. So delicately conceived are the sweeping lines of the black hulls, with their carved stem and sternposts, that they give from ground level the impression of being quite small craft. Ascend to one of the galleries, however, and you will be amazed at the breadth and depth, the sheer capacity, of these long-ships. Not so long ago a modern long-ship was rowed across the North Sea and up the Thames by a crew descended from the men who sailed *Oseberg*, *Gokstad* and *Tune*—what a lovely name for so lyrically conceived a craft!   We saw this modern long-ship amid the grey stone of a bombed site in Manchester. Even there she had a loveliness that made one forget the ugliness about her.   How much more entrancing was this ancient vessel, quietly lying beneath the white vaulted roof of her permanent home.

We were not the only sightseers.   Swarms of schoolchildren had been brought to Bygdöy that afternoon, and every vantage-point was occupied.   For schoolchildren they were remarkably quiet; only very rarely did we hear a word of mild admonishment from one of the schoolmasters in charge. Elizabeth and I, picking our moments, wandered at leisure alongside and beneath the long low hull of one of these lovely craft, noting the skilful manner of laying plank upon plank, the method of bolting the timbers, the knowledge of stress and strain and balance that was evident at every turn, and wondering at the soaring stempost with its carving and challenging dragon-head.   Such craft as these had crossed the same North Sea over which we had lately and in such ease and comfort passed in m.s. *Venus*; had crossed it in all weathers, and often to unknown and unsuspected landfalls.

I wish now that we had gone a little farther on than the Viking Ships to see the Kon-tiki, which was on show at that time.   I had not, then, read Thor Heyerdahl's remarkable book, or I certainly should have done.   Now it is too late, and I suppose I never shall see that balsa-wood raft with its crazy superstructure which made that unforgettable Pacific voyage. I have a foolish dislike of commercially exploited sights or I probably should have gone; but, after seeing the three long-ships in their beautifully designed home, I felt, as I know Elizabeth did, that anything else would be almost certainly anticlimax.

We took one of the small ferry-steamers from Bygdöy to the quayside at Pipervika beneath the Town Hall, almost the only adult passengers among the horde of schoolchildren. Most were in ordinary dress—frocks, knickerbockers, hand-knitted jerseys and the little woollen caps with tassels like nightcaps. One child, however, was in native costume: a tall, slim girl with a winsome little face.   She stood out among her schoolfellows like a semi-precious stone among a lot of trinkets, and I asked her teacher if I might take a photograph of her.

The woman was delighted. "It is Aga's thirteenth birthday," she told us. "That is why she is wearing her native costume."

Aga stood a little self-consciously on the landing-stage while her schoolfellows were whisked to one side so that they should not come into the photograph. As soon as she could she melted away among them, and I turned to find my hand seized by a lanky individual in a tight-fitting brown suit who was stuttering at me in a mixture of English and Norwegian. While he pumped my hand up and down, gazing earnestly into my face at very close quarters, he talked so rapidly and incoherently that at the end of his tirade neither Elizabeth nor I had any very clear notion what it was all about.

Evidently something had deeply stirred him. Evidently, too, he was an Anglophile. I think he may have been in the Merchant Navy during the war; perhaps have enjoyed hospitality or sanctuary at our hands. Now, at any rate, he was seeking to repay something. He knew we were English, he had noted the interest we were showing in the child's national costume, and he wanted somehow to reward our interest. He told us he wished there was something he himself could do to make our visit to Norway yet more enjoyable; Norway, he assured us, was a lovely country, filled with beauty and interest for visitors like ourselves. England was a fine country, too, and one that he had visited and remembered with affection.

I do not now recall one single phrase he used; but I do recall the intensity with which he spoke, his earnestness and sincerity; his anxiety to convey to us something important to him. He was the most articulate Norwegian we met, and I can still feel the rough clasp of his hand on mine. We were so taken aback by this unexpected greeting that I doubt whether we succeeded in conveying to him how truly happy we were to be in his country and to have met someone who loved England and wished to say so. A little overcome, perhaps, by his own impetuosity, he melted away into the background, and we lost sight of him. I wish we could meet him again: we could tell him more adequately now what Norway came to mean to us both.

OSLO TO LILLEHAMMER

The last impression we had of Oslo was as we were making our way to the bus that would take us from the outlying suburbs and give us a springboard into the hinterland. Revolving slowly in a corner of one of the big squares was a Ferris Wheel. It carried on its perimeter balancing seats, but these for once were not occupied by fun-fair goers seeking a bird's-eye view of territory they ordinarily knew only from ground level. Instead, each of the seats had been transformed into a giant window-box or miniature garden of bright flowers, and the flowers were revolving high above our heads against a background of grey stone, red brick, concrete, tram-cables and chimney-pots.

Oslo we thought a gay, clean city, and we said so to a friend at whose house we spent one evening.

"Oh, no," was her reply. "A dingy city, when you compare it with the Swedish capital. Stockholm is a clean and bright and lovely city."

It was surprising to be told this, above all by a Norwegian girl living in one of the pleasantest of Oslo's suburbs. If she considered Oslo dirty and dingy, what must have been her reaction when she visited, as she did some years ago, some of our own big industrial centres? We did not ask her, and she was too polite to tell us. Perhaps the fact that her Canadian husband is one of Oslo's more enlightened and progressive architects may have produced this diffidence. For us, however, Oslo remains, after Paris, the loveliest capital city we know.

We left it by the big main road that makes for distant Trondheim, Norway's third largest city. Tall blocks of flats, spacious squares, steeply rising streets—these we left behind us, to approach the rolling open country which, though warm

and lovely with its big fields, its copses and spinneys, its undulating skyline, might have been Berkshire or Wiltshire but
for its buildings. This is Oslo's hinterland, for sea and fjord
lie to the south of the city, and the Norwegian thinks in
terms of salt water. Beyond it, far ahead beyond Lillehammer, lie Gudbrandsdal, Ottadal and the Jotunheimen
for which, now, we were bound.

Hitherto, all our main travelling had been eastwards or
southwards from Bergen. After we had left Oslo we were
embarking on the second "leg" of our journey, north and
then north-westwards to the highest point in Gudbrandsdal;
the third and last "leg" would return us to Bergen by way of
Sognefjell and Sognefjord. Lillehammer was now our first
important landmark. To reach it we had some fifty miles of
road to travel to Minnesund at the southernmost extremity
of Norway's largest lake, the 60-mile-long Mjösa. This is a
curiously shaped inland water, sharply pointed at each extremity and never more than nine miles across. It reaches
its greatest width roughly midway up its length, between
Gjövik on the west bank and Hamar on the east; there the
island of Sund lies like a great raft just off a square tongue of
land projecting outwards and downwards to split the lake
into two narrow arms. Lillehammer lies thirty miles farther
north still, at the uppermost extremity of the lake, and is
really the threshold to Gudbrandsdal.

We left our bus at Jessheim, one of the most attractive
small villages we saw. The broad road cuts through it like
a blue-grey blade, and alongside it are white-painted houses,
the model petrol-station, clean and spruce as a dairy, the café
and bookshop and general stores and post office, strung out
like trinkets on a ribbon. We bought ice-cream and ate sandwiches beneath a broiling sun; much as we had enjoyed the
sights of Oslo, we were glad to be in open country once more,
foot-loose and bound for the unknown. Then we stowed our
ice-cream cartons in a hole in the bank on which we had
lounged, shouldered our packs and set off northwards.

A lorry rolled up alongside us, slowed down, halted. A
blond driver leaned out, made an inquiring gesture with his
thumb, and was out of his cab in an instant to seize Elizabeth's

rucksack and give her a shoulder on to his cargo of milk-churns. A moment later I was up, too. We settled ourselves with our backs to the cab, wedged our rucksacks behind us to prevent roll on corners, locked our sticks beneath our knees for greater security, and sat back to enjoy the run.

Milk-churn tops make hard, unyielding seats. We tried every variant on our basic position, but the lorry was travelling at a steady forty miles an hour on a wide, undulating road, the best we had seen since the stretch between Hönefoss and Oslo, which, also, we had travelled by lorry. We got some slight relief when we stopped a second time and two young Danes carrying enormous rucksacks were boosted up from road level on the driver's sturdy shoulders. In the sixty seconds needed to take them on board we stretched first to one side and then to the other, easing our half-paralysed rumps, and toyed with the idea of sitting, turn and turn about on one another's knees. Then we settled down to another stretch of discomfort. Minnesund was our destination, and at this rate of progress it could not take more than another quarter of an hour or so!

The Danes were perhaps more accustomed to this sort of travel than we were. They made themselves surprisingly comfortable, spread-eagled on the flat-topped lorry, their centre of gravity as low as possible. Only their heads rolled from side to side as we took first a left-hand, then a right-hand turn without reducing speed. At Minnesund there was a squeal of brakes and the lorry stopped. The Danes handed down our rucksacks and we exchanged good wishes. They stayed on board, and we were to see them twice later on, bound for Trondheim and going strong, walking in two pools of shadow cast by their enormous rucksacks, the sun beating down upon their bare brown necks.

"Left bank or right?" Elizabeth queried, as we sat in a wayside café studying our well-worn map.

The lorry had taken the right-hand road, clearly the better of the two that defined the banks of Lake Mjösa, and the one likeliest to carry frequent traffic. It made for Hamar and, sixty miles from Minnesund, our own objective, Lillehammer.

"There's nothing in it, so far as distance goes," I answered. "Our best chance of a lift will be on the right bank. But——"

"Let's take the left bank, then," said Elizabeth; and we did.

There was another reason for choosing the left bank, and she knew it as well as I did. It was now mid-afternoon. If we had taken the right bank our view across the water to the fine wooded slopes on the left would have been straight into strong sunlight. If we stuck to the left bank we should have the sun behind our left shoulders as we walked, and a view of hills and trees and blue water lit for us by the sun behind us. I have more than once planned a trip, either on foot or by car, in such a way as to have the country lit for me by a sun that shines above and behind.

We had certainly said good-bye to passing traffic. The road was a dust road again, and the dust was an inch thick, fine and powdery as flour. Even a passing cyclist could raise sufficient of it to make breathing uncomfortable for a minute or two, and the occasional car or van that passed drove us into the hedgerow, our faces turned away, our mouths tight shut and eyes screwed up. We were glad to enter a belt of trees, even though they grew so close to the road that for considerable stretches we could only just discern the bright waters of Lake Mjösa, lying far beneath us to our right. Across the water we could see now and then the road we had decided against; on it at intervals we spotted a car or lorry which could have been ours if we had taken that route. But we had been too much surrounded by vehicles and petrol-fumes and the hurly-burly of business and the movement of people on pavements to want any more for a while; we were happier to walk, in spite of the dust.

We had one short lift, again unsolicited. This time it was a private car, an elderly one at that, driven by a middle-aged to elderly man who had with him his 85-year-old father, white-whiskered and blue-eyed. He was, too, surprisingly garrulous. There was no doubt that those who had told us that the eastern districts of Norway contained more communicative people than the western were right in what they said.

Had we, the old man asked us, been to America? No. Well, *he* had. Yes, he had made the Atlantic crossing, he assured us, when he was still a boy. He had gone by Cunarder. Her name he could not now call to mind, but he did remember that the fare for the single trip was five dollars and took a week. We did not like to challenge him; but was it ever possible, we asked ourselves, to cross the Atlantic by Cunarder for five-and-twenty shillings?

After a few miles the driver stopped, got out, shook us both by the hand, regretted that he had now to turn off the road, wished us well and drove away. We walked for a very long time, the country becoming lovelier with every mile we covered. Our road rose and fell, but in general maintained a sufficient height above the lake for us to have a fine view across its increasing width to the tree-clad hills on the farther side. There was no snow in sight. In fact, it was difficult to believe, in this shimmering heat, that anywhere in all Norway at this moment snow might be found. Yet only a few days earlier we had been walking well above the snow-line, and soon we were to enter a region of snow and ice again, as we climbed out of smiling Gudbrandsdal into the Jotunheimen.

I do not suppose we walked much more than twelve or thirteen miles that afternoon, and the walking was easy, except for the dust, because the road was firm beneath our feet without being hard enough to jar our heels, and there were no stiff gradients. Thirst was our main worry, for the road was almost void of wayside cottages or farms and there was no running water visible. To clamber down to the lake for a drink would not have been difficult, but the steep climb back to the road would have created thirst anew. So, we were not sorry to come at length to Kapp, a tiny hamlet on the bank of the lake a long stone's-throw from the island of Sund. We entered the only *pensjonat*, found running water and a first-class plumbing system in full working order, and a meal second to none we had been offered until then.

It was a curious *pensjonat*, tenanted almost exclusively by men employed at a small works down by the lake. We ate our meal on our own, the others having had theirs earlier; and we ate it to the music of Grieg played over the air from some Oslo studio. Only the previous evening we had visited

Oslo's Broadcasting House. I myself had not been much impressed by its exterior, but the interior is a palace of wonder where stone and steel and glass and figured woods combine to present beauty at every turn. There was, too, a much greater sense of freedom within its walls than ever you will find at Broadcasting House, W.1.

From the window of our bedroom, at the top of the house, we had a fine view across the breadth of Lake Mjösa, across the low island of Sund, to the hills and trees in the distance lit by the warm rays of the westering sun. The *pensjonat* was white-painted inside and out and seemed for that reason less substantial than some houses we had entered. It was perched on a steepish slope that fell away from the road towards the lake, and was thus a storey higher at the back than at the front. We were at the back, overlooking the lake (though not near enough to have a balcony, as at far-off Norheimsund, overhanging the water); we had thus an added sense of height. It felt to us as though at any moment the lightly built framework with its white-painted weather-boarding might take to itself wings and sail at bird-height across the still waters, ourselves its delighted passengers.

"And here," said Elizabeth, "is our anchor-rope, in case of need!"

She indicated the neatly coiled hank of thin strong rope which constituted the fire-escape. We had met this before. The Norwegians, with such a high proportion of wooden buildings, are more on guard against fire than those countries which build in stone and brick. At every upper window there must be the strong hook, the systematically coiled hank of sufficient rope, that the occupant trapped by fire may throw it out and save himself. If he can! There was, so far as we could see, no loop or cradle or other gadget in which he could fasten himself. It is not everybody whose grip on a thin rope is adequate to enable him to descend two, let alone three, storeys to safety on the ground. Perhaps fear lends not only wings but grip.

"If we once took off I think I'd be content to remain in the air," I said. "I doubt whether there's a single corner of Norway over which we would not be happy to hover."

"Or happier still to alight and explore," said Elizabeth. "But *after*, rather than *before*, a night's rest, if you don't mind."

We had washed the dust from our eyes and hair and the pores of our skin, but it lingered still in our throats. This was an evening when the Export beer of Hönefoss would have been welcome again: it was strong enough to wash away the last clinging film of that fine, inescapable dust. But Hönefoss was the other side of Oslo and belonged to main roads leading into capital cities; we, here in Kapp, were heading for empty spaces again, the untried splendours of Gudbrandsdal and the loneliness of Norway's highest hills. We contented ourselves with a boiled sweet apiece, stripped off our hot clothes and spread ourselves on the cool sheets of our narrow beds in a dusk that never entirely surrendered to the darkness of night.

Ever since I had made the discovery that matches in Norway were *fyrstikker* I had looked forward to the moment when I could walk into a shop and ask for a box of fire-sticks. At Kapp next morning I was able to do so. And as I walked out of the shop I found myself repeating an absurd rhyme of which I could recall only a fragment, about some reckless young boy who had played with matches and burnt himself to death. It was not, I think, one of Belloc's *Cautionary Tales*, though that entrancingly horrific volume appeared when I was a very small boy. No, I think it was the extempore verse of a young and poetically minded uncle, who used to recite:

> "He lit Wax-vestas, lit Tand-stickers,
> Lit fire-sticks that burnt his knickers. . . ."

What happened to him I cannot remember (the small boy of the poem I mean), but I suspect that with his knickers on fire his number, so to speak, was up. And I realize how Nemesis is come upon me, for I smoke a pipe and all too often a piece of burning ash falls from the bowl when I am unaware, and makes a small, neat, black-edged hole in trousers or coat.

The morning surprised us with a threat of rain and we had not walked more than a couple of miles before the rain began in earnest. We were beginning to extract our oilskins when a car drew up alongside us, a door opened and we were bidden to enter. Two silent men in front, both smoking pipes, drove stolidly ahead after a monosyllabic greeting. There was no alternative road, so they knew we must be bound for Gjövik, ten miles or so distant.

Unexpectedly, they came to a halt near a copse and I then noticed that one of the men had a gun between his knees. The engine was switched off and both men got out. They indicated that they would not be gone long, and vanished gun and all among the trees. Elizabeth and I sat and waited for the shot we expected, but it did not come. It was most odd.

"They're wanted by the police for carrying lethal weapons, and have gone to bury it in the heart of the forest," I said. "At any moment now the police will turn up and we shall have to choose between playing dumb-clucks and spinning some-convincing yarn."

"With *our* command of Norwegian?" Elizabeth asked. "Anyway, there just aren't any police in Norway—or only two or three at most. They're not needed. No, the truth is that they've gone to see a man about a gun, if you ask me."

It may have been so, for they returned soon afterwards, walking in silent single file through the trees. They no longer had the gun, however. For the twenty remaining minutes of our journey we speculated individually as to what the story was, but we never found out.

At Gjövik we disembarked and, noting that the rain had eased up a good deal, set off for Lillehammer in good heart. The road was pleasant without being exciting; the lake had been at our right elbow for more than thirty miles and was now a familiar friend. The map showed nothing of importance between Gjövik and Lillehammer, and it was beyond that town that our real objective lay. So, when a big American car slowed down beside us and its driver beckoned we accepted the invitation willingly enough.

For a little while I was at a loss to place his accent. He

spoke English more fluently than any other Norwegian we met, but his accent was neither English nor American. It had a rather ugly, hard quality to it which I had met before, but still could not for the moment name. Then I knew: Australian. And very soon he confirmed my surmise: he had spent most of his life out there on various engineering jobs and had not been back in his native country a year yet. He was extremely knowledgeable, but preferred straight talking to answering questions. As a result, a host of queries we should have liked to raise went unanswered. He would interrupt the steady stream of his talking with sudden, irrelevant and often startling fragments of information. I remember that as we swung round one bend of the road he pointed across my face (I had taken the seat beside him and Elizabeth was crammed among his luggage and gear on the wide back seat) and remarked: "Last winter I ran into a bunch of elk just here. Shot three of 'em." Just like that. And then resumed his more deliberate narrative.

He dropped us in the heart of Lillehammer amid torrential rain and we had hardly time to thank him and then dart for shelter before he had shot off across the road and into the parking-ground of Lillehammer's swaggerest hotel.

"Whew!" said Elizabeth. "After that I think I'd like to get back into Norway again. What about a pot of coffee and something to eat?"

While the rain poured down outside we sat in the restaurant feeling very small and little-travelled. We had not been lost in the out-back of Australia; we had not fished for tunny off Australia's dramatic coast; we did not know the Great Barrier Reef; we had not been present at the opening of Sydney Harbour Bridge; we had not kept kangaroo on our estate, did not have a collection of boomerangs, had not had black men for servants or almost died of thirst in the great inland deserts. We had not even had our car held up by a herd of elk between Gjövik and Lillehammer and felt compelled to shoot two or three of them before going on. In fact, Norway was about as far afield as we had been jointly; before meeting him we had been content with our record to date.

"And we are still," Elizabeth said, or words to that effect, having read my mind as usual like an open page of bold print.

"Certainly we are," I assured her, and we went to the counter and renewed our pot of coffee and rang further changes on an excellent display of *smörbröd*.

FOLK MUSEUM

There was a promising break in the clouds soon afterwards, and we left our packs in a cloak-room and set off along the road to the Sandvig Open-Air Folk Museum.

About the time Gustav Vigeland was having his first exhibition of those sculptures which were to astonish Norway a young Lillehammer dentist of his own age to within a year or two returned from his annual tour of Gudbrandsdal, where he had been practising his dentistry among the scattered farmsteads. He had been paid for much of his services not in cash but in kind, and among the baggage he brought back with him was the first of what came to be an extensive collection of old-time beakers and cooking and other utensils. Thus was the germ of a great idea born: he would, he told his friends, begin to amass a collection of those objects large and small which were native to Gudbrandsdal, and, as he was intelligent enough to foresee, were likely in time to be superseded by other and less picturesque articles. His name was Anders Sandvig. The Sandvig Open-Air Folk Museum is his memorial.

What was begun in a modest and unassuming fashion swiftly grew in scope. Beakers and pots and old-world cooking utensils were followed by articles of furniture and eventually by whole buildings. The Lillehammer authorities were enlightened enough to recognize that here was something new and well worth fostering. Having seen the first erection of buildings in Anders Sandvig's own garden and orchard they decided that it was time they rallied to his support. So, soon after the turn of the century, a new and spacious site was selected and given the name Maihaugen— May Hill, after Norway's National Day, the 17th of May—

and the Sandvig Collection was purchased outright for the then gigantic sum of 79,000 *kroner*.

To-day there are, I suppose, upwards of a hundred separate buildings in this tree-grown and well-watered sloping estate. To wander there at will is to enter truly into the traditional life of the Norwegians of Gudbrandsdal, typical of all that is best worth preserving in rural Norway. It is carefully divided into four main sections: a collection of homes from the earliest settled times to about the mid-eighteenth century; a collection of farmhouses and outbuildings; a collection of some fifty different work-buildings clearly demonstrating the work and tools known to the old craftsmen; and, finally, a yet-incomplete section showing the principle of the *saeter*, or mountain-plateau "out-farm".

Owing to the natural features of this sloping site and the imagination and good sense of those responsible for its lay-out, this Folk Museum gives a remarkably convincing impression of having grown, rather than been transported, there. Reason tells the visitor that every building large and small has been dismantled at its own distant site, conveyed to Lillehammer, rebuilt, with necessary reinforcements and, so to speak, planted where now it stands. But reason takes a back seat when confronted with so skilful a presentation, and you may wander as we did for hours among the trees, along the gravel paths, across grass and skirting ponds and small lakes, ever more and more convinced that this has always been, that this is not artificial but natural.

There was, of course, too much to take in all at once, but there was no sense of overcrowding. From any one building or small group of related buildings it was usually possible to see the next; but you did not walk from one group busily adjusting your receptivity to the next set of impressions. It was a restful place and its spell lay persuasively upon you. Occasionally a woman's figure, a guide in native costume, would emerge from a building, take the air for a minute or two, and then retire again within. The interiors, as we found when we followed, were dim: whatever we may think about the contemporary Norwegian passion for light and fresh air, their forbears lived a great proportion of their lives in semi-darkness and doubtless an atmosphere of warm, clinging smoke.

The oldest building in the Sandvig Collection is the Stav-kirke from Garmo, near Lom in Gudbrandsdal. We are told that it was originally erected by Torgeir the Ancient (what a story lies in a name like that!) at about the time William the Conqueror was invading England. It would doubtless have been a very primitive building, probably not much more than a small, low, square chamber containing an altar. But it was added to and elaborated, with balconies and, eventually, an elevated roof. It fell into disrepair, was repaired in Shakespeare's day and thoroughly renovated a hundred years after that. The timbers the Norwegian craftsmen used had a life hardly less durable than stone.

The story of this ancient church then enters a sad chapter. Not many years before Sandvig began his research in Gudbrandsdal the church was dismantled and, strangely, put up for auction in separate lots. The less important lots, being heavily impregnated with tar, were sold for fuel and vanished for ever. But a Vågå man who eventually earned the nickname "Scrap Trond", with Sandvig himself, set to work to collect from the scattered buyers the various lots that had once been Garmo Stavkirke. Bit by bit it was reassembled; parts irretrievably lost had to be replaced by other ancient parts that would conform to its pattern. Eventually, the disintegrated church was rebuilt. It was consecrated in 1921, on the Saint's Day associated with St. Olav, who had, nine hundred years earlier, preached the Gospel in Gudbrandsdal and called upon Torgeir the Ancient to build him a church.

There are, I believe, not more than a score of these *stav-kirkes* still to be found in Norway. One is near Bergen; another can be seen in the Folk Museum at Bygdöy; a third is here on the outskirts of Lillehammer; we were to see a very fine one soon afterwards, at the upper end of Gudbrandsdal, where it becomes Ottadal, all the more attractive because it is still in use and stands on its ancient site. We saw yet another at Vågå, but a stiff price was payable for entry and it had not, for all the publicity it receives, quite the air of that other, the lovely timber church at Lom.

I have never seen an explanation why the traditional Norway church, the *stavkirke*, should have the oriental flavour which marks it—for it can hardly be denied that the immediate impression is of a Chinese pagoda. It is a complicated arrangement of steep, shingled roofs and gables, tar-black, out of which you would expect at any moment some quaint (but not malevolent) creature to appear, black-winged, and make off among the trees whose ancestors provided the massive timber framework, the great interior galleries and fitments, and the myriad small fish-scale shingles that are so steeply pitched that no weight of snow could ever cling to them.

There may be a steeple—the *stavkirke* at Lom has a particularly fine octagonal one set about with four small and beautifully proportioned baby pinnacles; there may only be a sort of turret such as might house a school bell or act as a dove-cote above a stable; but the cross will stand on the highest point of the architectural whole. The cross, however, is not the symbol that first catches and holds the eye; rather, it is the array of dragon-heads that face outwards from gable-ends in all directions: long-jawed, curving-jawed, rather sinister, stylized dragon-heads, whose origin is immediately recognizable by anyone who has seen even a picture of a Viking long-ship.

It may well be that men were building ships as soon as they were building houses: the two forms of timber building grew up together and many a man thought himself safer ploughing the stormy seas than scratching a livelihood on the stony mountainside down which at any moment bears and wolves might sweep to carry him off as legitimate fodder. And the dragon-head which was their challenging symbol on the stempost of their ships came to be associated with enterprise and triumph and the very essence of life; why then should it not be placed at gable-ends on their churches, the most permanently conceived buildings they were to erect on land? Experts in joinery will confirm that in these ancient churches the workmanship is that of a shipwright every bit as much as that of carpenter and joiner.

Unhappily, like so many of Norway's ancient buildings, they have been largely destroyed by fire. Not so very long ago there may have been as many as a hundred *stavkirkes*; to-day there are not a quarter that number, and it is an excellent thing that some at least should be preserved and safeguarded in such places as the Sandvig Museum. The strong smell of tar strengthens the impression one has already gained that there is much in common between ship and church; and the massive tree-trunks that form the main pillars of the framework inside are to all intents and purposes ships' masts supporting, not yard-arms and sails, but transverse beams and an immense spread of solid timber roof. What I have said about the lightness of timber building in an earlier part of this book, and repeated in connection with the *pensjonat* at Kapp, certainly does not apply to the *stavkirke*.

Most primitive of the dwellings on show is the *årestue*, not far from the church, a building rather more than five hundred years old and hailing from Vågå. The double word breaks up easily enough: *stue* is room, and you will find it in hotels and elsewhere—*spisestue*, for example, the dining-room; and *åre* is the square brick or stone fireplace which, in these most ancient dwellings, occupied the centre of the floor, so that the occupants of the house would, most literally, sit "round" the fire. The smoke rose from this central fire and escaped (if the occupants were lucky) through a hole in the roof immediately overhead, assisted by a draught from two low apertures at floor level. If the fire was not in use a thin animal-skin was stretched tightly across the hole in the roof so that rain was to some extent kept out and a little light admitted.

The fire was truly the centre of family life; the nearest we can come to it to-day is in the old-fashioned ingle-nook fireplace where, if the architect has been clever enough with his dampers and flues, one can crouch against warmed brickwork and scorch one's eyebrows at the leaping flames. The remaining fittings in this primitive dwelling are a tree-trunk chair, perhaps the oldest form of shaped chair known to man, and a row of crude benches built against the walls. The benches have one odd characteristic: they used to be box-shaped and filled with earth as extra insulation against the bitter cold of a Norwegian winter.

Other and more "modern" dwellings include the *rökovn-*

stue, or "smoke-stove house", which is a couple of centuries or so later than the other and shows a development particularly in the placing of the fire, which now stands back against one wall of the house, the timbers protected by a massive, stone-built guard. Later, the fireplace came to be situated in the corner of the living-room, often separated from the timber wall sufficiently for fuel to be stored and kept dry there. In some of these buildings the fireplace was far enough away from the wall for a narrow bed to be sandwiched between the two: I can hardly imagine snugger lying than such an arrangement would afford! In fact, we experienced something of the kind ourselves some days later among the Jotunheimen when the room we were given proved to be backed against the immense stone fireplace of the living-room; the wall was almost too hot to touch even in the morning when the fire had been out for six hours or more, though deep snow lay about us and a cruel north wind had whistled through the pass all night.

The list of these buildings is too long to enumerate, but a couple must be mentioned. One was the *lökrestue*, a substantial mid-eighteenth-century house whose most attractive feature was a spacious little attic reached by a narrow staircase and remote from the rest of the rooms. This is known as the *jomfruburet*—the Maidens' Bower. Here you will see all the feminine fripperies, the tapestries and spinning-wheels and carding-frames and treasure-chests that were used by the young girls of such an establishment.

It was in this room that, until comparatively recent times, say the middle of last century, a girl would be visited by her young man, and always at night. Day-visiting was, curiously enough, deemed not quite respectable or proper, but Saturday night was the occasion when the young men of the district were permitted, indeed expected, to pay their calls on any or all of the young women in whom they were interested. If there were many callers at one house the visits were necessarily brief; they took place at night, in subdued light, and it was understood that both parties should be modestly dressed and decently behaved. The custom was known as "Lying together in trust", and I do not think that the same precaution was taken by Norwegian fathers as was taken by those in Orkney when the young men came courting their daughters. For these made a practice of tying the girl's knees firmly together with knotted cords, lest the fire in the young blood got out of control.

The other building that I would describe is perhaps the strangest of all. It is, now I come to think of it, the most explicit illustration of my point that in Norway the buildings, in the country at any rate, are living things. For this is the famous "King of Dyringsli", a fir-tree which came to the Lillehammer saw-mills some sixty years ago and proved on examination to be such a remarkable tree that it was presented to the Folk Museum instead of being hewn into planks.

It is not only remarkable as having a girth of some twenty-five feet; it was found to have been opened skilfully, hollowed out and used as an entrance to an underground coiners' den in the heart of a forest. Hunters found it when seeking a wounded fox; the ground gave way beneath their feet and they found themselves in a cavity large enough to contain a score of men; their coining apparatus was bricked up in one corner. Counterfeit notes were found, dated in the early part of last century; there were dies and plates of zinc, tin and lead, ink-pots and rollers and presses. Surely it was one of the most imaginatively conceived hiding-places any gang of coiners ever thought of? My secret hope is that their ingenuity brought them some measure of success at least for a time, before they were brought to justice.

The famous fir-tree trunk now stands in the pathway, neatly capped with a cone-shaped shingle roof, its door padlocked, slightly reminiscent of those rare country cells where sturdy rogues and vagabonds in a more intolerant age were shut up to cool their heels and await the pleasure of the local magistrate. Not far from it is an object, admittedly not a dwelling, though it is very necessary to those who lived in the less well-watered regions: an irrigation system of hollowed logs on trestles that carried running water along gently falling channels from source to consumer. We were later to see these still in action in Ottadal.

As we walked back into Lillehammer our ears caught the

strains of brassy music and we turned off our route to locate
it. The town stands high above the lake, the head of which
is spanned by a wide, straight bridge. It was from that direction that the music came, and we tracked it down to a little
jetty close to the bridge at which a crazy-looking paddle-
steamer was just tying up.

The jetty was packed stiff with sightseers, and the narrow
deck of the paddle-steamer was packed stiffer still. She
was, we learned, a hundred-year-old pleasure-steamer that
regularly made this trip between Hamar or Gjövik and Lillehammer. She was dressed over-all with bunting, flags waved
from every possible vantage-point, brasswork gleamed in the
almost non-existent sun, for rain had begun again to threaten;
many of the passengers appeared to have dressed themselves
in clothes to match the boat. How the band contrived to
play in such a press of tourists only they themselves can tell,
and perhaps not even they; but play they did, and martial
air and alien waltz took turns under the baton of the conductor.

The band took no notice when the gangway was run up
from jetty to deck and everyone on board but themselves
surged uncontrollably to the side nearer to land. Looked at
end-on, the angle of the little boat was alarming; her port
paddle left the water completely, and looked like becoming
an autogyro-screw if something was not done to prevent the
slow upward lift. Perhaps something was, for the disconcerting movement ceased, and the boat remained at the quayside
in a position absurdly reminiscent of a dog lifting its leg
against a wall.

South of the bridge the water we had been following ever
since we left Minnesund was, even beneath a greyish sky, a
satisfying blue; but as we turned to look upstream into Gudbrandsdal, to which this was the true threshold, we could see
an immediate and remarkable change in its colour. Once
again we were looking at ice-water, water which reminded us
immediately of that we had followed during our unsuccessful
attempt on Buarbre and Folgefonna, or alongside the mountain road from Haugastöl to Geilo. The water we were
looking at had flowed off the vast snow- and ice-plateaux

of the Jotunheim Mountains, and, in spite of its long journey down Gudbrandsdal, had not lost its deathly greenish tinge.

A lovely pattern of timber rafts and timber barricades, however, gave a sense of life to the great sheet of green-grey water above the bridge. Here was a wide expanse of floating timbers, upright stakes and wired enclosures not unlike a vast empty cattle-market in which, all in good time, sheep and cows would be penned in their several stalls. We were to follow this water for more than a hundred miles before we were even within sight of the Jotunheim Mountains, and we were to see it not only as a broad sheet of almost still water, as here at its junction with Lake Mjösa, but as a furiously foaming river plunging through rapids and riding swiftly through close-set walls, widening suddenly almost to lake breadth, where its travelling logs seemed to float inert and aimless, and narrowing again to a bottle-neck through which these same logs shot like great arrows glinting in the sun.

With the arrival of the tourist boat, Lillehammer took on a different aspect and we decided it was time for us to leave. We collected our rucksacks from the cloak-room, bought a bar or two of chocolate at great expense, for chocolate is a luxury in Norway, cashed a travellers' cheque at one of the hotels, for all banks were closed, and then set off along the hard Trondheim road, heartened by a break in the sky that was wider than any we had seen that day, and with a wind behind our shoulder that gave added impetus to our walk.

Små Mus!

As the valley narrowed it became more beautiful; it was, in fact, the exact opposite of Hallingdal, where we had descended the valley into ever widening and flattening country. Here, when the last outskirts of the bright little township that is Lillehammer had been left behind, the road began to climb steadily but not arduously, leaving the river flowing far down beneath us on our left. On the far side the trees were thick on the gentle hills, above which white clouds had now taken the place of the grey ones that had followed us all day; on our own side there were correspondent hillsides carrying fields and farmsteads, fewer trees, a tumbling burn or two and outcrops of rocks to break the contours. A hidden railway-line—the important Oslo-Trondheim line—followed the road, below us and out of sight among the nearest trees, close to the river's edge. Later it crossed to the other bank and as we ascended the valley we could see it threading its bright way among the trees that came to the very water's edge, for mile after lonely mile. If you miss the Trondheim train one morning you do not, I imagine, remain seated on an Oslo platform seat till the next one is ready to leave; there is time and plenty before that!

The old problem confronted us: how much were we disposed to walk, how much to travel by car or lorry if one came along; how much (if any) by train or bus? The conditioning factor, of course, was time, and we knew that, with only a week to go, and our main objective the Jotunheims, there was little point in indulging our pride just to be able to say that we had walked "most of it". Yet to travel by train or bus would mean missing the "feel" of the road and the country it passed through. It was Friday evening, and within a week we must be in Bergen. Between Lillehammer and Bergen we must cover some three hundred and fifty miles. We had so far covered between six and seven hundred.

The best country, we knew, lay at the upper end of Gudbrandsdal, where it merges with Ottadal; then there were the Jotunheims; then there was the famous Sognefjell road, over which we were determined to walk; and, finally, there was the easier stretch down to Voss and so back to Bergen. Common sense, then, dictated that we should not be too resolute about walking this early stretch of Gudbrandsdal; and as if to confirm our decision a butcher's van came up behind us, slowed down, and took us on board.

It was a very short lift, for the driver was merely visiting a farmer and then returning to Lillehammer, but it took us well clear of the town and gave us a good start. He turned off up a side road, beyond the point at which tarmacadam had been replaced by dust damped down by the afternoon's rain. We walked on a mile or two, and were overtaken by a most ancient American car. Its noise preceded it in such fashion that before we turned round we assumed that it must be a travelling hardware-dealer's van. Or perhaps even two together. A grimy individual with splendid teeth and a shock of dark hair gripped the wheel with one hand and signalled to us energetically with the other. We hopped aboard.

It was one of the oddest lifts I have ever had in a long experience of this sort of thing. The car itself, though it bore a famous name, would not have looked out of place among the earliest Mack Sennett comedies; indeed, neither Elizabeth nor I would have been in the least surprised if a Keystone Cop had popped out of the petrol-tank or from beneath the dashboard with its row of empty instrument-sockets. It was capacious as a van and about as bare of upholstery. There was a cushion on the driver's seat, but Elizabeth and I sat on the inverted spring framework of the wide back seat, from which the covering had long vanished. We could watch the back axle bobbing up and down beneath us, and we were prodded in the most embarrassing fashion by loose ends of wire coil-springs and clips that had come adrift.

No sooner were we in, and the door slammed loudly behind us, than we were off. There was less noise inside than outside; or rather, one noise dominated the whole interior to the exclusion of all extraneous rattles and clankings: the roar of the six-cylinder engine which drowned all else. It seemed that the bulkhead between driver's seat and engine had been removed bodily, and we looked forward alongside the enthusiastic young man at a mass of rusty iron, brass pipe-lines, twisted and knotted rubber cables, plastic caps and loose wires and lengths of flex which would have puzzled even Heath Robinson.

Not only noise, however, came from the engine through that vanished bulkhead; intense heat came, too. Why the driver's trousers were not scorched and his eyebrows sizzling we did not know; even behind the comparative protection of the front seat the temperature was more than we could comfortably bear. Elizabeth unzipped the front of her windbreaker and I undid the last button of my shirt. We mopped our brows. The windows were all closed and, so far as I could see, hermetically closed at that; and handleless anyway. Something of our discomfort must have made itself apparent to the driver, for without warning he fumbled in his pocket, reached backwards over one shoulder and handed me a chromium-plated and incongruously new-looking window-handle. He pointed at the window nearest to me, and indicated that I might open it.

I turned round on my uncomfortable seat to do so—and found that it was, in fact, open. Not merely open, but vanished altogether: just a jagged upper edge of thick glass sloped diagonally across its frame, a menace to anyone who might be so foolish as to put his arm near it. Gripping the handle he had so obligingly offered me, I cautiously thrust my bare arm out through the rectangle of the window-frame; the effect of my gesture was to reduce him to almost hysterical mirth. His hands alternately gripped and surrendered the wheel, he appeared to be playing tunes on brake and clutch and accelerator pedals, and the car responded like a thing possessed. Until, without warning, the engine gave a violent cough and stopped dead. The young man's foot being for the moment on some other pedal than the clutch, the car stopped in its tracks almost as suddenly; the appalling din ceased; the wave of blast-furnace air was stilled; the driver muttered something unintelligible to us, and got out on to the road.

Elizabeth and I seized the opportunity to insert something between the sharp spring-ends and our own lacerated selves. How far was this fellow going, we wondered, and should we be in one piece on arrival at his, or our, destination? Our speculations were interrupted by a stupendous roar from the engine and the slam of the car door as the young man leapt on board. Releasing a wire he had been holding between finger and thumb, he pressed his foot on the accelerator and, with a jerk that practically dislocated our necks, the car shot forward again, seized with a new and terrifying energy.

The energy expended itself in less than twenty yards and in a matter of seconds all was silence again save for the muttering of the young man who had this time stripped off the bonnet, tucked it behind the spare wheel on the running-board, and was only visible from his waist downwards. He plucked at wires—we heard them ping as they came adrift; he snatched at distributor-caps and snapped them on and off; he twiddled at a pipe-union loose enough to undo without a spanner, and blew mightily down a thin copper pipe so that a jet of fine fluid sprayed out into the still evening air and made him rub his eyes with the back of an oily hand. Then, bending to the starting-handle again, he gave a wrench that might well have lifted a lesser car clean off the road; the engine burst into frantic life once more and a moment later we were on the move, the engine racing at its maximum revs., the car gaining speed as he slipped and slipped the clutch. We knew he was doing this heinous thing, for not only was the motion of the car erratic and unpredictable, but the most distressing fumes rose up from beneath the floor-boards to augment those that came from the engine itself. And twenty yards farther along the road we came once more to a sudden halt.

This time I too alighted, if only to show our host that though we appeared to be a couple of Jonahs one of us at any rate was anxious to help. I pointed to the carburettor, scrabbled with my toes in the dust of the road and so gave him to understand that possibly some of this might have caused a stoppage in the fuel supply. Perhaps he was managing to inject just sufficient petrol into the carburettor to get us along those twenty yards each time, but no more? He shook his head and rapidly removed a set of sparking-plugs, not one of which appeared to be more than finger-tight. His finger-tips must have been of asbestos to hold them. He shook his head complacently over each and replaced it casually; such was the variety of patched-up plug-leads that I doubted very much whether he had connected the right one to each.

My doubts were confirmed when he motioned me to climb in again and began to swing the engine into life. I shudder to think what shocking sequence of explosions went on within its bowels, for there were a very large number of possible false connections among those six sparking-plugs. Certainly the engine would not do more than turn over once or twice in the most spasmodic fashion and the comedy of diagnosing the trouble began all over again, this time with new variations on the original theme.

Four more times altogether he got the engine to go, leapt aboard with myself neck and neck beside him, and shot off for another twenty or so yards; four times the engine died upon us in the same inexplicable fashion. The last time we were both standing beside it, staring hopelessly at the tangle of wires and the inadequately coupled pipes, the long, dark stains where water had leaked out of the cylinder-block and rusted the once spruce metal, and the general confusion of rods and ties and spring-loaded joints that conveyed to this recalcitrant engine the will of its master, when all of a sudden he broke off what he was doing and pointed to the dusty edge of the road a yard or two ahead of the car.

"*Små mus!*" he exclaimed delightedly, all his troubles apparently forgotten. "*Små mus!*"

And a small mouse it was: a diminutive self-sufficient creature travelling at high speed with all its mechanism in perfect working order, totally unconcerned at the mountainous feet which it had had to dodge on its journey, the feet of two men probing the entrails of this ancient, irresponsible car.

Even now I do not know quite how Elizabeth and I made our getaway. We did not want to offend the man by pointing out that we could make our way along the road, if not quite so fast as the small mouse, at least a good deal faster than his six-cylinder car. Yet clearly we had nothing to gain by remaining with him, and equally clearly there was nothing at all that we could do to get the wretched thing going. Possibly, too, he might know the story of Jonah and for all his cheerful air be wishing to goodness we would clear off and take the hoodoo with us. After all, had not the car been running well enough before he was so ill-advised as to take us on board? Perhaps when we had vanished into the distance it would once more remember its obligations?

Our command of Norwegian, though greater than when we first set foot in Bergen, was not yet adequate to express the gratitude we felt for his initial offer; the regret we felt that we had to leave him now; the sympathy we felt for him as he wrestled with this stubborn engine; the hope we entertained that both his journey and ours might soon be successfully resumed; our mortification that we were not sufficiently mechanically minded to solve his problems for him. He never ceased to smile as we fumbled for words—a smile of pure good-fellowship without *arrière-pensée*. When I had stumbled to a conclusion he held out a large and oil-stained hand, grasped mine and shook it spiritedly, wiped his hand on his trousers and seized Elizabeth's hand afterwards, and continued to wave to us as we walked away along the straight dust road into the distance.

He never overtook us. We walked seven or eight miles, leisurely, stopping at intervals to sit by the roadside and contemplate the great mass of turbulent river that flowed in the opposite direction to ours, great baulks of timber tossing like match-stalks on its surface and being catapulted by impact with hidden boulders so that they shot through the air, dripping spray, to fall again with a splash that could not be heard amid the furious tumult of the water.

The sides of the valley closed in little by little and, because we were on the east side of it, we had to look into the sunlight, at masses of trees that were black rather than green. Far behind us lay the wide waters of Lake Mjösa, fed by this same striding river, and the pleasant township of Lillehammer. Somewhere along this road was the car we had so cravenly abandoned. We hoped—not because we particularly wanted a further ride—that we should be overtaken by it again; that it would draw level, its engine running steadily instead of staccato, its driver lounging triumphant at the wheel. If so, we would remove our Union Jacks from their straps and wave them heartily at him, bidding him good speed. But we had reached the *pensjonat* at Åsletta before he overtook us; if he did overtake us it must have been during the hours of night.

We found ourselves the only occupants of this large *pensjonat* and once more congratulated ourselves on having taken a position in the van instead of the main body of the tourists who would soon be flooding the country. Had we been one night later, however, we should have found ourselves two

English people in a gathering of between twenty and thirty Finns who had booked for the week-end. We sat within easy reach of the *kold-bord*, which was spread as usual as though for a whole roomful of diners. Hungry, we were beginning to help ourselves when the door from the kitchen opened and a tray of ham and eggs and fried potatoes appeared. When we had dealt with that, and actually been offered a second tray-load, we turned to the cold table. There was still room for the inevitable sweet: rhubarb in syrup.

If we remember Åsletta for that meal, and for the equally good breakfast next morning, we shall remember it also for something else. We had hardly finished our meal when a party of four Norwegian business men turned up. We thought little about them, though we did notice that for Norwegians they were surprisingly talkative and hearty. They were at table for a long while after we had left the dining-room and we could hear them bantering one another and laughing with considerable abandon. Four friends on a week-end's fishing trip, we guessed, having left their womenfolk behind them.

For a tiny place like Åsletta the *pensjonat* is remarkably large. The upper floor is one long corridor with rooms opening off it on each side from end to end. Twenty rooms at least, possibly more. And all had been empty until we came and took one of them. Now another party had arrived, so presumably two more rooms were engaged. We went early to bed, for we were tired and the air was too cool for a stroll that evening. We had not been asleep more than an hour before the four men also came up to bed. We found that the two rooms allotted to them sandwiched ours.

I have written appreciatively of the sense of space and lightness which characterizes these Norwegian timber-built houses and in general I would not go back one whit on what I have said. But this was the other side of the medal. Every sound, every hint of a sound, from the unbuckling of a sock-suspender to the tinkle of toothbrush on tumbler, percolated through those thin wooden parti-walls from fore and aft to our small room amidships. Two deep voices were in incessant exchange on each side of us, swapping stories, may be, exchanging hopes for fishing (as we imagined) over the week-end, perhaps discussing exports or market prices. It did not matter to us what the subject was: all too sufficient was the fact that they were there at all, and there to stay. Of all the rooms in which they might so well have been put on that long corridor, the two chosen adjoined ours!

I suppose we did sleep that night. Elizabeth certainly did, for she has that childlike and blessed gift of slipping off to sleep as easily as she slips into a swimsuit. But I lay and tossed and turned and thought unkind thoughts about my neighbours and prayed for darkness, forgetting that we were in a latitude where in June darkness never quite makes the grade, and went back on my delight in timber-built houses, wishing for thick stone walls such as the limestone uplands of England can show—anything but the paper-thin sound-boards through which every rustle of sheet and snore of contented sleeper attacked me without pity or remorse.

I must have slept, for I was awakened at some unearthly hour by one of the men, not six inches removed from the head of my bed, apparently reading aloud from some excruciatingly funny collection of anecdotes, every one of which, though unintelligible to me, evoked the hearty guffaw from his fellow that he anticipated. It went on for a quarter of an hour, for half an hour, for three-quarters of an hour. May be they exchanged roles and the other read the stories while the first reader did the laughing, but the effect on me was the same. I listened in growing fury for an hour, for more than an hour, and finally got out of bed, went to the window and found that the grey twilight of night was giving place to another of those blue-gold mornings which we had come to look upon as our right.

I went across and shook Elizabeth, sound asleep, her dark head invisible beneath the sheet and the beloved *dyne* curling intimately about her. She emerged, opened one eye, blinked it sleepily and said, "Is it really time to get up?" She had not heard a thing, from the moment we said good night till the moment I roused her, nine hours later.

AUSTIN "7"

It was between fifty and sixty miles from Åsletta to Otta: a two- or three-day tramp if we did it on foot; and that, of course, would mean that we should have to scramble through the last lap of our journey.

"Perhaps those four men would give us a lift on the way?" Elizabeth remarked.

If she had been feeling about them as I was she would never have suggested such a thing. I told her so.

She smiled. "Probably they're nothing like so objectionable as you make out, you know," she said, with the sweet reasonableness of someone who has not listened throughout an interminable night to four unco-ordinated, deep-throated snorers.

We set off on foot, walking through some of the loveliest stretches of pine-bordered road we had seen in all our wanderings. The river was far below us, visible only at rare intervals when our road dipped to some small hamlet and we came to a bridge that spanned it, linking this road with the railway-line that still clung obstinately to the farther side of the valley. Then we rose again and the water was hidden from us for a while, though it still glinted brightly enough to penetrate the trees when they thinned out and remind us that we were travelling towards its source, while it was running swiftly down to Lake Mjösa and beyond, to the flat country that lay behind Oslo, and ultimately to the sea itself. It was Saturday and there was no traffic at all. The heat was considerable and at intervals we sat by the roadside, telling ourselves that since we could not hope to walk all the way to Otta we might just as well wait till something came along. Surely, on this main road between Oslo and Trondheim there should be some long-distance traffic?

"There are always our fellow-guests from Åsletta," Elizabeth reminded me, a little maliciously, I felt, for she had not suffered as I had.

We had left them at breakfast, cheerful as ever, fortified by the excellent food, the long night's rest and the early morning

171

entertainment in reading aloud. We had established the fact that their car was large enough for two extra people, even with rucksacks as bulky as ours. But they had not overtaken us.

We heard the unmistakable tinkle-tinkle of an Austin "7" approaching. There was no point, we thought, even in sitting up and flagging it, for even if it had only one person on board there was hardly room for the two of us and our baggage. And even if there were room, what driver of a car so small would be willing to take aboard unnecessary cargo?

It approached us as unobtrusively as the *små mus* of the day before. And furthermore, it stopped: a small maroon car with tyres little larger than those of a motor-cycle, a man at the wheel, a woman at his side, luggage and a big bunch of flowers spread over the back seat.

As it had stopped it was only polite on our part to walk across the road and say thank you and wave it on its way. We tried to do this, but the couple in the car would not hear of it. They both got out; the woman began to reorganize the clutter on the back seat and the man opened the microscopic boot and began to try to make room for one rucksack. They would not take no from us, and before long we were sitting on the back seat, nursing between us the other rucksack, several small and one large parcel, the flowers, a thermos flask and a picnic-basket, a handful of books, our two walking-sticks, a car rug, two light raincoats and the man's wide-brimmed trilby hat.

We stayed in that diminutive car the whole way to Otta, and anything I may at any time have thought or said about the smallness of that particular model can be written off against its performance. The tinkle remained with us—an excellent free advertisement of the make, as doubtless the firm is aware; but the car itself, as we bedded down, seemed to expand and for the best part of two hours we spun merrily along the climbing Trondheim road engaged in brisk conversation with the driver and his wife, both of whom spoke tolerable English.

Only once did we stop on that fifty-mile run, and that was when, with an immense flurry of hooters and hammering on windows, we were overtaken by a large black saloon which proceeded to cut in in front of us and force us to a standstill. Our driver and his wife got out and we, with a struggle, got out too, to stretch our legs. The occupants of the big car were the four men from the Åsletta *pensjonat*, bound for a conference of telephone managers at Kristiansund, well on the way to Trondheim—whither also the Austin "7" was bound, and for the same purpose. They were, all six of them in fact, buddies. And in the good cheer which resulted from this chance meeting I forgot my peevishness and resentment of the restless night, and everybody shook hands with everybody else and wished everybody else the best of everything.

Then the occupants of the two cars, one so large, the other so small, dispersed to their several seats; the large car drove off in a cloud of white dust, its occupants hammering on the rear window, and after a few minutes of furious driving the smaller car overtook it, sailed by with a derisive toot on her absurd horn and left the other to suck her dust for a matter of twenty miles and more. Elizabeth, when she was not chewing at a stick of chocolate which had been thrust upon her by the woman in the front seat, wore a most absurdly complacent smile, as of one who might be saying, "I told you so!"

At Otta the road divided and our friends went directly forward while we were to turn off to the left, into the mountains. We were not a little astonished to find ourselves, soon after noon that day, so very much farther on our route than we had ever dared to hope. Though the sun over our heads was hot there was a strange nip of cold in the air. We unfolded our map on the parapet of a bridge beneath which greenish-white water flowed silently, and noted that the Jotunheimen were appreciably nearer than they had been. The nip in the air was their silent greeting.

There are quarries and other works at Otta. Arriving at such an hour, we found ourselves surrounded by workmen packing up for the week-end and there was a sense of industry which we found depressing after so long in a rural landscape. Having crossed the bridge, near which the Otta's green ice-water joins the bluer water of the Lagen, we found ourselves in a huddle of petrol-stations, store-yards and workshops.

There was a café near by and we went to see what we could get to eat.

There was coffee—if we could find a table among the crowd of workmen who filled the little room—and there were biscuits. There was no prospect of a cooked meal, however; and that, for once, was what we craved. Though Otta is barely two thousand feet above sea level its temperature is many degrees lower than Åsletta's and the rest of Gudbrandsdal had been; the wind had shifted to the north-west and would be in our faces as we climbed towards the snow-capped mountains whose presence, even there, we could unmistakably feel.

"Isn't there a hotel where we can get *middag*?" I asked the man who served us with our coffee.

He shook his head positively, took the price of the two cups of coffee and the two unappetizing biscuits and vanished into the back regions. We ate and drank in some gloom.

Ten minutes later we realized that he must have completely misunderstood my question. Having paused to admire and photograph a most captivating lych-gate with a pattern of carved figures along its ridge-pole that might well have stepped straight from the drawing-boards of Walt Disney, we turned a corner and found ourselves outside a real hotel. Inquiries revealed that in less than half an hour *middag* would be served; and our noses told us very convincingly that the meal would be well worth waiting for.

It was. We ate an excellently served meal in a spacious dining-room where only half a dozen other guests were at table. The soup was good enough to interest even a non-soup-lover like myself. When the main dish was brought to us it consisted of a large oval dish—I do not think we once saw a round dish during the whole of our stay—of sliced beef of a quality we never expected again to see: there was a negligible amount of fat to it; it was perfectly cooked, neither under- nor over-done. Slice after slice we ate, marvelling, reminding ourselves that now or never we must stoke up for an arduous journey. For once, too, we had vegetables—a distressing rarity in Norway, except for the potatoes, which the Norwegians have not yet learnt to prepare and serve well enough to satisfy even the uncritical English palate. The sweet was delectable: cool and luscious fruit and cream.

Fortified, we left for the hills. Between Otta and Vågå, about twenty miles distant, our map showed only one halting-place, a tiny hamlet which might or might not have a *pensjonat*. The road was uphill most of the way, the Otta flowing strongly alongside down the steep cleft with an impetus derived from Otta Lake and Vågåvatn.

We climbed steeply the narrow road which hung over its tumbling waters, river and road crowded into uneasy juxta-position by the high, rocky hills to right and left of us which seemed to be jostling us together as we walked. In the hour we had spent at the hotel the population of Otta seemed to have vanished. There was no sound of life or movement behind us in the village we had left; no children called to one another, no more cycle-bells were rung as friend passed friend, no engine coughed or gears whined on the long hill that we were following.

We walked steadily, in the teeth of a wind that already had a bite in it. It funnelled down the narrow gorge, cold and stern and a little menacing. Though the sun shone overhead from a clear sky there was now little warmth in it. The road levelled out for a while in a belt of trees and we were just beginning to find walking easier when a light van swung round the bend of the road behind us, stopped, and we were offered a lift. It was an irony that we should have completed the really arduous part of that walk and now be offered trans-port on a level stretch, but fortunately we accepted the lift; this was the last vehicle we saw that day.

At Vågå, where the two men had business to transact, we dropped off, grateful to be already so well on our way. For me the fifteen miles of that lift remain almost a blank, for there was room for only one passenger in the front and Eliza-beth occupied that seat, crushed between the driver and his friend. I crouched low in the back, on the floor, surrounded by a mass of gear, beneath a low roof which prevented me from seeing more than a glimpse here and there of the wooded and well-watered hill country through which we sped. It is the one stage of our whole journey which I cannot recapture on the screen of my mind, though I have Elizabeth's word for it that it was lovely indeed.

There is a *stavkirke* in Vågå, alleged to be the oldest building in all Gudbrandsdal. It was heavily locked, and the key had to be sought at some distance. The charge for entering was high—two shillings or so, if memory serves—and the hours during which visitors might have the key and go inside were severely restricted. Here, as so often in Norway, we were struck by the stiff charges made for such sight-seeing. Because we had been able to wander in and out of one fine *stavkirke* already we did not feel disposed to go in search of the key and spend two shillings each to enter this one, even if it could claim to be the oldest building in Gudbrandsdal.

We lingered in Vågå only long enough to take a photograph of one of the most attractively sited *gjestgiveris* that we saw. It fronted on to the lake along which we were to walk for the remainder of that memorable day. It carried a large, glass-ball-topped flagstaff, and in the shelter of one of its balconies there hung the most appetizing hams. The temptation to stay overnight was strong, but by now we were feeling we had perhaps accepted car-lifts over-often, and it was time we earned bed and board by our own unaided efforts. By English standards it was tea-time. The afternoon was fine and there were some hours of it left to us. We were feeling gloriously fit, as indeed we did from the first day to the last. The road ran close alongside bright water for at least as far as we could hope to walk that day.

VÅGÅVATN

I think we shall remember that walk as long as we remember any single stretch of walking we have ever done. There was a magic quality about it, compounded of many subtle ingredients. For one thing we were this time walking almost into the light, for our road alongside Vågåvatn ran north-west-by-west. It did not matter, for we were on the south-west side of the long, narrow lake which bears this name, with the steeper side of the valley beside us. So, we could look

ahead and to the right to slopes more gentle, warmed by the
radiance of the sun, their feet dipped into the clear, ice-green
water. And over our right shoulders, behind us a little, were
the higher hills that shelter Vågå from the north-east. These,
blue and green and gold in the warm light, had snow near
their summits wherever there was a gully or an outcrop of
rock that had screened the noonday sun. Perhaps the view
would have been lovelier had we been walking in the opposite
direction, but I am not so sure. For here we had the gradual
unfolding of shoulder upon shoulder of ever-rising hills,
beyond which were the true Jotunheimen and the great
plateaux weighted down by the permanent snows and glaciers
of the Jostedalsbre.

The hollow in which this lake is held possesses a quality of
intimacy and welcome which made our later experience
among the high hills all the more vital by contrast. Small
farms lie snugly among trees, with well-trimmed fields carved
out of the rougher turf of the foot-hills. Men and cattle
could be seen, giving life to the wide landscape. And almost
everywhere there were to be seen little isolated water-
sprinklers of the type installed on golf-courses, whose silvery-
white plumes fanned the air and were dispersed on the little
unexpected breezes. Now and then the angle of the sun was
such that small private rainbows were born and lingered
momentarily over one or other of these fairy jets, and the
green of the fields took on scraps of Joseph's coat-of-many-
colours.

As we came closer we saw how these numerous small water-
sprinklers were operated. Long, sinuous pipe-lines came down
the slopes from among the trees on higher levels where we
supposed there must be a head of water trapped by a dam,
gravity giving sufficient power to turn the rotary spray. There
was something quite fascinating about these little machines
working away leisurely in field after empty field. Some of
them were on our side of the lake and as we came near to
them we could hear the rhythmic hiss-hiss-hiss as each jet
in turn came up against the baffle-plate that broke it and
spread it far and wide. We wondered whether, in the absence of human attention, the sprinklers had been taught to

pick themselves up and transport themselves at specified intervals from point to point, so that every corner of every field got its share. In the magic light of that evening we should not really have been surprised to see them do this!

Another sort of irrigation-system we saw alongside Vågå-vatn for the first time since leaving the Sandvig Open-Air Folk Museum. Descending the easy slopes of the hillside near the road were sections of hollowed-out tree-trunks, perhaps as thick as a man's thigh. They were not joined together, but, halved, lay one below the other, each lipping the one below and the one above in such a fashion that water could flow uninterrupted from the supply up the hillside to its destination among the fields below. Where they had to be carried to fields on the lake side of the road the wooden channels were held aloft on timber pylons. In some of the fields to which these channels carried water a pretty comb-like system of irrigation-ditches had been dug and the water, delivered into the main ditch, spread out along the wide-spaced teeth of the comb, to reach the whole field. It was the perfect contrast to the use made (or not made) of water in the wilder parts of the west coast of Ireland: there, with more than sufficient water available, no attempt has been made to turn it to account, and a glass of milk is more readily come by at any farm than a glass of drinking-water.

We came at last, round a bend in the road and still close to the lake, to our first glimpse of the Jotunheim Mountains, the 6,000-foot eastern advance-guard named Hvitingskjölen, snow-capped, aloof. We were, of course, skirting the main Jotunheim group, for to cross them, if it is possible at all, can be done only by those prepared to use both skis and ropes. The map shows tracks running off the road which we ourselves were following, some linking up with others, some petering out on the higher contours. But they were not practicable yet, in early June; the road which skirts them, the road we were beginning to walk, can be strenuous enough at times, and for long periods actually impassable. These mountains lie in the area bounded to the north-east, north and north-west by this road out of Gudbrandsdal, and by the long, tortuous eastern arms of Sognefjord, Lusterfjord and

Årdalsfjord to the west; south of them is the complicated system of interlocking lakes such as Tyin and Bygdin and Vinsteren.

We came in due course to Tessand, another hamlet with a *gjestgiveri* of modest pretensions so far as exterior is concerned, but outstanding in interest within. Here we stopped for the night.

The *patron* and his wife were clearly taken aback at receiving visitors as early as the second week in June. It was much earlier than tourists were wont to arrive, in these parts at any rate, and so decorations inside and out were still in progress. A smell of paint and distemper and strong carbolic pervaded everywhere, rather putting-off to people who had been in the open air all day, far from all but country smells since leaving Otta at any rate. But there was the usual smile of welcome, that air of being glad, even if not entirely prepared, to see us which almost all countries save England seem to offer spontaneously.

Let it not be thought that I of all people decry the English way of hotel- and inn-keeping. I do not. I have never fared better, nor been better catered for in little things and big, than here within our own shores. But I have moved about enough not to rely on such treatment. If I get it, I am delighted; if I do not get it, I am not very surprised. We in England have a long way to go yet before we learn to confront our guests in such a way as to make them feel immediately that there is no one in the whole wide world we would rather have beneath our roof, at our table. I have been hotel-keeper as well as guest, and therefore know something of both sides of the picture.

Here at Tessand we knew before we were more than half-way up the bare wooden stairs that not only was this a well-run *gjestgiveri* (and we wonder now whether there are any in Norway which are not well run): it was run by someone with imagination.

It was the smallest thing in the world that gave us the hint. Half-way upstairs there dangled on the wall a curious little piece of wood which was evidently the work of an enthusiast with a penknife, a piece of glass-paper and a little varnish. I cannot name it, for it does not fall into any precise category. Someone had picked it up in a wood, or broken it off a tree, and placed it there to delight others as well as himself. Except that it was twisted and asymmetrical it might have been a boy's catapult-stick. It was vaguely Y-shaped, but none of its three arms could be said to be straight, none of its angles equal to either of the other two. It was smooth to the touch: a diminutive forking tree-trunk, or two-fingered hand-and-wrist, of warm brown wood, serving no useful purpose whatsoever, unless to give a sudden start of pleasure to two strangers is justification for its existence.

It reminded us of two similar objects we have on the wall at home: an alleged toasting-fork which is nothing more than a dead branchlet picked up by some poetically minded individual in the New Forest and smoothed lovingly with glass-paper till its tips are sharp and smooth as black ivory and its handle an affair of gaunt dark bones that might be the wasted arm-bone of a pigmy. It has a faintly surrealist quality to it, but I have had it for twenty-five years and it still gives me pleasure to look at and to touch.

The other is a slighter thing still: a piece of firewood picked up at random from a pile of kindling and shaped as the result of a jesting challenge that that piece at any rate was worthless. With a penknife and a piece of glass-paper the artist whittled away even as he walked along, and out of that sliver of cheap wood there emerged a dolichocephalic creature who grins sardonically from his wall-perch over a book-case: proof that it is not only from the finest materials that the true artist can produce the masterpiece.

Along the landing at the head of the stairs at this Tessand *gjestgiveri* were more of these little wooden figurines, this time serving a utilitarian purpose as a row of coat-hooks. I should have been reluctant to hang a coat on any of them, for each was a little treasure of natural design and no two had any features in common save their originality. They were linked each to other, however, by a long, slender, split-cane fishing-rod that lay there high up out of mischief till its owner should have occasion to use it.

We found a basin and taps in our bedroom, but the

running water had not yet been installed, though it was on the way, for we could see the stack of copper piping on the landing floor. The wide windows of our bedroom opened, not over the lake we had now followed for so many miles, but towards the mountains that were our objective; dark now because the sun was setting behind them. In the morning they would be lit for us by the sun as it rose over the far side of Gudbrands-dal. We should walk towards them with the warmth of the sun on our backs, its brightness reflected on the coloured hills with their caps of snow for which we were making.

At Åsletta we had been waited on by a bright Norwegian girl who had just returned from a prolonged visit to a relative in America and now spoke fluently in the accent and idiom some of us are inclined to deplore. But here at Tessand there was no second Agnes. The girl was silent, puzzled, quite evidently uneasy; though we tried to chat with her in our own brand of Norwegian she took refuge, when she was forced to reply, in a flow of words that silenced us.

After our evening meal we went through to the *årestue*, the fireplace-room, a most enchanting room, snug and homely; we were surrounded on all sides, intimately, by lovely things. It was the first fireplace we had seen with a fire burning in it. While we had been at table the shy girl who had served our meal had come through by a different door, piled split logs high against the wall, placed kindling on the stone slab of the fireplace and brought light to it. By the time we arrived the fire was blazing and only then did we realize how cold the air had become in the last half-hour since the sun had dropped behind the mountains.

This fireplace was neither in the centre of the room, as in that ancient dwelling at Lillehammer, nor against one wall, as in the later dwelling we had seen. It was built in the corner, so that two walls at right angles made its back and a massive square-in-section twisted iron pillar supported the heavy stone slab through which the smoke rose to the corner chimney and so through the roof into the open air. The slab on which the burning logs were placed was not yet more than gently warm. Elizabeth and I rested our feet on it, at right angles to one another, and were selfishly glad that we were the sole occupants of the *årestue*: this was luxury, and one we had no immediate desire to share with anybody else.

Braced against the iron bar was a bracket which could be swung, lowered and raised like a spit over an old-fashioned fireplace here at home, though all cooking in this *gjestgiveri*, as usual in Norway, was done by electricity: in the smallest and most out-of-the-way corners we came to cooking and lighting were by electricity, and current was evidently cheap because lights burned through the day as well as throughout the night in porches and on balconies and landings where no one bothered to switch them off.

When the girl came in with another armful of logs we offered her a cigarette in the hope that this might persuade her to linger with us and talk. She accepted it reluctantly, lit it without skill from one of my *fyrstikker*, smoked it without pleasure and thrust it behind her when, unexpectedly, the door opened and the owner of the place came in. He had hardly sat down before she had vanished through the doorway and we did not see her again till she served *frokost* next morning.

For the next hour we had one of the most exhilarating conversations I can remember having had for a long time. Yet, if you were to ask me what it was all about I should be hard put to it to give you a summary. Our visitor, a man in his middle fifties, had not a word of English, but he had an extraordinary alertness of mind and gift of interpretation. He had, too, if I may use the phrase, a most articulate face. He was swift to guess when we were stuck for a word, swift to turn the conversation when we were properly bogged down, swift to complete a sentence for us, whether question or answer or comment.

Why then did we find this so exhilarating? I think because our minds, all three of us, were at full stretch. It was exhausting, but that often goes with exhilaration. When my inventiveness failed Elizabeth's took on a new lease of life; when hers failed I was ready to step into the breach. We may have talked at cross-purposes, but the impression we had was of a full-bodied triangular conversation in which all three of us

took our full shares. We talked of the differences between
Norway and England, of tourists and sight-seeing, of different
kinds of country through which we had passed, of things seen
and enjoyed, of the differences between ourselves and the
people we had met. We heard the long, exciting tale of the
moose he had shot and carried home down the mountainside;
their two fearsome heads and extravagant horns adorned the
room we sat in, piercing the tobacco-laden air.

He explained to us the origin and purpose of two pieces of
furniture which fascinated us. They were, or rather had
been a century and a half ago, saddles. They were mounted
now on blocks and served as additional semi-upholstered
chairs. Each consisted of a long broad inverted-U-shaped
leather pad which fitted over the animal's back and was held
in position by girth and crupper. Built on to each was a
wooden framework consisting of a curved back-and-arm-rest-
in-one, so designed that it would embrace the waist and support one elbow and forearm. Small swinging foot-rests on
adjustable straps gave additional comfort. It was padded with
leather and studded with a fine bold pattern of brass-headed
nails. To ride on such a saddle, provided one were confident
in the sure-footedness and goodwill of one's mount, would be
to ride in comfort indeed. The leather was tooled and beautifully sewn and the proportions of the whole were, as seems
always to be the case with traditional and ancient things, completely satisfying to the eye.

Perhaps they appealed even more to Elizabeth than they
did to me. But, then, I do not ride, whereas Elizabeth knows
the satisfaction of horse-flesh between her knees and her feet
in stirrups. It is a pleasure to which from time to time she
encourages me; but hitherto, foolishly no doubt, I have
remained adamant. I suspect that it is a pleasure I now shall
never know.

Tessand was the farthest north we reached. I remember
that there was no point throughout the whole of the night at
which I was unable to read the time by my wristwatch, still
on my wrist and not even held up to the window for better
light. I think some folk in Tessand did not go to bed at all.
Between half-past two and three I was awakened by a lorry

and voices outside. Curious, I slipped out of bed and crossed to the window to look out. Just across the road was a petrol-station and drawn up outside it was a petrol-tanker. The proprietor was out in his shirt-sleeves and the driver was filling his tanks from his truck. They exchanged cigarettes, one or two cronies, including our landlord, ambled up to talk of this and that. Half an hour later the truck went on down the valley, presumably to unload further supplies at Vågå and Otta and beyond. An amusing thought that this was at three o'clock on a Sunday morning!

Tessand was, perhaps, the cheapest place we stayed at. In the morning we had bacon and eggs as well as the usual cold table. It was our fault, not theirs, that we did not eat the bacon. It was served raw, and neither of us could face it. Fish, of course, is regularly eaten raw in Norway, as elsewhere, and no doubt it was our loss that we did not sample it and come to appreciate the taste. We had met this raw fish at Oslo, in that astonishing little *pensjonat* where I had ten rashers of bacon, three eggs and an omelette stuffed with, of all ingredients, cauliflower. But there the choice had been so abundant that we could afford to look hostilely at the raw dishes and turn elsewhere.

There was enough and to spare at the Tessand table, and we ate well. An ample supper had been ours the night before; we had been excellently housed; a fire had been lit for our exclusive benefit in the fireplace-room; we had enjoyed the vigorous conversation of our host for an hour or more; we had breakfasted well in the morning; milk had been "on tap" for both meals—and milk, at any rate in the cafés and restaurants where one buys it by the glass, is not cheap by any standards. And the total bill presented to us as we left was a few pence over nine shillings each!

TESSAND TO BERGEN

INTO THE JOTUNHEIMS

WE walked for a long while next morning, still alongside
bright water, with the high hills ahead of us lit by the powerful sun. The slopes of the hills were steeper by far than they
had been the previous day, and they plunged into the lake
at times almost vertically, so that it was more like fjord scenery
than anything we had walked through since Hardanger.
Small farms were wedged into the folds of the hillsides almost
at the water's edge. Lom, our next objective, was a considerable distance away and we were not sorry when the only
vehicle we were to see until evening overtook us and we were
offered a lift. The car had two men in front and an extremely
elderly woman in native costume on the back seat, nursing a
great armful of flowers and a basket containing cakes and
pots of jam.

The two men were in their Sunday suits of sober black, the
old woman in black, too, save for some bright embroidery
and her flowing headgear. She squeezed herself into one
corner as Elizabeth and I, feeling gross interlopers, climbed
in beside her, trying to compress our awkward rucksacks into
manageable form. She did not speak one word, but when
on the bridge over the Bövra at Lom we thanked our driver
and his companion, and her, too, for accepting the incon-
venience we had caused her, she gave an odd formal bow,
moved her lips in silence; that was all.

The Lom Stavkirke may be twelfth century or it may be a
little later: there seems to be some doubt about its precise
date. But we saw no church that was more finely posed
against a background of great hills and fast-flowing water than
this. Its dragon-heads challenged the filmy clouds that were
beginning to lace the blueness of the sky and there was a fine
alternation of light and shade on the many-faceted steeple that

187

soared away triumphantly from the dark pattern of its shingled roofs.

At Lom the road divides. One fork bears away west-by-north-west and comes eventually, after skirting the northern limits of the Jostedals glacier, to Nordfjord. The other fork, the one that we were to take, responds to the magnet-like Jotunheimen and curves west and southwards, ultimately to cross Sognefjell and drop steeply down to Sognefjord. Close to the fork of the road stands the *stavkirke*; and close to that, one of the lych-gate type gateways the Norwegians so dearly love: two massive tree-trunk pillars and a shingled roof with ornamented ridge-pole. We posed three Gudbrandsdal women in their native costume within this fine timber frame, and afterwards persuaded two of them to pose for a close-up photograph of the workmanship of their dresses.

Then we entered a trim little café, drank coffee and ate cakes and studied our map, while a small party of four twelve-year-old boys drank from bottles boldly labelled "*Öl*"—or ale—without the slightest apparent effect. There is, I believe, less than one per cent of one per cent alcohol in that popular beverage or the Norwegian authorities would never allow its sale to children.

One other photograph I took before we left the quiet upland village that is Lom. It was a close-up of some of the wooden staddle-stones, the *stabbur* from which these rural store-houses derive their actual name. Dark as chocolate, weathered by generations of wind and snow and blazing sun, they supported the great timbers of the building for which they had been fashioned, and the play of light and shadow beneath and among them was intricate and wonderful. I had seen nothing better of the kind even in the Sandvig Collection, so many of which had come from the villages and open country within short hail of the elongated lake that is called Vågåvatn.

Then, because time pressed, we set off uphill, away from the lake side, with the tumbling ice-water of the Bövra for noisy companion. On our right, standing sentinel between the two forks of the road out of Lom, was the 6,ooo-foot mountain Lomseggja. Ahead of us, and very near to us now, were the Jotunheims whose chill breath we had been conscious of ever since we reached Otta, just twenty-four hours before.

We climbed almost without break for the remainder of the day. Not steeply, except for small stretches, but steadily. The wind blew increasingly cold in our faces and before mid-afternoon the strength of the sun had diminished noticeably. When the road dipped close enough to the river at one point I crossed over and put my hand in. It was shockingly cold. Out of the wind there was still some warmth in the air, but it was a hesitant warmth, a warmth which said unmistakably: Don't expect too much of me, I've precious few reserves; and when they're gone—well, you can expect the worst! We ate a snack in the shelter of a low bush, drank from a trickle of water that almost froze tongue and lips, and then set off once more.

The entrance to the Jotunheims from any direction must be dramatic. This cluster of high peaks, among which is the highest peak in northern Europe, Galdhöpiggen, 8,100 feet high, is well named Home of the Giants. The translation from comparatively unspectacular heights and contours to this close-set Alpine region is so relatively swift: at one moment you are tramping along a steadily ascending slope; at the next you have entered the narrow gateway and the Giants' Homes surround you on all sides. Nor does it seem, as you stand and look about you, that there need necessarily be any way out on the farther side. You enter at your peril.

The hillsides closed in about us, the vegetation became more scant, the rocks more prominent. Though there was still water alongside us it was ice-water, forbidding, hostile. Now it ran viciously over tumbled boulders in a narrow bottle-neck, its fall precipitate; now it widened temporarily, to slide with treacherous smoothness over mud that had been formed by the age-long grinding of detritus from the mountainside. Where the road ran almost at the same level there was a thick carpet of silt where the river in spate had burst its banks and flooded widely. A degree or two's drop in temperature and this would become a frozen river.

There came a point at which the rocks rose sheer on each side of us, as they had done at the approach to Buarbre and

Folgefonna: boulders were perched dangerously on bastions and massive crags, and thin courageous trees had found precarious footing, their roots threatening in time to loosen these boulders and send them crashing to the bottom. It would be a perilous defile indeed when those roots had thickened. How long this road would wind upwards among these menacing crags we did not know: our map gave only the most casual indications of distance and we had long learned to accept the fact that a place-name need not imply more than a single, and perhaps evacuated, dwelling-house.

Somewhere we had seen that there was actually a bus service along this road, once daily each way. We did not find this easy to believe, yet we knew that the Norwegians, whether building railways or planning bus services, are not men to be put off by topographical considerations. The recollection of the Bergen-Norheimsund trip was vivid in our memories yet. But if, in fact, a bus did run along this forbidding route, where did it go to and whence return? Where was it at this moment, anyway? If behind us, then it might be safe to linger till it picked us up and took us to some place where we could rest for the night and get warm and eat; if it was ahead of us, approaching us, how far must it travel before it turned back to overtake us? And how long could we dawdle in a wind-swept canyon like this before our marrows froze and our lips were finally sealed with the ice of our breath?

"There's a man in the road," Elizabeth said. "He might be able to tell us something about it."

The first human being we had seen for a long time, he was presumably the occupant of the small cottage planted on the only level site to be found between these high, rocky cliffs. He was standing in the middle of the road, leaning on a long, bent stick, considering the immensity of a waterfall which, right opposite his home, was plunging sheer down a precipice whose height I could not begin to compute.

"Living in such an isolated and end-of-the-world sort of a place as this," I said, doubtfully, "he probably talks some weird dialect that will be incomprehensible to us even if he can understand our standard Norwegian."

We drew nearer, half expecting him at any moment to turn about, retreat to his timber cottage and bar the door firmly behind him.

"I'll speak slowly," I said. "Basic, simple words and nothing more. Cut out all the frills of 'Would you be so kind', etc. . . . I'll state the main word we're after. *Rutevogn* —that's Norwegian for bus. *Til*—he can hardly misunderstand that word for 'to'. And what's the name of the place we're making for, again?"

"Elveseter," Elizabeth reminded me. It was a name that had rung in our ears ever since we began checking over the route into and through the Jotunheims. There was a cool, clear, musical ring to it: Elveseter.

We drew level with the man. He was an elderly, decrepit-looking individual in the shabbiest of clothes, with an expression on his lined face that seemed to belong to this uncompromising mountain region and the bleak winds among which he lived. His eyes were pin-points beneath heavy lids and shaggy brows. My heart sank. However, he was our only hope of information.

"*Rutevogn*," I began, enunciating clearly and distinctly. "*Når går det til Elveseter?*"

That was a simple enough question. I had put the essential word first, so that his doubtless simple mind could grasp the picture of the route-wagon. Then, spacing out the four monosyllables with equal emphasis and lifting my voice at the end of my question as I stressed the place-name, I had presumably made it clear that we wished to know at what time the bus went to Elveseter.

I have not often been more taken aback. He answered me promptly, in fluent English corrupted by the usual American accent: "The bus for Elveseter ought to be along in about two hours' time," he said. "It may be a bit late to-day as there was a landslide last week and some stretches of the road have been weakened and it has to travel slowly. But you can rely on it all right: the driver has never once failed to get through on schedule." He gave that last word the horrific American form, *skedjule*.

Elizabeth and I stammered our thanks and hoped to

goodness his hearing had not been keen enough for him to catch our speculation—or my speculation, rather, for as usual it was I who had voiced the tactless queries—about his ability to understand basic Norwegian. He nodded pleasantly and hoped we would have a good trip. He had vanished when next we looked round, two or three hundred yards farther along the road; probably gone indoors to tell his wife how competently he had answered a couple of sceptical British tourists.

It was four o'clock. The bus, if it ran to schedule, would presumably be coming along soon after six. If we waited here for it we should probably freeze to death. If we walked on we might manage to keep warm; we might even (though we hardly dared to hope for this) come upon some place where we could get a cup of coffee. It was a comforting thought that, if we should drop by the wayside, there was every chance of our being eventually picked up by the bus and delivered somewhere in safety. With that comforting thought we stepped out again with new enthusiasm.

The road climbed more steeply, higher and higher hills crowding in upon us. The river ran whiter, and in the chill wind little balls of foam were whipped off it and sent scudding across the road between our feet. We came to a minute cluster of huts. There was no smoke or other sign of occupation, but set against two boulders in the river bank were some scrubbing-boards, and we realized that the occupants, Spartan women, these, must do their weekly wash in this same ice-cold water! Elizabeth shuddered at the thought and we increased our rate of walking to raise our temperature, which had dropped a point or two at the very idea.

Then, just as the road steepened again considerably and we realized that our easy steady tramping must now change to determined foot-slogging, a flat-wagon came speeding up behind us with a bunch of workmen on board. I flagged it, and to our relief it stopped. Elizabeth hurled her rucksack into a pair of waiting arms and was dragged up the side by another waiting pair. I scrambled up behind her, and we had hardly dropped to the rough and gritty floor when the lorry jerked off again and roared up the ever-steepening slope till the river had vanished from sight below us.

It was no time or place for ceremony. There were no sides to this lorry, so I thrust Elizabeth against the most solid-looking of the men and wedged her myself on the other side. We rocked as one unit and swayed to every spin of the wheel as the driver took us round bend after bend. A cloud of thin white dust hovered in the air immediately behind our wheels, to be dispersed by the wind that had been in our faces all day long. The road dipped violently and our lorry dipped with it, plunging downwards like the best of Giant Racers; it rose again and dipped again, switchbacking alongside the roaring river. Suddenly and without warning the lorry braked, swerved off the road, nosed into a narrow quarry-approach that looked too steep for anything but a tracked vehicle, and came to a drastic halt. The men tumbled off to right and left, and with them Elizabeth and I and our rucksacks, shaking at every joint, but exultant at our luck.

We walked on a mile and came to another tiny cluster of solid timber huts. Outside one of them was a high trellis on which dozens of pairs of bleached antlers had been arranged —an alarming spectacle to be confronted with as one turned the corner walking alone at night. A little farther on another shanty, with smoke coming from a stove-pipe chimney, proclaimed itself a café. Gratefully we left the road, tapped on the door, walked into a small, snug room where half a dozen men were playing cards over cups of steaming coffee, and called for cups for ourselves.

I do not think the Norwegians can make bad coffee. It is rationed over there, or was at that time, and so one would have expected to be fobbed off with some poor substitute such as one is offered in our Milk Bars to-day. But we never were. Only aboard *Venus* and in the lovely Utne hotel did we taste more delectable coffee than here. Yet it was a place too small to have a name even on a map such as ours which gives large-type names to almost non-existent congeries of huts. Dark, rich coffee, and cream so thick that it stood for a moment in a blob in the centre of the coffee till it was broken by the spoon and stirred into its heart; a warming, heartening beverage that ran through our whole system and made us wonder why we should at any time have felt misgivings about our ability to penetrate these unknown hills. We were, jointly, more than twice the man we had been when we left the road a quarter of an hour before!

The gradient stiffened and the rocks closed in upon us from each side; the rushing, tumultuous Bövra, far from being a smaller stream than it had been far down the valley, and by all known laws should, in fact, have been here, seemed to be greater in volume, more substantial, more furious than at any time during the day. It was own cousin to the swift, impetuous stream that had plunged down from Buarbre into the lake in the hollow of the hills above Odda. Where the gorge through which it travelled was at its narrowest a cloud of white spray hovered over it, continuously dissipated by the wind, continuously augmented from beneath. It was so solid-seeming that it might well have contained not only particles of water whipped to atoms, but particles chiselled off the rock-faces through which the river had been charging headlong down.

We walked and walked, but Elveseter seemed to come no nearer. There were no milestones to encourage or discourage us, and I am not sure whether in general they would have been a good thing. Marked in kilometres they would be deceptive, for with each successive stone we should know that in effect we had walked but five-eighths of a mile; and if they had been marked in "miles" they would have been Nor- wegian "miles"—which are, like the unofficial Irish mile, just six times as long as English miles.

"I shouldn't think there are, in fact, any villages up here, small or large," I said to Elizabeth at one point, as we leaned against a boulder to gather our forces for another stretch of this hard walking. "Who would build a hamlet, however small, in such a place as this?"

"I would, for one," she answered, surprising me. "I'd like to build a hamlet here of stoutest timber cottages, and settle in them all the people we like best. We wouldn't live here all the year round, of course; but just think of being able to retreat here from time to time and live surrounded by all these moun- tains, with a river like the Bövra flowing beneath our door- steps! Think of the books we'd write!"

I was not so sure. But then, though I myself can be carried away in poetic fancy, I had by then begun to realize that, excellent as that coffee had been, we had really had nothing to eat since breakfast but a snack in the early afternoon. There had been for some time past an insistent rumble within me that was a danger-signal I could not ignore.

"I must eat, and soon," I said prosaically in answer to her flight of fancy. "And much," I added with some emphasis.

I deserved a rebuke. Instead, Elizabeth shot me a sympathetic glance which showed me that she, too, could do something with a well-spread *kold-bord*.

"Come on," she said. "Let's find a place to stay."

It was, in such surroundings, an improbable remark. In all directions save the one by which we had come our view was limited by an almost sheer mountainside, snow-capped, inexorable. Where there was a dip between two mountains a more distant peak filled it; we knew that there were higher and yet higher peaks beyond even the horizon we could see. This region was not called the Home of the Giants for nothing. As for anyone establishing in such a region a place where one could stay: the thing was unthinkable. Elveseter, it is true, appeared in bold print on our map. But so did Galdhöpiggen (8,100 feet); and there were other *piggen*, or peaks, only just less considerable, within hail of where we stood.

ELVESETER

So when we came round a bend in the steep road to find ourselves confronted by one of those great lych-gates we had so often seen and admired, and a banner proclaiming the Elveseter Hotel, we were astonished. More practical and intelligent tourists than ourselves would have taken the precaution of inquiring at Bennett's Travel Bureau whether there was in fact any chance of accommodation in such a spot as this. We had not done so, and were naturally astonished to find so large a hotel just here of all places. We were a little dismayed, too, because clearly this was no ordinary hotel, no *pensjonat* or *gjestgiveri* such as were accustomed to: it was something quite out of the ordinary run of hotels, even of tourist hotels, and we could guess that its hidden courtyard and garages would be filled to overflowing (provided the place were open at all) with opulent cars bearing transatlantic and Continental number-plates and badges too numerous to mention.

"Here," said Elizabeth firmly, "we eat."

"Impossible," said I. "Not here."

I rapidly computed what currency remained in our possession and how much longer it had to suffice us. We were a very long way yet from Bergen, and though we had our return tickets safely in my wallet we had to eat and sleep for several more days, to preserve a margin for enforced travel and leave a little over for spending-money before we sailed from Bergen.

"Impossible," I repeated, with what sounded to me like conviction, and I turned my gaze resolutely up along the climbing road that vanished among the trees a hundred yards ahead of us.

Elizabeth smiled. "I'll go and do some reconnoitring," was all she said. Dropping her rucksack at my feet she departed through the gateway and up a flight of wooden steps beyond.

For my part I sat down on a log by the roadside to await her return. Part of me, the part that hankers after the flesh-pots, would have been delighted to put up here for the night and leave the rest of the trip to chance. To bathe, and sleep in the sort of bed they would undoubtedly have in such a hotel as this, with something kindlier than the accursed *dyne* over me, and sup well and breakfast well and sit long over a great log-fire: that would be a fitting end to such a day as we had had. But at what cost? Common sense said that such reckless extravagance would put paid to more than the hotel bill. Empty of pocket, we should have to beat it rapidly for the coast, cancel the room in our Bergen hotel and seek out some cheap lodging-house instead. It would be good-bye to any chance of purchasing a few souvenirs of Norway.

Elizabeth returned, the look on her face untranslatable.

It seemed that she had entered the home of some member of the hotel outdoor staff and learned that there was quite literally no other roof of any kind for many miles of snow-bound road. If we did not spend the night here at Elveseter, we should spend it on the roadside, and we should not be alive in the morning. The road itself, they had stressed, was not officially opened for two days yet after its long winter sleep of deep snow and the iron grip of ice.

"In brief," Elizabeth said with the utmost cheerfulness, "*ici nous sommes!*"

In moments of great emotion Elizabeth has the habit of breaking out into basic French or German. To these utterances she has now added certain useful and expressive Norwegian ones; these will doubtless stand her in good stead when (and if ever) we go to Italy, or Spain, or the United States of America, an even more improbable chance.

"So be it," I said, rising to the occasion. "And *ici nous restons*, my sweet."

The Elveseter Tourist Hotel is, I would say, the most immediately prepossessing hotel we have ever seen. It has been planned and designed and to a large extent equipped on the lines of a substantial Gudbrandsdal farmstead. Round an open courtyard are grouped the main and auxiliary buildings, all in massive timber, with trees interspersed among them and the slope of tree-clad Leirasfjell beginning quite literally on its doorstep. Immediately opposite, on the other side of the road, rise the even greater mountains culminating in Galdhöpiggen and its peers. Thus it lies broad-based on a small plateau, itself well over two thousand feet above sea level; steep mountainsides rise from it in all directions.

We walked, Elizabeth and I, through the gateway and into that spacious courtyard, our steps shortening as we walked, for most clearly this was not the sort of hotel we ordinarily patronized. What its prices would be we hardly dared to speculate: certainly high by ordinary standards; and to two people who had alternated for the most part between *pensjonat* and *gjestgiveri*, quite formidable. Yet we really had no choice. The road through the mountains, which we were to know later as the Sognefjell Road, was not yet officially opened, and what lay beyond the hotel would be interminable miles of ice and snow and wind-swept rock. The only alternative to it was one that we just could not accept: to turn back on our tracks and hope to find something down the Bövra Valley. But we had been walking through that ever since we left Lom, and neither Elizabeth nor I make a practice of turning back.

We entered an L-shaped, low-ceilinged, panelled lounge. An enormous fire blazed in a fireplace of the sort we had first sat by in the little Tessand *pensjonat*, but this time conceived on so giant a scale that most of the Tessand *årestue* itself could have been contained within its glowing hearth. The lounge had the usual highly polished floor, but a number of thick peasant-weave rugs lay upon it, so that one could cross the floor without once setting foot on bare waxed boards. The walls were panelled in the wood that was to be found in every house large and small, but panels here and there had been decorated with bold, almost garish, painted designs similar to those we had seen in the Hallingstua, in far-away Nesbyen. On the floor, too, were various pieces of traditional furniture, in particular great painted wooden chests as large as blanket-chests, with semi-domed tops, curiously shaped and decorated wooden chairs, stools, and other such things.

The fire was so built into the room that it faced outwards, not inwards, into the long and the short sections of this great capital "L", and the heat from its high-piled logs penetrated into every corner. There were snug and deep arm-chairs, round and square tables, deeply upholstered window-seats, squat occasional chairs which one could draw up and squeeze into the glare of the fire if one wished to crouch and cook oneself to a turn. And behind a discreetly planned reception desk there stood a very friendly looking woman awaiting us.

We put our cards on the table. We had been foolish and taken no steps to ascertain whether the Jotunheimen could offer our sort of accommodation. We had arrived, to find no alternative to this grand hotel. We had not come by car but on our own four feet, with the assistance for a mile or two of a ballast-lorry. What were our prospects here?

The woman smiled. It was true, she said, that this was a

Tourist Hotel. Even now she was awaiting the arrival of a number of guests, the first of the new season, by car and by bus and by jeep. Among them there would be an organized English party travelling under the aegis of a famous travel agency. But she thought, she felt pretty sure, that if we would seat ourselves by the fire while she went and had a word with the Proprietor, Hr. Elveseter himself (how delightful, we thought, to have one's own name on the map!), all could be arranged.

And it was so. She returned soon afterwards and led us, not upstairs to one of the forty or more bedrooms that open off the various landings and corridors, but across the lounge to a door which was one solid panel painted in Gudbrandsdal style, and through the doorway into a ground-floor bedroom whose wide, double-glazed windows opened straight over the foaming rapids of the Bövra.

"I think," she said, as she began to close the door behind her, "that you will be happy here."

We for our part knew we should, and told each other so.

It was not often on that trip through Norway, or indeed on any of the other trips that we have made together at home and abroad, that I leave such matters entirely to Elizabeth. In the ordinary way it is I who make the initial contacts with landlords and receptionists and people like that. I had done so, of course, at Elveseter, if it comes to that. But the true initial contact in this case had undeniably come through Elizabeth, who described to me later how, with far more trepidation than I had suspected, she had climbed that wooden stairway to the house by the gate, looked in vain for bell or knocker, and eventually had to enter, unannounced, the living-room, where owner and wife and children and two adult friends and several dogs had been congregated round a fireplace, deep in conversation. She told me how she had stood there, and I could imagine her coughing modestly, and then a little less modestly, and finally with a certain aggressiveness, until someone or other had turned round from the fire and the moment had come for her to explain why she was there.

I could have kicked myself afterwards when I remembered

that during that day's walking Elizabeth had spoken very little because the previous night at Tessand she had accepted a cigarette of some unknown brand and smoked it to the acrid end in the full knowledge that she was rasping the skin off the inside of her throat. In the morning she had wakened almost speechless, and she had spared her voice all she could throughout the day. Yet I had chosen this of all evenings to let her loose on her own, in circumstances much more complicated than usual. I wish now that I could have been there, watched her standing, a little uncertain, a little hesitant, behind the throng of strangers in that firelit, timbered room, with only a few seconds in which to explain her presence. Things had been made no easier for her by the fact that an immense dog, an elk-hound, she felt convinced, had been nuzzling about her legs as she stood there, and for all she knew it was merely indulging in a reconnaissance in order to select the tastiest mouthful of flesh!

At any rate, here now we were. Within a few minutes Elizabeth had slipped out of the room and up the stairs in search of a bathroom, from which she returned, glowing and radiant, to change into something rather more suitable for the dining-room and lounge of the Elveseter than boots and tweed skirt and a reversible blue-and-fawn wind-breaker.

I took her place, and enjoyed the first bath I had had for long enough. Drying myself was complicated by the fact that, attached loosely to the wall within thirty inches of where I had to stand, was the most sinister electric-heater I have ever seen. It was like the elements of an electric kettle on a grand scale: a series of white-coated elements which radiated an almost intolerable heat, but no red glow or anything to show that it really was alive. In that small, hermetically sealed bathroom, with boiling water from the tap and this fierce heating-element on the wall, only a salamander could have remained alive for more than a matter of minutes. Throwing modesty to the winds, I opened the bathroom door and took my bath and dried myself that way, in full view of all the newly arrived guests if they should happen to come to the top of the stairs and be shown this way to their rooms.

We dressed leisurely, with that satisfying awareness that our

day's walking was done, that a roof was over our heads, two
real beds were ours for the night, and *middag* would be served
within the hour. After which, we could sit all evening if
we wanted to, basking in the radiance of the log fire. More
suitably clothed, now, we jotted down a few notes on our
day's walking and then emerged into the lounge to find it
swarming with people, most of whom seemed to be speaking
English with the strongest of North-country accents.

The majority of them had come in on that same bus which
we had once contemplated waiting for, far down Bövredal;
we wondered whether, if we had waited for it, there would
have been room for us. Quite probably not. A few others
had come by private car, and we particularly noticed a
Swedish number-plate on a big car drawn up outside. All
these had come from the direction of Gudbrandsdal, as we
had done. But one party of four elderly people, two men
and two women, muffled to the eyes in fur coats with high
collars, and blankets still pinned round them, appeared to
have arrived from the opposite direction in a jeep belonging
to the hotel. From conversation overheard later on it was
evident that this had been a quite spectacular journey, as we
were to discover for ourselves next day.

We ate that evening at individual tables in a spacious
dining-room of which almost the whole of the wall-space on
three sides was window. We looked down into trees and over
the rushing turbulence of the Bövra. Ducking our heads, we
could look upwards at the remote peaks of the mountains
girdling the hotel. On each table was a small flagstaff set
firmly in a wooden cruciform base, and at the top of each
there hung the Union Jack, or the Swedish, or Danish, or
American, or Swiss, or French, or Belgian flag. The dining-
room filled up by stages and from our vantage-point in the
middle we could overhear snatches of conversation from all
directions. Only the two Swedes were silent: a man and a
woman of middle-age, who had nothing to say to one another
and registered no interest in their voluble table-companions.

Middag was a more stereotyped meal here than elsewhere,
as might be expected in a hotel which caters mainly for
tourists, but we were not sorry to be served with soup and

meat and sweet and cheese for once, after so many meals of a more unusual sort. We descended in twos and threes to the lounge, where excellent coffee and most tasty biscuits were served to each of us, a continual supply of both coffee and biscuits being available so that we drank far more than normally we should have done, and time passed like a dream.

We had heard already that the famous Sognefjell Road was not yet officially opened, and now there was corroboration. The party in the jeep, the two elderly English couples, had much to say about this, but were unfortunately somewhat incoherent. If they were to be entirely believed, the driver of the jeep had virtually told them to shut their eyes, hold their scarves about their faces, hold their breath as long as they could and, in capital letters, SIT TIGHT. This they seemed to have accomplished, for all were alive to tell the tale and they had now reached that comfortable state in which, dangers being past, they could exaggerate indefinitely without frightening themselves. Even whittled down to its bones, however, it must have been quite a drive. Though the road would not be open to traffic officially for two more days, the early spring sunshine had made it just possible a day or two before the usual date, and the jeep had apparently been the first to risk a passage along it.

The bus which we had at one time contemplated taking had come from the direction of Otta, perhaps from the rail-head there; it was now to turn about and go straight back: there would be no bus service over the remainder of that road, the highest sections of it, until word had come through from the crews on the big power-driven rotary ploughs that they had cut a carriage-way at last. Such word might come by phone at any time, direct to the hotel.

It was along this road that we must travel on the morrow, if we were to get to Sognefjord, and then to Voss, and ultimately back to Bergen and *Venus.* I turned to Elizabeth after a further instalment, with variations, of the tale, and raised an eyebrow.

"Sufficient unto the day," she said, somewhat sententiously. "What about bed?"

This, however, was out of the question until the lounge

emptied, for our bedroom opened off the lounge within three yards of the fireplace. Already several people, prowling about, had opened it, wondering what was on the other side of the painted panel, and we had noticed that, as usual in Norway, there was neither lock nor bolt to it. So we sat and looked about us instead. Looked particularly at the silent, self-contained Swedish couple, man and woman, who sat nearest to the fire, the man smoking, the woman playing a solitary game of patience. They never smiled, they never looked up at us, or about the room; they looked as dull and depressing as melting snow on a dirty lawn. And there was, we felt, a certain selfishness about the way in which the woman took the whole of a table for her game, drawing it close up to the fire so that several who might have sat nearer than they did had to remain at a distance. I was annoyed with myself for feeling, amid such pleasant surroundings and when Fate had been so kind to us, that slight antagonism towards them which their behaviour evoked.

Gradually the lounge emptied. In twos and threes the other guests went upstairs. Men lit a last cigarette, women took a last close look at some of the exquisite embroidery and tapestry on the walls, and a tall dark youngish man appeared silently at the reception counter. It was Hr. Elveseter himself, the quite perfect *hôtelier*.

He spoke, as we might have known he would, excellent and idiomatic English. He knew very well that we were not occupying his best suite, that we had not arrived by car or bus, that we carried two travel-stained rucksacks and had come to his hotel not from choice but from necessity. Nevertheless, he contrived to make us feel that, out of all his guests present and to come, there were none in whom he felt more interest, for whom he would like to do more, than our own two selves.

It was late in the evening of the first day that his hotel was officially open and he had been badgered, to our certain knowledge, on and off for more than an hour, by a difficult couple who had decided at the last moment to reverse the order of their organized tour and had found themselves here without the necessary reservations for the next few days' travelling. On him, they made it very clear, devolved the responsibility of sorting them out, telephoning through to the hotels they ought to be staying at to say that they would not be arriving till later, and to the hotels where they were not expected for days to say that they would be arriving to-morrow, or the next day, or the day after. All this he under-took with a ready smile, complete sympathy, and a subtly concealed patience that may well have made the two people think they were actually doing him a favour by pouring out on him their self-induced worries.

He confirmed the fact that the road was not officially open, but said he could guarantee that a small, sturdy bus would make the journey on the morrow. It would be leaving the hotel at such and such an hour, with a small party on board at most, perhaps none at all, if those who had arrived felt that a journey so soon over such a route was more than that they could face. Word had come through from the snow-plough crews at Krossbu that there was now a single-track line open through even the biggest drifts, though vehicles would take the Sognefjell Road at their own risk.

We realized then, Elizabeth and I, how incredibly foolish we had really been, to set out like this, unprepared, to take the road through the Jotunheims, which is annually snow-bound for more than half a year, which was not even opened at all until just before the war if memory is not at fault, and which rises to a summit only a few feet short of 4,700, the highest mountain-crossing by road in all Norway. Why, we might have arrived at Elveseter from Tessand only to find the hotel still closed after its long winter sleep and no means whatsoever of attaining the far side of the Jotunheims save by returning the way we had come and then trying some other and less mountainous route. We felt, in spite of the sense of triumph we had in achieving this much, and Hr. Elveseter's courtesy, very small indeed and deserving of the strongest reproof.

He had any number of suggestions to make. He wanted us, before we left in the morning, to climb at least a little way up the mountainside on which his hotel was built, so as to get an uninterrupted view of the major summits on the other side of the narrow valley. After which, if we so desired, we could travel on by that bus. Or we could set off on foot ahead of the bus, leaving our packs to be put on board by the hotel porter, so that we could travel light, conserving our energies for the stiff climb that lay ahead of us. We turned in that night, our heads filled with all sorts of attractive plans, each of which had almost everything to commend it to us.

Our room was beautifully warm and snug, for the great lounge fireplace backed on to it and the wall was almost too hot to touch. I threw open the window at the head of my bed and was met by a blast of ice-cold air that made me shut it speedily and securely. I knew then why there were double-glazed windows to the rooms of this hotel. If it could be like this in June, what might it be like in late autumn, in winter, in early spring, for those who lived here all the year round?

For it was indeed a home, a house that was lived in. I had for a time been a little sceptical. Those massive pieces of traditional furniture, those painted panels, those tapestries and rugs and embroidered thises and thats: were they really genuine Gudbrandsdal? Or were they not just perhaps a little too "Wardour Street"? Had they not been cleverly manufactured and planted here, to give atmosphere to this hotel that was modelled on a Gudbrandsdal farmstead?

Well, they had been manufactured; and they had been planted here. But the manufacture was of olden time and the planting had merely been the transference from one Gudbrandsdal home to this. For Hr. Elveseter quite convinced me when he spoke to us of how he and his father before him and their intimate friends and relations had scoured the valley for pieces of furniture to place in this hotel, thereby endowing it with a spirit and atmosphere like that in which the pieces had passed the hundred or two hundred years of their lives already. It was all genuine enough.

I may never again see the Elveseter Tourist Hotel, though I should like to be there in winter, if such a thing were possible, and to know that only its sturdy timbers and massive roof, its double-glazed windows and the comfort of its beds and chairs and rugs, stood between me and the whirling blizzards that are the storm-play of the Jotunheim Giants when their bleak world is abandoned to its rightful inhabitants.

THE SWEDES

We slept soundly and woke to brilliant sunshine, but we knew that if we opened our window and put our heads outside we should know something other than the warm caress of a gentle breeze. Appearances were deceptive, and we were well content to wash and dress and stand beside the relit fire in the lounge until the gong sounded for *frokost*.

During the meal Elizabeth said to me, "I don't know about you, but I feel very strongly indeed that to walk on ahead of the bus, leaving our rucksacks to be put on board by someone or other at the hotel, is a risk. They might be forgotten. The bus might not start. Or it might get stranded before it overtook us. Then where should we be?"

I had been thinking along the same lines myself, but the prospect of a few hours' walking without a pack on my back had been very seductive. We knew how steep the road was, how long the miles would be; and there is quite an expenditure of energy in carrying even a twenty-five-pound pack, uphill. On the level, and downhill (unless it is very steep) a pack is a blessing rather than a curse; but uphill, NO. Nevertheless I could see a dozen ways in which we might be let down and I knew that Elizabeth was right.

"Let's stick to them," I said.

Before packing we scrambled for half an hour up the tangled trail above the hotel for that splendid view across to the mountains; then, having seen less than we had been promised, through mistaking the trail and so losing ourselves among thick trees, we descended again to ground level, went indoors to warm our hands, and then packed.

I have never understood how our account was made out. For the first few lines it was rather frightening: items of meals and bedroom and service and so on in figures larger than any we had so far seen. At the end there was a further percentage-figure, but this time it was deducted from the total. The ultimate figure would have looked high at Norheimsund or Tessand or Åsletta or Kapp; but in relation to the Elveseter Tourist Hotel it was ridiculously small. I think perhaps there was a twinkle in the receptionist's eye as she handed us the receipted bill, but there was nothing more specific than that. We left, still marvelling at our luck; the other guests, standing with their backs to that superb fire, waved us an unenvying good-bye.

Krossbu stuck in our minds as the one definite landmark we were to make for along this road. It was about seventeen miles from Elveseter—a long enough walk in normal conditions and not too heavily laden, particularly at this altitude. At Krossbu there was a *turiststasjon*—a very different thing from a Tourist Hotel, but something to make for. This was the point from which the snow-plough crew had telephoned the news that they had now opened the highest stretch of the famous Sognefjell Road to single-line traffic at its own risk.

We climbed steadily and it was only after we had been on the move for an hour or so, each apparently doing some silent calculations, that we realized the dilemma that was about to confront us. If we walked on until the bus overtook us and then went on board, we should miss our only chance of walking the best part of this spectacular road. If we let it go by we should miss our last chance of transport that day; we should then have to expend most of our energies approaching the summit, where we should almost certainly have to stop for the night, thus leaving the formidable stretch for the very day when by rights we should be well on our way down to Sognefjord if we were to reach Bergen as we had planned.

Looking back over some of the pages of this book I am inclined to ask myself whether, in fact, we really did very much walking on this trip, and whether we did not have more than our rightful share of luck in the matter of lifts. Remembering some of the stretches we did walk, the Haugastöl-Geilo stretch, for instance, and the Sognefjell Road stretch which we did eventually walk, I can answer the implied accusation with a clear conscience. By the time our round trip of roughly a thousand miles was over we had walked not far short of two hundred miles, much of it in the more arduous sections.

As to lifts, I cannot answer as complacently. We did have the most extraordinary luck. The long run down Hallingdal with the fishermen was perhaps the first, unless we count the Nesbyen Choir bus, which was in a different category altogether. The lift to Otta in the little Austin was another: it came just when we needed it, ended exactly at the right moment and place, and was unsolicited—the best kind of lift. And now we had yet another example of our special brand of luck: a lift which enabled us to fit into one another all the remaining scattered jigsaw-fragments of our trip so that they made a patterned whole. And, as though the Fates were gentler in their irony than usual, those who gave us this lift were the self-same Swedes whom, the previous night, we had been inclined to write-off as unfriendly and selfish.

Their big car slid to a standstill alongside us. A window was wound down and we were signalled to. Room was made for us on the back seat and Elizabeth and I settled ourselves down, our rucksacks on the carpeted floor at our feet, and relaxed. There was no fork in the road ahead: the car must be going at least to Krossbu, perhaps farther than that.

The couple in front were not communicative, but we hardly expected that. The driver sat impassive at the thin-spoked steering-wheel; his wife's gesture was to turn a few degrees in her seat so that we could see the side of her face instead of merely the back of her neck. After the initial greeting neither of them spoke again: our needs were manifest, their ability to meet them were not less so. In any case the road, if the track we were now riding upon could be so called, demanded the driver's undiluted attention.

I am always critical of drivers, though on the rare occasions when I have to take a back seat I successfully avoid the temptation to become a "back-seat driver". Two drivers stand out in my memory above all others. One was the owner of a Vauxhall 30-98 in which as a schoolboy-just-left-school I had one of the most exciting drives in my young life. We were bound for a rambling old farmhouse which a number of us had taken for a summer holiday, tucked away in a fold

of the Brendon Hills. The owner of the Vauxhall, a long,
open model, had gone to the nearest rail-head to pick up
provisions in bulk and we were returning by a devious route
that included Porlock and Countisbury and Lynmouth
Hill.

Porlock to-day is no sort of a hill at all, nor has been for
many years; its gradients have been eased, its hairpin-bends
widened and its surface improved beyond belief. But there
was a time, at the end of the first World War, when it held
terrors for many motorists. Its steepest gradients were at the
lower end, among the hairpins, set between high earth banks
on the upper side and a drop into the unknown on the lower
side. I remember how, part-way round one of these hairpin-
bends on an acute gradient, we found ourselves confronting
a descending vehicle, the driver of which was clearly unhappy.
I myself was perched, foolish boy that I was, on top of the
back seat, clinging to a crate of provisions put up for us by
some London store.

"Beaver", as we knew him, though he was and is clean-
shaven and had never dreamed of growing the beard which,
about that time, evoked that foolish cry, brought the Vauxhall
to a standstill and without hesitation backed her round the
hairpin we had just begun to turn, swinging the wheel over
till the back of the car quite literally overhung a sheer drop
down among the thin trees. Looking over my shoulder, there
appeared to be less than nothing at all between myself and a
bottomless pit. With the rear wheels just clinging to the
gritty edge of the road, we paused; the downcoming car, which
should have given way to us, slid timidly by, its driver far too
anxiously bent over the wheel even to acknowledge the sport-
ing gesture we had made. Then, without jerk or back-sliding,
we went forward again effortlessly, gathered speed and were
round the bend and approaching the next before I and my
schoolfellow-passengers had recovered our breath.

The other driver I shall always remember is the Swede.
Within a few hundred yards the road we had been walking
on degenerated into a rough and hump-backed track, barely
car width, its earth surface broken by the weight of snow and
the clenching hand of winter ice, so that the underlying

boulders had broken through and it might have been a dis-
used river-bed save that the level of the ground alongside it
was often lower than the road itself. Where the road ran
straight for a while its undulating surface presented problems
enough; where it began to serpentine, as for the most part it
now did, the undulations presented problems even more
exacting. Where it dipped to some watercourse swollen by
melting snow, it appeared to be heading for disaster and
taking us along with it; where it rose, it rose uncompromis-
ingly, and our radiator was tipped to the mountain-peaks
and sky.

I have never sat behind a more impassive driver, nor one
in whom I had more complete confidence. Two large gloved
hands lay lightly but firmly on the wheel; shoulders were
squared and if the neck was tense with strain we did not
know it. From the casual air of the woman beside the driver
we could tell that our confidence in him was not misplaced.

He stopped once, when we saw looming ahead of us a
board announcing in bold red letters that the road was
CLOSED. It was, I think, near the spot marked on the map
as Bövertun—the "Town" on the Bövra. We stopped. The
Swede beckoned to a man standing in the snow not far away
and asked him a question in the minimum of words. The
man answered as briefly. The road was not, he said,
absolutely closed. There *was* a passage through to the other
side of the Jotunheimen. The Swede pointed to the notice;
the man shrugged, then jerked his head towards a building.
Standing there was a car: an old, battered but sturdy car.
It had been driven, he said, last night to Bövertun, and from
the west, the far side. That was enough for the Swede. Our
engine, which had been running silently all the time, took
charge; we slid forward, heading for the pass that would take
us to Krossbu.

The road became wilder. It dipped and rose and plunged
about in the pass like an untamed thing, narrow, tilting,
undulating, broken, rock-beset. If the car had not had
independent suspension it might have been an uncomfortable as well as a spectacular ride; as it was, the solid, warm
and well-upholstered saloon rode those bumps and hollows as

though they were not there; only the swift, sure movements of the gloved hands on the steering-wheel and the occasional changed angle of vision told us what the car was being called upon to do.

There were narrow bridges, flat, concrete and steel, with low parapets or none at all, most of them set at an angle to the line of the road. Water flowed beneath them, so close to the road level that we half expected our tyres to splash through it. Banks of snow lay to either hand, scooped out underneath by the passage of the water, leaving high con-cave-curved sides beneath which a dark stream swiftly flowed; and on the convex side there was the stippled effect born of the movement of wind alternating with strong, un-filtered sunshine.

We stopped once more. Ahead of us a lorry was drawn up, blocking the entire width of the road. We all got out, wrapping ourselves as best we could, to see what was going on. In front of the lorry a set of sheer-legs had been estab-lished, and from a block and tackle at its apex there dangled a rounded and ice-smoothed boulder weighing certainly not much less than a ton. It had been rolled down the hillside at some time since that ancient Bövertun car had passed by the previous evening, had blocked the road, settling itself deep in the soft surface, and was now being man-handled out of the way. We saw the lorry backed cautiously beneath it, the endless-chain of the tackle run through strong, gloved hands, and the lorry settle to its new load like a pack-animal bending at the knees to take its hampers. Somehow the lorry was then manœuvred to a rocky ledge. Having taken our photographs we climbed into the car again and, with a wave of the hand responded to by the hard-bitten road engineers, we drove on to Krossbu.

The timber building stands high, well clear of the road. In front of it was one of the big rotary snow-ploughs which had cleared our route. Its work was immediately evident, for the road under the lee of the mountain hut ran straight through a snow-drift twelve feet high and hard as rock. It had been carved by the snow-plough wide enough for a car to pass through if driven with skill. The Swede's big car, sliding through the cleft between the ice-walls, was dwarfed to a mini-car in a moment.

Here we said good-bye and wished our host and hostess well on their journey over Sognefjell to Skjolden and, eventually, to Sognefjord, where we too hoped later to arrive. For a moment we were tempted: we could, they said, travel with them the whole way, if we wished. We knew we should be comfortable and warm if we did so; but we should never be able to say, as we hoped to do, that we had crossed the highest mountain summit in Northern Europe under our own power.

It is easy to see how fortunate this lift had been. Not only had it brought us fourteen miles on our way, it had allowed us to drop off at the very beginning of the most famous stretch of the road with our energies in hand for this crossing of the Sogne snowfield. Gaily we set off, the only signs of previous traffic being the outsize tyre-marks of the snow-plough's wheels and the lesser ones of the Swedes' motor-car.

THE SOGNEFJELL ROAD

We climbed steadily for a long while, each new stretch of the road offering us a new horizon. The mountains that had beset us so far dropped away behind us and we seemed to be approaching a plateau. At any rate it was a vast undulating expanse of virgin snow very often hardly to be distinguished from the low cloud-filled sky which had unhappily replaced the bright sunshine we had awakened to at Elveseter. Then it dipped till it became a tract of melted ice-water, broken floes such as we had seen by the roadside for mile after mile between Haugastöl and Geilo. It was desolation indeed.

We might have approached the highest barren levels with more hesitation had it not been that we had been assured that there would be a small bus coming up behind that we could hop aboard if we liked. We found ourselves hoping that it would not come too soon, for it would be too great an irony to have come thus far and then have to do the actual summit in a bus.

We need not have worried. Having seen the road over

which it would have to pass we could imagine how long it would take. A bus was heavier and less manœuvrable than a car and there might be more boulders on the road by now: melting snow can play dangerous pranks on mountainsides.

As we approached a distant signboard marking the actual summit we found we were not entirely alone in this vast field of whiteness. Not far from the edge of the road and approaching us confidently was a diminutive figure on skis, who had unexpectedly loomed (if such a word can be used of so small a personage) out of the emptiness of the snow.

She was a small girl, perhaps twelve or thirteen years old. She wore a grey woollen scarf and helmet in one piece, a gaudy knitted long-sleeved cardigan with mittens to match, a sort of woollen pinafore that escaped below her cardigan and nearly covered her bright tartan skirt, thick woollen stockings covering her thin legs and knees, and ski-boots. Her small ski-sticks steadied her as she stood there, her face upturned inquiringly at us while I took a photograph.

It was perhaps a pity that she should have been so unprepossessing in appearance: a missing tooth drew attention to a rather large mouth. But her eyes were bright and there was a remarkable air of self-possession about her. Where had she come from, alone like that, we wondered, and whither was she bound? She must know the district pretty well to be allowed out alone on such a waste of treacherous melting snow and ice. However, mature enough to travel on skis alone among the mountains, she was child enough to slip quickly into her mouth the sweet Elizabeth found for her; when we turned a little later she was again a diminutive figure slithering away into the mist in the direction of Krossbu.

The mist turned to fine rain as we continued silently on our way and as the ground rose the rain turned to sleet, to a thin, vicious snow. It blew icily into our faces and obscured the fine summits that ring the plateau. It was still some twelve miles to the next stopping-place, Turtagrö, and a farther nine miles to Fortun, by which time we should have left far behind us the heights on which we were now uncomfortably facing the driven snow.

Its strength increased, and its density, too. Very soon we

could hardly see more than a few yards to either side of us, where snow lay thickly, and perhaps twice as much along the darker surface of the road ahead. We came to a little hut, not much bigger than a night-watchman's hut. It contained a miniature stove, a small pile of kindling and two or three split logs. Into the hut we darted, and pulled the open door to behind us. We were now at about the highest point on the road.

"And therefore," said Elizabeth, picking small ice-flakes out of her eyebrows, "we've done what we set out to do: walked a stretch of the highest Norwegian road, the Sognefjell!"

We looked about us through a gap in the top of the door. What we could see was not encouraging. Our horizon was now limited to a matter of a few yards in every direction. The sky seemed to have lowered until it was not so much a distant all-embracing vault as a concentration of snowy mist that beset us on all sides.

We waited, growing increasingly chilled and depressed. Even the thought of what we had achieved did little to compensate for the onslaught of this driven snow. Then, very faintly against the wind, we heard the hum of an engine. Realizing, fortunately, that it was probably much closer than it seemed, I darted out. I was just in time to flag a small, squat, blue bus travelling quite empty but for the driver along the narrow ribbon of the Sognefjell Road.

He stopped, more surprised to see us than we were to see him. We went aboard, settled ourselves amidships, between the wheel-bases for greater comfort, and took a whole side of the bus each. Then began a drive which eclipsed the Bergen-Norheimsund drive, if not in beauty at least in dramatic quality.

As soon as the road left the highest contours the snow turned to rain, the rain in due course to mist and in time the sun made a half-hearted attempt to appear through the cloud. The road here was better than on the other side of Krossbu, wider and harder surfaced. The bus ran steadily, with very few changes of speed, for mile after mile, the driver smoking cigarettes alternately out of his own and Elizabeth's packet. As the road descended we came into view of the great peaks and canyons and valleys and watercourses which till then had remained obscured for us by mist or snow. Near Turtagrö, which was little more than an isolated hotel, is the great cluster of high peaks known as the Horung, among which is the Great Skagastöl which, at 7,900 feet, is little less high than Galdhöpiggen himself.

I have written earlier of the skill of the Swedish driver and that of the Vauxhall owner with whom I climbed Porlock as a schoolboy; I said that these two men stand out as the best drivers I have known. I was speaking of drivers of private cars. It would be less than fair to the driver of this bus not to pay tribute to him. He may have had the advantage of a more powerful engine and a set of lower-ratio gears; but on the other hand by the very nature of a bus its driver is more remote from the road surface he travels on and the attendant dangers alongside. I would much rather take my own car up or down the famous Stalheim hairpins, or the hardly less spectacular hairpins this man negotiated as we dropped off the Sognefjell heights down to Turtagrö and Fortun, than be at the wheel of a bus.

Many of these hairpin-bends were too close-set to be negotiated in one lock; to watch this imperturbable driver run forward and backward, locking round angle after angle, was to be filled with admiration for the exactness of his judgment, the control of those steady hands and his sure-footed way among the pedals. If final tribute is required, let it be said here that Elizabeth, who is less phlegmatic about heights and corners and things mechanical in association with them than I, was sufficiently convinced after the first half-dozen or so to take the remainder, so to speak, in her stride. Thereafter she concentrated in ever-growing wonder on the peaks and waterfalls and sheer rock faces that met us at every turn.

One thing we had again omitted to do, and that was to take sandwiches with us when we left Elveseter. We had had a substantial breakfast, but so long before that it was now forgotten, and the keen wind in which we had walked those miles of snow-beset country had wrought havoc with our appetites. There was, however, no solution. Though we stopped at

Turtagrö and at Fortun and elsewhere on our route it was for a moment only, not long enough to dash into any restaurant and demand food. Hunger grew upon us with alarming strides; a time came when we were so conscious of our empty bellies that we could hardly have cared less about the beauties that were sweeping past us on either hand.

In vain I pleaded with the driver to hasten along one stretch of the road so that he would have a margin of time in hand at the next stop and thus enable me to jump out and snatch at something to eat. He was inexorable. Whether it was against his principles to vary his fixed schedule for two casual passengers when he had succeeded in adhering to it against the challenge of snow and landslide and falling rock I do not know.

He became human once, for a moment, the last moment. We had reached, after four hours' travelling, the little fjord-side village of Sogndalsfjora, and here his journey ended. As I sidled past him to step down on to the road he prodded me suddenly and violently in the stomach, and with a hearty guffaw remarked that now at last I should be able to fill it. Such was the penetrative power of his finger-tips, however, that it was some time before I could be absolutely certain that they had left space for the food I so much craved!

THE NAERÖYDAL GORGE

The mountains lay behind us; for the last several miles of the drive we had run alongside still serene water. We slept in another of those satisfying and reasonable *pensjonats*, the Loftesen, wandered leisurely round the village in the evening, and sniffed the alluring smell of fishing-boats and their tackle, fish-scales, tar, old rope and new paint, among the jetties and small warehouses which lay almost beneath our bedroom windows. On the wall of the lounge, which we had all to ourselves, there hung an oil-painting of the exact scene we looked out upon. Elizabeth coveted it and we debated during the evening whether it would be all right for us to ask if we might buy it. Laboriously, phrase-book in hand, because this was an inquiry for which we had no precedent, we worked out the form of our request, carefully wording it so that there should be a nice blend of appreciative comment and genuine stated desire.

There was one snag: the picture was framed. But if we were allowed to buy it we could easily remove it from its frame, leave the frame behind and roll the canvas carefully for the all-too-short remainder of our trip. It was only when, word-perfect as to what we proposed to say, we were about to embark upon our request I happened to take one more look, a rather closer look this time, at the coveted picture. Then we met the really insuperable obstacle: the picture was painted on plywood, not canvas after all! That was, unhappily, that. We consoled ourselves with the reflection that in all probability we should not have been allowed to take it away with us in any case.

We crossed the little ferry to the other side of this arm of Sognefjord and set off to walk to Kaupanger where, all being well, we were to pick up the boat for our last fjord trip, to Gudvangen. There we should take the road to Stalheim and Voss and then the railway back to Bergen, where we were due to arrive next evening.

It was eight miles exactly to Kaupanger: the first four miles on a gently climbing road among trees, over a shoulder of the mountain, with water on our right for most of the way; the second half gently downhill to sea level and the Gudvangen boat. We walked briskly, anxious to catch the boat, which left in exactly two hours and ten minutes' time. We knew that these boats left promptly; we knew, too, that the Kaupanger bus would overtake us, but we wanted to be independent of that.

Rain was falling before we had walked the first mile of the uphill road. We kept a careful check on our walking and estimated that if we kept on at this pace we should arrive with a few minutes to spare. Long before we came to Kaupanger we could see the fjord, backed by mountains, the water grey beneath the rainy sky. It looked very near, but distances are deceptive among hills and water and curving roads.

"D'you think we ought to hop on to the bus when it

overtakes us?" I asked Elizabeth. "If we miss it there isn't another."

For answer Elizabeth quickened her step and I shortened mine to accord with hers. We strode out. We heard the hum of the bus coming up astern and I wondered whether Elizabeth would waver. She did not turn her head. So be it, I thought, and we let the bus streak by.

By the time we arrived at the Kaupanger wharf its passengers had gone aboard. I glanced at my watch as we went on board, too: one hour fifty minutes for the eight-mile walk. And we had even stopped long enough to take a photograph or two of one of those white-painted churches with sharply pointed steeples which belong to this countryside. There was something very satisfying about that; and when a few minutes later the ship's bell sounded and we cast off we sat down to a cooked meal in the trim dining-saloon feeling that we had earned it.

We had thought Sörfjord narrow, but compared with the needle-like proportions of the branch of Sognefjord which ends at Gudvangen it is open water with limitless horizons! To our great disappointment the weather conditions during the three hours we were on board were the worst possible: torrential rain, a thick, grey mist that obscured the mountains from their summits almost down to water level, and water so grey that it could not carry reflections. Just now and then there was a temporary break in the rain pall and we caught a swift glimpse of the quite fantastically close-set hillsides, steep as precipices, off which waterfalls tumbled sheer for hundreds of feet into the fjord itself. An occasional tiny farmstead crouched on a handkerchief-sized plot of sloping turf and rock, hardly above water level, its occupants able to communicate with those of other farms only by water. Every such farm had its own tiny stone and timber jetty and small boat tied alongside.

The most astonishing thing about this arm of the fjord was its narrowness. It almost seemed as though one could reach out to either side from the deck and toss a stone ashore. Opening off it at intervals were even narrower branches, up which we supposed no steamer could ply at all. These were not

fjords but clefts in the mountainous rock masses which constituted this region; up them it was not unreasonable to surmise that monsters unseen of men lurked in dark caves and
the Kraken's tribe spawned in the deeps of the water, "Win-
nowing with giant arms the slumbering green".

The craft on which we were sailing was a car-ferry. In
addition to one or two private cars there was a bus, empty but
for a golden-haired conductress, who throughout the three
hours of this romantic journey slept curled up, her face buried
in a rug, on a padded bench alongside the driver's seat. Perhaps it was a familiar trip, holding no wonders for her at
eighteen.

At Gudvangen the water runs to a fine point. Indeed, had
it not been necessary to step aboard the waiting bus that
would take us to the summit of Stalheim (which we should
have walked but for the torrential rain) I should have been
tempted to stay and see how the captain contrived to turn his
boat round for the trip back to Kaupanger.

After a level stretch of narrow, winding road running south-
west out of Gudvangen between high earth and stone walls
the flat valley floor turns abruptly into a canyon. A hundred
years ago only men on foot, and the sturdiest of horses, could
ascend from Gudvangen to the uplands leading to Voss. Then
an enterprising engineer planned and chiselled a roadway
the whole eleven hundred feet out of the bottom of the
Naeröydal gorge to the summit where now the hotel stands
which is all there is of Stalheim. There are innumerable
hairpin-bends most skilfully graded to take motor traffic. Up
these the bus, travelling at little more than walking-pace in
drumming bottom gear, climbed relentlessly the steep side of
Stalheimskleiva, while behind us there unrolled the stupefy-
ing panorama of the gorge, set between mountains rising to
nearly five thousand feet, part-way up which masses of cloud
clung like cotton-wool eyebrows to a Father Christmas's
face.

At every turn I hurled myself (the bus was practically
empty) from window to window, hoping for a moment when
it would be steady enough, and the window unobstructed by
tree or bus, for me to record the scene. That I did so seems to

me little short of a miracle, for the stretch of road between angle and angle was very short, and the bus seemed to be almost perpetually swinging round one or the next or the next.

One thing I failed to discover, and that is what precautions are taken to ensure that no vehicles should meet between the base and the summit of the Stalheimskleiva, for assuredly nothing could pass anything else on the hairpins, and the lengths of road between them are hardly wide enough either. Possibly there is a standing arrangement whereby, as on some single-track lines, a baton must be passed from vehicle to vehicle and only the holder of the baton be permitted to use the road. If so, I did not see it. It may be just a matter of timing; but how in that case is the private traveller introduced into the pattern?

At the hotel we got out and walked back for a last view over the astonishing hill which we had just climbed. Preparing to descend it was a man on a bicycle, heavily loaded with kitbag and panniers. I am not sure that, even in the days when I preferred cycling to all other modes of travelling, I should have cared to make that journey, at any rate without a fixed wheel in addition to the brakes.

The Stalheim Hotel stands superbly on the flat summit of the hill, girt about by other and greater summits. It is not a lovely building to look at, like the Elveseter one, but it can take a hundred and fifty guests, and from the look of it when we were there it was pretty full. It was not our intention to stay, however, and we walked briskly away downhill in intermittent sunshine, the rain having been cut off at source about half-way up the hairpin hill.

On the way we encountered two Scots who hailed us, seeing our flags, and entered into conversation. They were members of a large organized party which had its base at Stalheim. The shortage of tobacco was distressing them. They could not obtain anything they considered fit to smoke at the hotel, and they were stranded there tobaccoless for two or three more days. Their gratitude when I handed over to them my last unopened packet was pitiful to behold. I warned them that it had been bought in England well before we had sailed,

that it had lain in a pocket of my rucksack for weeks of sun
and wind and would probably be as dry as cork-shavings.
They did not mind. A slice of potato, if they could persuade
the chef to produce so humble an article, would bring back
something of the natural moisture! They were already lighting up as we said good-bye and set off again down the long
hill to the valley that would bring us to Uppheim.

SIGNE

The last of the spectacular country now lay behind us,
though much remained that was quietly and impressively
beautiful. We walked along a level road among trees for
many miles, through stretches of gated roads, alongside a
narrow lake beyond which were the foot-hills of those mountains which we had skirted on the railway between Voss and
Myrdal. We came to more frequent clusters of little houses,
schools, farmsteads, churches; even a post office—the first we
had seen for a long time. And we came at length to the last
small *pensjonat* we were to stay at, just short of the white-
steepled church of Uppheim. For the last few hundred yards
of our walk the road had been bordered by a high stone wall
turfed over and sown thick with small pansies and other graceful flowerets. After the wildness of Sognefjell it was a little
intimate fairyland of warmth and colour and peace.

The *pensjonat*, like so many others, was in the throes of
preparation for the tourist season and there was only one room
available, one that did not, unfortunately, overlook the lake
and the mountains. But it was distempered, like the rest of
the house, in delicate pastel shades, with built-in cupboards
and a view up the hillside to the belt of trees that hung upon
it beyond the field. A little *stabbur* stood alone in the field,
its dark, weathered timbers contrasting strongly with the
cream and yellow outside paintwork of the *pensjonat*.

Signe served us: a smiling, soft-spoken, enchanting twenty-
year-old daughter of the house, her school English still fresh
on her tongue without the pollution of imported Americanese.
She was the most unsophisticated Norwegian girl we met on

our travels, with soft brown eyes, broad smooth brow from which the naturally waving hair was drawn back behind her ears, a snub nose and a short upper lip.

Again we were the only guests. We sat at a corner table overlooking the lake and the hills, a table to which she brought continuously replenished trayloads of good things. In addition to the usual dishes there were fried eggs and beautifully fried potatoes. And when we had taken the edge off our appetites with this she appeared again and laid before us a large dish of trout taken from the lake within fifty yards of our window and not half an hour before. It was to be our last evening meal in the real country, and it was one which we shall long remember.

There were books about the house, books that had certainly been read and were being read. Sigrid Undset's *Kristin Lavransdatter* in a characteristic Norwegian binding lay on a table near ours. Picking it up, we were pleased to find that what a few weeks before would have seemed little more than a page of Sanskrit now glittered with words and phrases we had made our own. It was no longer an entirely strange country or foreign tongue.

Signe was twenty, and her proudest possession had but newly arrived: the native costume which, now that she was no longer a child, would be hers to wear when occasion offered; hers, incidentally, to wear on her wedding day. We asked her if she would put it on so that we could see her in it, and she was overcome with distress because, since the costume still lay in the drawer, it would show crease-marks. We assured her she had time to have it ironed out, and went off to pack our rucksacks. Next time we packed these it would be to go aboard ship for England.

When we were ready she was ready, too. We stood her in the small field behind the house, near the *stabbur*, and there photographed her in that lovely native costume, the handiwork of her own mother: black skirt, long and full, snow-white apron, belted with a belt of beautifully embroidered workmanship; embroidered bodice and coatee and white, long-sleeved blouse with embroidered cuffs. Beads played a considerable part in the embroidery her mother had done for her, and the lace on her apron had been handed down to her from her grandmother. Signe was an appealing little figure, standing there with her hands at her side in the dewy grass, and we promised her a photograph on our return to England. Perhaps even now it stands on the dressing-table of her little bedroom.

DOWNHILL TO BERGEN

Then we left for Voss some fifteen miles away down the valley, walking once more in bright sunshine with a pleasant breeze in our faces all the way. The road wound among trees, alongside water, beneath steeply overhanging cliffs and then again through wide open country. Silver-birch trees abounded, bringing a lightness to the landscape in contrast to the darker pinewoods of the hills. Close beside us for several miles of the way a stream tumbled hurriedly, tripping over itself, dodging among boulders and under log-bridges, trapped every now and then into small leats which ended in unexpected turbine-houses producing electric current for some undertaking hidden away among the trees.

Saw-mills had been built here and there. Not the great saw-mills of Hallingdal and lower Gudbrandsdal, but baby saw-mills, with saws spun by water-power or by these small electric motors. The sawyers worked leisurely, handling the baulks of timber with apparent pleasure and treating each new operation as though it presented a new problem which it would be their pleasure to solve. Here was no working to schedule: so many logs to be sawn into so many planks of such-and-such thickness by such-and-such a time. There was cool shade beneath the heavy plank roofs, spray from the water lifted into the warm air and hung there lazily, a dog slept beneath a saw-bench, a lad stacked planks on end against a wall, and someone with an open-mouthed sack collected saw-dust and carried it to the stream to tip it in and then stand watching the thin brown carpet disintegrate and vanish down-stream.

"And this time two days ago," Elizabeth said as we lingered

once more, watching the easy motion of the sawyers, who nevertheless got through such an amount of work in a long working day, "we were plodding along the top of Sognefjell in a waste of snow and ice! "

It really was quite hard to believe that things could have changed so much in a bare forty-eight hours. In that time we had been picked up by the silent Swedes, had walked the plateau to its summit and just beyond, had been carried off that plateau in a bus that brought us down to sea level from about 4,600 feet; we had walked from Sogndalsfjora to Kaupanger, had taken ship to Gudvangen, had been carried up the famous hairpin-bends of Stalheimskleiva, had then descended the valley to Uppheim and were now bound for Voss, some dozen miles away.

It would mean hard walking if we were to reach Voss in time to catch the train for Bergen; and comparatively uninteresting walking too, for now the mountains were behind us, the landscape was opening out, the streams and rivers dispersing. We came to a closed gate near a quarry-approach, and on the hither side of the gate was a truck. We passed through the gate, closing it carefully behind us. Perhaps the truck would have to be driven through it; if so, we would open the gate for the driver, and climb on board.

There were signs of movement. Someone swung the engine to life, tools were thrown in and the truck began to move. We watched it approach the road, ready to dart to the gate and open it. But, alas for our hopes, the driver turned back the way we had come and vanished round a bend among the trees. We had hardly recovered from our indignation when there was the roar of a much more powerful truck and it appeared round the bend heading ponderously for the gate. We opened it, looked a question at the driver and at his nod climbed up and settled ourselves down back to back. Half an hour later we were in Voss, our journey done.

With the buying of our tickets for Bergen at the station a faint persistent melancholy settled upon us. Last time we had placed our money in this same neat gadget and seen it twiddled round we were taking in exchange our tickets for Haugastöl, on the dramatic section of the Bergen-Oslo railway.

This time it was in the other direction, the last short trip that would end on the water's edge. Then—embarkation, the crossing; and Norway would be a memory only.

Yet with this melancholy there came also a sense of release. We had been living at high pitch, confronted at every turn with things that were new, sights that were strange, experiences that made demands on us. There was, we were coming to realize, a limit to the amount we could take in without surfeit, and that limit had been pretty well reached. We talked of this during the slow 70-odd-mile run to Bergen.

It was an attractive enough run, without being spectacular. There was deep water on the right-hand side of us almost the whole way—an extension of that strange and fascinating fjord-pattern which lies about Bergen itself. The train pottered—there is no apter word—leisurely alongside the water, lingering at some small halt to collect a passenger or two or drop some shopper from the market at Voss, dodging behind some mass of rock, cutting through some small dark tunnel, slipping quietly enough over some bridge or gateless level-crossing, with a discreet warning note from time to time.

We came now and then to some small industrial centre built on the solid rock between railway-line and water's edge. At a jetty there would be tied up a squat cargo-boat and a few men would be leisurely at work loading or unloading. For a few hundred yards the clear sky and bright sunshine would be obscured for us by smoke drifting from a tall chimney, then the train would nuzzle into a cleft in the rocks and emerge into open country again, the industrial scene behind us. We ran thus into the outskirts of Bergen, drew parallel with the road by which our first bus had taken us away from the city, over the pass and down the other side to our first glimpse of smiling Hardanger; then we came to a halt in the station.

FLESH-POTS

We alighted seasoned travellers, shouldered our rucksacks and set off along the cobbles of Kong Oscar's Gate. It would not be necessary this time to ask, as we had now asked so many times: *"Har De et vaerelse med to senger for oss i-natt?"* We had booked in advance before leaving Bergen, for we knew that our return would coincide with the beginning of the true tourist season and *Venus* would just be landing a full complement of passengers before taking off those of us whose holiday was at an end.

A warm rich patina lay over Bergen; the buildings and boats and open spaces, the tiled and coppered roofs, looked as though they had been dusted over with powdered light. Grey cement took on a gilded hue, steel tram-lines wound among the cobbles like thin silver ribbons, and all yellows and reds and blues and greens were enriched. We had said good-bye to Bergen in torrential rain; we were seeing her now anew, as we had seen her on our first arrival, in her gayest attire. Remembering how quickly, here in Bergen, skies that were alight with laughter could turn to weeping, we wasted little time over a meal but took camera and film and filter and set off to capture all that we could of this lovely little city to which we had lost our hearts.

We walked along the wide Tyskebryggen by which we had first entered the city on disembarking, and turned about to see it anew. It was nearly seven o'clock and the sun, shining from across the water, was lighting up the quaint gabled wooden buildings which the stern Hanseatic League merchants built five hundred years ago; lighting up, too, the more modern timber warehouses that backed on to the Torvet and C. Monsen's *Bok & Papirhandel*, Books and Stationery, in which we had seen so many English books in translation, finely bound, stacked in the broad double windows, and bought our maps that had served us so well.

Pottering about, looking for the best vantage-point for a photograph that would include all this, I was tapped on the shoulder by a man in seaman's rig. If I walked this way, he suggested, I should get a better photograph. He was right. Standing at the spot he indicated I found just the balance I was seeking, took my photographs, dodged the bus that was bearing down upon the three of us, thanked him and went off to find other subjects. It is impossible to go wrong, of course, where there is water with ships large or small afloat upon it.

When, some weeks later, I went along to collect my three hundred "contacts" made from the $2\frac{1}{4}''$-square negatives I had handed over to the expert who does my developing and printing, so that I could begin to make my selection for this book, I was met with an odd smile and tentative manner. Would I, he asked me, accept——? He withdrew from a large envelope a photograph some twelve inches by ten, mounted and framed. It was this scene from the Tyskebryggen. It had so taken his fancy that he had masked down the negative from the square to better proportions, and then enlarged it to these noble dimensions. It hangs on the wall now above a row of travel books, and the hand on the clock indicates that the photograph was taken at twenty-five minutes to seven.

Having taken all the photographs we wanted on ground or sea level we turned to the mountain-railway, *flöibanen*, from the summit of which we hoped for an almost aerial photograph of the city lying nearly a thousand feet below. And so it was. Standing on a terrace, we could look over the whole expanse: railways and sidings, beautiful rather than sordid from such a view-point; tall buildings with the narrow stone canyons that were the intersecting streets; sharply gabled wooden buildings in the older quarters; open Squares with their trees sheltering the statues of the Composer Edvard Grieg whose music had followed us throughout our travels, and the violinist, Ole Bull; the great and small lakes that lie in its heart and the quays and dockyards and slipways and engineering-shops that lie beyond, their lines softened for us by the heat-haze that rose above the whole.

Behind and beyond all this there were the little scattered buildings, the close-set trees and modest fields, the white ribbons of the dust roads; then the valleys, the blue mountains rising beyond them, and here and there the gleaming fingers of the fjord, turned now to silver-gilt by the westering sun. I know of no other city on which one can look down at once from so high aloft and so intimately, as Bergen.

Next morning it was grey and rain threatened, though it never actually broke upon us. We turned our thoughts to shops. We would like to furnish a whole house with Norwegian products. It is not just that the wood their craftsmen use is so pleasing to the eye and finger-tip, it is the workmanship that has gone into its translation into beds and chairs and tables and bookcases and boxes and stools. We did not once see a single piece of shoddy workmanship. Accustomed, though by no means reconciled, to an enforced lowering of standards in materials and workmanship here in post-war England, we never lost our wonder and delight at products which bore the unmistakable stamp of pride and artistry. The simplest fitments, the wooden spoons and rolling-pins, the shelves and meat-safes, the housewife's tools-of-trade, as well as the more elaborate pieces of furniture, all possessed this quality.

They were not cheap by our standards. In general we would have said that whether we were looking at garments and textiles or furniture and china prices in the shops were much the same as those at home. So far as clothing was concerned, and certainly in regard to boots and leather goods, there was nothing in those shops which we would have wanted to buy even if the prices had been lower. But with furniture and articles of wood it was a different story. Even though the prices were high and, because they were marked in terms of *kroner* (almost exactly the equivalent of a shilling to-day), often rather frighteningly high until you reduced them to pounds, the quality was vastly superior to anything we could buy in England in the same price range.

Only when the craftsmen had been set to work in an alien wood was there something lacking. It is curious but true that if we looked at a piece of furniture made of wood not truly belonging to the country there usually seemed to be something basically wrong with it; the men who had worked to the designs laid before them seemed to have been aware that they were working in a foreign material. A piece of pseudo-Jacobean oak in a window full of spruce and pine and birch was as out of place as a chromium-plated, glass-topped table in a monks' refectory.

We bought a few pieces: a beautifully simple box in un-stained, lightly varnished birchwood, with a fitted tray that would take Elizabeth's sewing-silks, her buttons and hooks-and-eyes and press-studs and needles and pins; beneath it was ample room for her darning-wools and the oddments without which no woman feels that life is complete. It was of the simplest design, without frills or flourishes or ornamentation of any sort; but the workmanship was quite perfect and the tray with its varied rectangular sections possessed real beauty.

We bought a birchwood bowl or two, a few plates of elm, chosen after we had worked our way through a stack three feet high until we had got those with the most pleasing grain. Then we turned to china, and the choice again was to be difficult. In the end we contented ourselves with a narrow-necked bulbous jar with a small handle, of a pale duck-egg hue with thin vertical stripes of oatmeal showing through the fine glaze, and a little set of four stippled green fruit-plates, two with male and two with female figures, ornate, improbable, Norwegian: a man with a rake, a woman with a broom, a man with a fish in either hand, a woman with a basket and an umbrella. They were gay, insouciant; now, when we sit at table and look at them, we remember the shop where we bought them, the friendliness of the young assistant behind the counter and the care with which she packed them when she learned that we had only our rucksacks in which to carry them.

It turned cooler still that evening and Elizabeth said: "Let's spend our last evening in Norway luxuriously. Let's go to one of Bergen's crack hotels, order the best dinner they can offer us, and sit drinking coffee afterwards in the lounge and watch our fellow-men!"

We spruced ourselves up as best we could: Elizabeth in her better skirt, somewhat crumpled from long journeying in her rucksack, I in my other pair of grey flannels and a reasonably clean shirt. I wore a tie; but I also wore my nailed *Veldt-schoen*, for otherwise I had only a pair of light gym-shoes with me. Together we made for the best hotel.

Dinner was about to be served and we were shown to a table by the head waiter. We sat down a little self-consciously because at all the other tables people were looking tremendously respectable in evening gowns, in well-pressed suits and highly polished shoes.

The menu offered us soup, chicken and a sweet. The soup had a name on the menu which meant nothing to either of us. Its taste meant less still, and to this day we do not know what it was intended to be. It was not disagreeable, merely negative. There was no alternative to the soup. The chicken may have been the light of its mother's and father's eyes and a gay and sprightly member of a well-knit family, but that had been a long time ago and the cares of the world had saddened it and hardened its sinews since then. The portions that appeared on our plates, small as they were, defeated us when we came to deal with them. With the chicken there was a small helping of boiled potatoes accompanied by two very limp lettuce-leaves. The sweet which followed consisted of two prunes and an unnamed plum-like object in a thin, tepid syrup. Coffee was not served in the dining-room, but was obtainable in the lounge. In paying our bill for that meal, 17/6, I had our only moment of satisfaction.

The waiter had spoken English to us with emphasis and some arrogance. It was a curious experience, after weeks of making ourselves understood by a variety of Norwegian girls in simple, homely surroundings. The waiter most clearly did not approve of our travel-stained tweeds, our heavy boots, our ruddy and bronzed complexions. It was doubtless petty of me to resent him as much as I did. Some foolish pride, too, was no doubt involved. I know I ought to have allowed him the satisfaction of speaking his faultless English to us, but I was childish enough to want him to know that we were capable of getting around on our own, and indeed had been doing so for some time past.

"Ask for our bill and let's go," Elizabeth said, recognizing in me the restlessness that sometimes leads to friction. "Don't let's have coffee here."

"We won't," I said, relieved. "I will."

When the waiter next came within hail I caught his eye, waited till he came up to our table, and then, in quite unnecessarily elaborate phrasing, did so: "*Vil De vaere så snild å la mig få min regning*," I said to him, with considerable emphasis.

He hesitated only an instant; then, with an urbane

"Certainly, sir," he scribbled the shocking total on his pad and thrust it beneath my plate.

We had hoped to spend the evening drinking Norway's excellent coffee in a well-warmed lounge watching other people, but we had by now changed our minds. Instead, we crossed the Plass, making for the Torvet, and very soon were ensconced with our coffee in a window, able to look out on the comings and goings of ordinary folk. This was more like it, we said to ourselves. How silly we had been to think it worth our while to spend an evening in a four-star hotel! It was our own stupid fault and we had no one but ourselves to thank for the experience.

There was nothing really wrong with that hotel. It was filled with tourists, mainly English, great numbers of whom we had watched disembarking from *Venus* that very afternoon. We had not felt any of the envy we might have expected to feel at seeing so many people just beginning a holiday while we were just ending ours. If we envied anyone it was the scattered rucksack bearers who broke the monotony of ordinary passengers streaming ashore with their porters loaded with heavy and much-labelled suitcases, to await their cabin-trunks in the Customs Shed. There were only a few of these lighter travellers, for it was still mid-June and the schools and colleges were still in session.

No, the hotel served a definite need. At every table except ours there sat groups of two and three and four who were just beginning their visit to Norway. They had security, a base, somewhere to return to whether from a shopping expedition, a trip up the mountain-railway, a trip into the country by *drosje*, or a more protracted trip by bus or railway into the interior. They would be eating food not unlike the food they would get in Scarborough or Brighton or Newquay or Keswick, and if they had a question to ask someone would give the answer in their own language. When they went upstairs to bed it was my guess that they would have beds more like the ones they were used to, with sheets and blankets that tucked in, not the native *dyne*.

We met a number of our fellow-passengers during the return crossing to Newcastle. The majority of them may have welcomed that form of security, but there were certainly some who did not; some who were wondering whether they had, in fact, seen anything much of the real Norway. It was difficult to resist the temptation to tell them what they had missed; to describe the Hallingdal farmstead at Nesbyen and the many wayside *pensjonats* where we had been made welcome and had felt immediately at home, far removed from waiters in dress-clothes, hall-porters in braided uniforms, and lurking *drosjes*. Elizabeth and I had been lucky enough to have been able to fulfil a desire to go through Norway in the unorthodox fashion which suits us best wherever we go.

Så Lange, Norge!

Next morning we packed our rucksacks for the last time, paid our *regning*, said good-bye to the receptionist and to the " Blue Girl "—her deputy who had once tried so hard to make us understand that if only we would be patient all would be well. Then, with our rucksacks swollen to bursting-point by our purchases of the previous day, we set out for the last time along the Tyskebryggen, the sun on our backs, the cobbles uneven beneath our boots. *Venus's* white-ringed black funnels towered above the wharf-side cranes and warehouses and Customs Shed ahead of us, and *drosjes* threaded their arrogant way among those of us who walked. Half an hour later we were on board, our packs stowed below, standing at the rails where we could get the best view of Bergen, that lovely city, when she should begin to drop away astern of us.

The two small, black-funnelled tugs, the same doubtless that had assisted us to find our berth at the quay owned by Det Bergenske Dampskibsselskab, fussed about us at stem and stern, their crews preparing to take us in tow. A bell or two tinkled from remote regions; hawsers were cast off; there was the grinding of one of the wharf-side cranes as it swung its jib clear and propelled itself along a section of its own private line; people waved and a car horn was sounded. Then the whole array of quayside and warehouses, with their backcloth of buildings, streets and tree-clad mountainside, began to turn as upon an invisible pivot. Punctual to the minute and with characteristic lack of commotion, m.s. *Venus* was heading down the fjord, bound for the open sea.

There was blue water all about us and the light was too bright for us to look long astern in the direction of Bergen itself, basking in the sunshine. A solitary gull hovered with motionless wings overhead. Then someone jettisoned a basketful of scraps through an unseen vent at water level; instantly, conjured out of the still air, a flight of urgent sea-gulls swooped down upon it and there was pandemonium as beak challenged beak and the tastier morsels were snatched by one after another, dropped and salvaged, torn apart, fought for and relinquished and greedily swallowed.

Then, the supply exhausted, the gulls took wing again and drifted effortlessly astern, bound for Bergen, where men with knives would be gutting fish in the Torvet and delicacies were to be had without the asking. *Venus*'s screws turned faster, her bows lifted to an incoming roller: we knew at last we were really homeward bound.

INDEX